Actor Training
The Laban Way

Actor Training
The Laban Way

An Integrated Approach to
Voice, Speech, and Movement

Barbara Adrian
Illustrations by Chelsea Clarke

ALLWORTH PRESS
NEW YORK

12   11   10   09   08   5   4   3   2   1

Published by Allworth Press
An imprint of Allworth Communications, Inc.
10 East 23rd Street, New York, NY 10010

Illustrations by Chelsea Clarke
Cover design by Derek Bacchus
Interior design by Kristina Critchlow
Page composition/typography by Kristina Critchlow
Cover photo by Scott Nangle
Models: Lindsey Liberatore and Jowan Thomas

Library of Congress Cataloging-in-Publication Data:
Adrian, Barbara.
Actor training the Laban way: an integrated approach to voice, speech, and movement/Barbara Adrian; illustrations by Chelsea Clarke.
     p. cm.
Includes bibliographical references and index.
ISBN-13: 978-1-58115-648-5
ISBN-10: 1-58115-648-0
1. Movement (Acting) 2. Voice culture. I. Title.

PN2071.M6A37 2008
792.02'8--dc22

Printed in the United States of America

A song for my father and mother

TABLE OF CONTENTS

ACKNOWLEDGEMENTS

Without the students who ventured into my studio, there could not be a book. In many ways, the students at Marymount Manhattan College have been my collaborators. Always openhearted and ready to experiment, they continue to inspire me to grow this process. The value of their feedback over the past years has been invaluable to the development of this integrated approach to voice, speech, and movement training.

I also wish to thank Marymount Manhattan College faculty and administration for their continuous support. The award of three Sokol Grants supported me in earning my CMA in Laban Movement Analysis and helped defray the cost of the illustrations for this book. Thank you to my department chair, Dr. Mary Fleisher, who from the word "go" encouraged and supported me with appropriate class time to develop this integrated approach.

I am particularly grateful for the artistic talents and generosity of Chelsea Clarke, who made an immeasurable contribution by creating all the illustrations for this book. Over the past two and a half years, Chelsea has been dedicated to getting it just right, and she did.

I was touched by and remain thankful to all who volunteered to read this book and offer their particular expertise during various stages of the writing. Thank you to Cheryl Clark, CMA; Kate Devore, MA, CCC-SLP; Ellen Goldman, CMA; and my colleagues at Marymount Manhattan College, Ellen Orenstein and Haila Strauss. Each of these individuals has specialized knowledge relative to voice, speech, and/or movement. Their experience in performance and training actors proved essential to a successful completion of this book.

Over the past thirty years, there have been many teachers who have influenced my work, but none more than the instructors from my certification program at the Laban/Bartenieff Institute of Movement Studies: Janis Pforsich OTR, CMA; Charlotte Wile, CMA; and Aliza Shapiro, CMA. Though he is no longer with us, I wish to acknowledge Raphael Kelly, who gave me my foundation in voice and speech training and encouraged me to teach.

Thank you to Ramona Tarkington-Deal who read every page more than once for clarity. Ramona does not make her living in the theatre; therefore, her feedback and editorial suggestions were priceless for making the content accessible to a wide range of readers.

Finally, for his profound knowledge of the human body and how it moves, and for his unflagging moral support, a special thank-you to my husband, Richard Sabel, MA, MPH, OTR, GCFP.

INTRODUCTION

My Journey

This is an age during which we are encouraged to learn more and more about less and less. Consequently, it is de rigueur to compartmentalize all manner of expertise. Regardless of your field of endeavor, after you have studied the "basics," you are encouraged to pick a "specialty." While this makes some legitimate sense in fields such as medicine, it has always seemed an artificial approach, particularly when applied to theatre training, and most specifically to voice, speech, and movement. That is because this triumvirate comprises the pillars that support the actor's craft of storytelling. Take any one of them away and it all comes tumbling down. As one might imagine, the approach described in this book is based on my experience as a student, performer, and teacher.

When I was an undergraduate student earning her BA in theatre, voice training was exclusively the domain of singing lessons. Likewise, the movement curriculum was modeled almost entirely on dance classes. In speech classes, we sedentarily drilled on diction exercises that tended to result in the talking-head syndrome. Nice diction, but no connection from the neck down.

While singing, dancing, and diction lessons are important disciplines, many students find the studies intimidating. Student actors can become inhibited as they strive to sing the correct notes, reproduce the exact choreography, or standardize their pronunciation. The concern about being "right" can create disconnection between the actor and his instrument, which prevents the actor from moving and speaking on impulse, one of the hallmarks of an excellent actor. I define "acting on impulse" as mastery of whole-body responsiveness to stimuli moment to moment. In this light, it is easy to understand how the potentially exacting natures of the three pillars could be alienating. And when you combine their prescriptive natures with the fact that they are compartmentalized from each other, it becomes clear how the trainings could ultimately fail to support the actors toward the goal of "acting on impulse."

At this moment, it may be useful to take a brief historical look at voice, speech, and movement training. In the sixties, seventies, and eighties, exciting models for voice training that moved away from traditional singing classes were developed by individuals such as Catherine Fitzmaurice, Roy Hart, Arthur Lessac, and Kristin Linklater. These individuals also recognized the importance of the whole body in the production of sound and each of their systems includes some movement training as well. While Fitzmaurice, Hart, and Linklater concentrated mostly on voice, Lessac developed some innovative approaches to diction. There can hardly be a student of performance dating from the 1960s to present times that hasn't been touched directly or indirectly by the processes developed by these individuals. In recent times, relative to articulation and pronunciation, Dudley Knight's Detail Model provides the tools for describing and producing dialects of English as opposed to learning a "correct" or standardized way to speak English. This is in direct contrast to the teachings of Edith Skinner, who was a diction teacher from the 1940s until her death in 1981. Skinner valued standardizing pronunciation, and her book, *Speak with Distinction* (first published in 1942 and revised several times), remains a popular text.

Before and during the time that Fitzmaurice, Hart, Lessac, and Linklater were developing their experiments with voice, a few unconventional acting systems integrated voice with extreme physicality. The ultradisciplined trainings initiated by Jerzy Grotowski, Vsevolod Meyerhold, Eugenio Barba, and Tadashi Suzuki all developed the use of voice as part of their movement vocabulary. But since philosophically these trainings do not support the American dedication to traditional "naturalism," they can often be relegated to special-topic classes.

Consequently, many American acting programs now include physical training modalities that are not exclusively embedded in the traditional dance model or in extreme, rarified physicality. Instead, the focus is on "body re-education," which can include the Alexander Technique, Feldenkrais Method®, Body-Mind Centering™, and Bartenieff Fundamentals. I find these trainings very useful to the actors because they help them identify habituated patterns of physical behavior and through this awareness develop functional ease with physical tasks. Additionally, these modalities do not fashion the actors to look as though they are trained in a particular technique or style. They train the actors to look more like themselves, which culturally supports the American ideal of celebrating the individual. In spite of all this innovation, the three pillars are still usually taught by highly skilled specialists during separate class periods, leaving the students to build their own roadmaps toward their acting goals.

After completing my undergraduate studies in acting, I studied speech with Raphael Kelly at the Shakespeare Studio in Manhattan. Mr. Kelly's approach to speech was based on the writings and teachings of W. A. Aiken, MD, a phonologist from the early 1900s. This information was passed to Mr. Kelly from J. Clifford Turner at the Royal Academy of Dramatic Art and Elsie Fogerty at the Central School of Speech and Drama.

From Mr. Kelly I learned a kinesthetic approach to diction that was steeped in early traditions. The precise movements of the articulators required a meticulousness that built strength and flexibility into my speech muscles. However "old-fashioned" the system was, what I learned then and what remains with me today is: *speech is movement*. Modifying the system for today's actors became the first step toward accomplishing my desire to integrate voice, speech, and movement. Modifying it meant finding a balance between the rigor of the muscular activity of the articulators for speech and the "modern" psychological approach to voice.

As my training continued, I felt encouraged but still unsatisfied with the existing integrated models. At that time, most current models concentrated on voice, through which the emotional life of the actor was revealed, but which gave little more than a glancing nod to articulation. Without intelligible articulation the emotional life had no shape or clarity; it lacked intention. Likewise, the bodywork attached to voice training seemed very general and was subservient to the voice work. I wanted a process whereby voice, speech, and movement were treated as equals in service to each other.

Relative to teaching voice and speech, I purposely sought positions where I could advocate for and teach them as one component. I was doggedly determined not to be the "voice lady" or the "speech lady", and I continued to believe that movement was critical. Consequently, I began to experiment with supporting voice and speech training with movement. I didn't have a clue what I was doing. I just knew that the three pillars should be integrated, so I continued to take workshops and experimented with synthesizing the material in the classes I taught. I was shopping for the right fit. In the mid-eighties, I team-taught with a movement coach who was teaching Laban Movement Analysis (LMA), and the connection to my goal was immediate. I found my home base for movement technique. LMA training, along with the incorporation of Bartenieff Fundamentals (BF), promised to provide the necessary functional and expressive physical skills that would clarify the actor's intent and thus create clarity of meaning.

Over the next eight years, in addition to teaching and training, I also continued to perform on the stage. I acted in a variety of plays that required different styles and was, therefore, fortunate enough to test out the practical applications of my synthesis. I was thrilled to find that my acting work had gained both clarity and emotional depth. As I gravitated more and more toward teaching and coaching, I felt compelled to enter the LMA certificate program. Since completing my certificate to become a Certified Movement Analyst (CMA) in 2000, I have been developing LMA as a support for voice, speech, and movement training for actors. Witnessing my students' imaginations and clarity of purpose blossom with this integration has been a joy. Likewise, my students have inspired and challenged me to dig deeper and take more risks as an artist and teacher.

By reaching back in time to retrieve the vital essence of speech training and uniting it with LMA, I am endeavoring to move actor training forward toward a fully integrated approach to voice, speech, and movement. As a teacher, it is my desire to help actors 1) learn what messages they are sending into the world when they move and speak, 2) identify their habitual patterns and how these habits can impinge on new expressive choices, and 3) develop both their functional skills and expressive capabilities in voice, speech, and movement simultaneously. Consequently, the principal purpose of this book is to describe a progression of exercises from beginning to advanced levels that include individual and group work. The exercises develop skills related to breath support, tone, range, articulation, dynamic alignment, balance, flexibility, strength, and stamina. These enhanced skills inspire the actor's imagination and are applied to building relationships to the physical space and strengthening communication with others through body, voice, and speech.

Rudolf von Laban

Born in Austria, Rudolf von Laban (1879–1958) was a choreographer, teacher, philosopher, and writer. He is still considered the most important movement theorist from the early 1900s to present times. Laban observed how the body moves as its physical condition, environment, cultural issues, communication with other bodies, and the universe at large affect it physically and emotionally. Through these observations, he was able to develop a theoretical framework called Laban Movement

Analysis to describe qualitative and quantitative changes in movement. He also devised Labanotation, a system of symbols with which to notate these changes. Through LMA, Laban developed a means whereby expressive movement can be explored by all, not just trained dancers. Laban's expanded vision for movement training led him to observe and notate how the body moves in the real world, accomplishing real tasks. Devoted to the development of an expressive and efficient instrument for the purpose of accomplishing work and play, Laban observed man in relation to nature, the workplace, religious rituals, and play, ultimately becoming the consummate teacher and mentor to individuals from all walks of life. Among Laban's famous dance students were Suzanne Perrottet (prior to her work with Laban, she was the star pupil of Emile Jacques-Dalcroze), Mary Wigman, Dussia Bereska, and Kurt Joos. Laban's teachings were the inspiration for his disciples to open Laban schools in Switzerland, Italy, France, Poland, and England.

Despite the deeply practical nature of LMA, Laban was also linked to the occult, a connection born of his interest in observing the relationship between movement and the rituals of many Eastern and Western religions. In his adolescence, he was introduced to the Sufi Dervish dances and their powerful trance-like states. This awakened in him an unshakeable belief in the magical potential of movement. In his adult life, his relationship with the occult is marked by his association with the Rosicrucians, who practiced a life based on the mystical properties of art and idealism. Additionally, he established a "movement commune" at Ascona, Switzerland (1911–14), which gave him a place to explore this mystical potential of movement with a group of students while living a free, bucolic life. Laban's Rosicrucian studies, the experiments that began at Ascona, and his strong mathematical and architectural background were synthesized in his theory of Space Harmony, which was finally published posthumously as *The Language of Movement* (*Choreutics*) in 1966.

Sensitizing the body to be receptive to inner and outer forces of energy, which Laban believed could lead to psychic experiences, was prevalent throughout his work. But also present was an effort to balance the practical with the spiritual. Classically educated in math and science, with advanced studies as an artist and architect, Laban's curiosity was insatiable. These qualities, along with his rich imagination and connection to nature, made him an ideal artistic explorer to open new frontiers in movement theory and application. As Laban formulated his theories, he was deeply influenced by Hermann Obrist, Wassily Kandinsky, and Arnold Schoenburg. He admired Isadora Duncan and Dalcroze for their groundbreaking approaches to movement and used their work as a backdrop to examine his own ideas. Laban was concerned that man's movement potential was being seriously compromised by industrialism, which was moving man away from the land and into factories. This fueled his all-inclusive approach to movement. Laban believed that movement for *all* would be man's salvation from the physically repetitive nature of factory work. This belief began his legacy of choreographing movement choirs with laborers of all types. In the instance of the Craft Guilds of Vienna in 1927, he choreographed 10,000 performers, of whom only 2,700 were dancers. Laban's fame grew and, during the 1930s, he became the head choreographer at the Berlin State Opera and choreographed for Siegfried Wagner (Richard's son) at the Bayreuth Festival and for Richard Wagner's opera *Tannhauser*.

With the rise of Hitler, Laban was embroiled in distressing times and had to make some difficult professional choices. Impressed with Laban's charisma and reputation in German dance as the father of German Expressionism, Dr. Josef Goebbels, Minister for Public Enlightenment and Propaganda, asked him to be director of the German Dance Stage; Laban therefore opted to stay in Germany. The regime soon turned on Laban, however, when in 1936 he prepared a movement choir of one thousand participants for the opening of the Olympic games. Dr. Goebbels viewed the dress rehearsal and banned the performance, accusing Laban of celebrating the individual. With increasing pressure on him to toe the party line, Laban finally fled Germany in 1937. Sponsored by Mr. and Mrs. Elmhirst of Dartington Hall, Laban arrived in England, where some of the students and teachers from his school, Essen Laban School, had taken refuge. It was during this time that he began his collaborations with Warren Lamb, resulting in the inclusion of **Shape** with the original three concepts of LMA: **Body**, **Effort**, and **Space**. Subsequently, during World War II, Laban was hired by the British government to conduct time and motion studies for the purpose of bringing greater productivity to factory output. Always pragmatic, Laban used this opportunity to further expand the applications of LMA.

In fact, there seems to be no end to the practical applications of Laban's theories. Its plasticity has allowed LMA to survive and grow, accommodating our changing world and many professional needs. While he used dance as a way of exploring and developing his theories, he never intended LMA to be just for dancers. Laban's ninety-seven published books and articles are impressive in their scope, and they contribute to the breadth of LMA's applications.

Irmgard Bartenieff applied his theories and concepts to physical and dance therapy, as well as dance ethnology and anthropology. Marion North, who applied LMA to psychology, became a renowned expert on the psychological effects of movement and nonverbal communication. Warren Lamb, Laban's assistant and collaborator in England, worked in business and industry, conducting Action Profiling for job suitability. Janet Hamburg has successfully applied LMA in her coaching of professional and Olympic athletes, and her most current applications include individuals with Parkinson's disease. Of extreme interest is the work of Martha Davis, who was a consultant for the United States government. She used LMA to analyze the movement signatures of notables such as Saddam Hussein to establish evidence of truth and lying. On the lighter side, during my studies at the Laban/Bartenieff Institute of Movement Studies (LIMS), I met a woman working for the Disney Corporation who was attempting to computerize LMA as a means to create more expressive cartoon characters.

I believe that these and many more applications were born out of Laban's commitment to education. Laban poured his energies into educating everyone who would listen: dancers, actors, occupational and physical therapists, grade-school teachers, psychotherapists, blue-collar workers, architects, athletes, and painters. Consequently, the material was interpreted and used by a wide range of students and Laban openly encouraged and supported this diversity.

Regardless of his rich legacy of movement theory and application, during his life he struggled to make a living. His efforts were complicated by the fact that he was often afflicted with ill health and bouts of depression. However, because of his pragmatic sense of survival, undying curiosity, and dedication to movement, Laban managed to continue to write, lecture, choreograph, and teach up until his death on July 1, 1958, at age seventy-nine.

Irmgard Bartenieff

Irmgard Bartenieff (1900–81) led a multifaceted career in movement as a dancer, teacher, physical therapist, dance ethnologist, notation expert, and movement therapist. With an insatiable appetite for learning, she was a lifelong student of art, music, and archeology.

In 1925, Bartenieff began her studies with Rudolf Laban. His theories and practices had a profound impact on her life and work. In addition to studying with Laban, she and her husband, Michail Bartenieff, toured Germany with their dance company, Romantisches Tanztheatre Bartenieff, until 1932. Both her studies and the tours were interrupted by the rise of Nazi Germany. Subsequently, she emigrated to the United States and brought Laban's teachings with her. In the U.S., she taught dance and began to explore the healing potential in movement. Inspired by the work she had done her last year in Germany (helping dancers with breathing issues and tension), Bartenieff began her formal studies to become a physical therapist, and graduated from New York University in 1943. Subsequently, she became an expert in polio rehabilitation and was the chief physical therapist for Polio Services at Willard Park Hospital in New York until 1953. During this time she began to develop the body re-education system now known as Bartenieff Fundamentals, which integrates LMA, kinesiology, and motor development.

In 1950, she visited Laban in England and, thereafter for three consecutive summers, she studied with Warren Lamb (Laban's assistant and collaborator), then briefly again with Laban before he died. The three of them together focused on **Effort**, and this study became a primary influence on her continued work in physical therapy, dance therapy, and movement research. With her interest in dance training reignited, she offered classes using LMA at the Turtle Bay Music School in New York and continued to develop what would become Bartenieff Fundamentals by working with injured and overworked professional dancers. From 1954-57, she worked as a physical therapist at Blythedale Children's Hospital.

Bartenieff's interest in the relationship between movement and psychology led to a ten-year position (1957-67) as a dance therapist and research assistant at the Day Hospital, a psychiatric hospital connected with the Albert Einstein College of Medicine. During 1964–66, her inquisitiveness about the ethnology of movement resulted in a collaboration with Albert Lomax (renowned folklorist and musicologist) on the Choreometrics Project, which studied dance and work movement around the world.

In 1978, Bartenieff founded the Laban/Bartenieff Institute of Movement Studies in New York City, where she continued to teach until her death in 1981. Her signature work, *Body Movement: Coping with the Environment*, was published the year before she died.

How to Use This Book

"My motto was always to keep swinging. Whether I was in a slump or feeling badly or having trouble off the field, the only thing to do was keep swinging."
–Hank Aaron (Baseball Hall of Fame)

This is a book that you read and *do*. The exercises and explorations progress from beginner through to advanced. At each level, the practices focus on both individual and partner work. The intermediate and advanced explorations include group work as well.

To avoid confusion, please take note that many of the italicized, capitalized, or bolded words are translations from the German words originally used by Laban to describe movement. They may also represent "newer" vocabulary that has been added by the Laban community for the purpose of expanding and clarifying the language of movement. In some instances, the LMA language describes what the body is actually doing, such as *widening* or *narrowing*. Other words describe a concept or theory, such as **Effort** and **Shape**. You will also see specific words such as "space" written in several ways. For instance, written as "space," the word refers to our generic understanding of the word. Capitalized (Space) refers to one of the Effort Factors and bolded (**Space**) refers to the concepts and theories of Space Harmony. Additionally, some of the speech terms describing consonants in chapter 9 are also italicized for ease of presentation; these italicizations do not indicate a relationship to the language of movement.

You do not need to read the entire book from beginning to end before starting your journey. It would be beneficial, however, to approach the book sequentially, one chapter at a time. This is to assure that you will have the physical and vocal experience from the previous chapters to fuel your understanding of the new material, both intellectually and physically. The lessons in this book take time and dedicated practice to absorb. If you follow the guidelines for practice, then the benefits to your functional skills and expressive availability will be assured.

You also do not have to do the whole book to gain benefit. If you are a beginner and want just the basics, Level One will provide them and you can stop there. The basics will enable you to improve your functional skill level, which in turn will reveal your expressiveness with more ease. If you are advanced in the area of voice and speech and have an embarrassment of riches relative to breath, tone, range, and articulation exercises, then incorporate your own amalgam of exercises with the suggested movement explorations. This book is not meant to *prescribe* but rather to *inspire* readers to use what they know in a new way and, hopefully, to learn something perhaps unexpected in the process. It is important to note that there is nothing magical about the exercises that I have devised. They are simply the results of my teaching and coaching experiences and they work for my students and me. In that spirit, they are suggestions. It is my hope that you will play with my suggestions and also devise exercises and explorations of your own.

At the start of each chapter, I have referenced a time frame for understanding and embodying the contents of the chapter. The time frames apply only if your practice is consistent. However, the time frames can only be approximations, as each reader will come with his or her unique background and strengths relative to previous training and experience. Additionally, like Hank Aaron, each reader will have a highly individualized relationship to the concept of practice. In this age of immediate gratification that virtually eliminates the need for "process" on the part of the consumer, I felt it would be beneficial to offer practical and feasible frameworks to ensure that the *expectations* of the reader and the *results* of the practice bear a relationship to each other. Each time frame includes a warm-up and review of previous lessons. You can draw on the previous exercises and explorations to warm up for the next adventure. A good warm-up prepares the body, voice, mind, and spirit for the task that is about to be undertaken. As you progress through the book, you will attain an embarrassment of riches relative to warm-up material.

Have at it! Enjoy the process and the results will follow.

Laban Basics

Laban Movement Analysis (LMA) is a theoretical framework for observing movement.
Major Themes: Mobility/Stability, Function/Expression, Exertion/Recuperation, Inner/Outer

- Mobility/Stability can be described as the "wings and roots" of movement. The body is always engaged along the continuum between stability and mobility during both movement and stillness.

- Function/Expression together create meaning in movement. Due to their symbiotic relationship, the functional aspects of movement have expressive consequences, and expressive movements have functional consequences.

- Exertion/Recuperation describes the natural ebb and flow between work and relaxation, which allow the body to become restored. They also refer to the body's natural inclination to seek relief from one quality or type of movement by engaging in its opposite.

- Inner/Outer governs the motivational aspects of movement. Inner impulses can manifest in an outer form. Conversely, stimuli from the outside will affect one's inner experience.

Major Concepts: Body, Effort, Shape, Space, Relationship (BESS-R)
Body represents the physical instrument and provides the mechanics for voice, speech, and movement.

Effort describes the manifestation of moment-to-moment impulses that relate to feelings or emotions. **Effort** reveals one's dynamic attitude toward investing in the Effort Factors called Time, Weight, Space, and Flow. Each Effort Factor contains two *effort elements* and each is revealed along a continuum.

Effort Factors:
> Time: *effort elements = quick ↔ sustained*
> Weight: *effort elements = strong ↔ light*
> Space: *effort elements = direct ↔ indirect*
> Flow: *effort elements = bound ↔ free*

Shape reveals and describes emotional investment. The changing shape of the body may be in relationship to the self or to the environment.

- Still Shape Forms are the most basic forms the body can make and include Pin, Ball, Wall, and Screw.

- Modes of Shape Change reveal how one feels about the changing shape of one's body. The Modes are designated as Shape Flow, Arc-like Directional, Spoke-like Directional, and Carving.

  ○ Shape Flow begins with the breath and is the underlying support for all movement.

  ○ Arc-like and Spoke-like Directional Movement are goal oriented. They form a bridge between oneself and the environment.

  ○ Carving describes cooperation, adaptability, and molding, for the purpose of accommodating the environs.

Space describes where the body moves in relation to the environment.

- Kinesphere is the distance around the body that the limbs can reach without taking a step.

- Pathways of the Kinesphere are called Central, Peripheral, and Transverse (CPT). They reveal one's personal kinesphere.

  ○ Central Pathway shows the distance between center and edge of your personal kinesphere.

  ○ Peripheral Pathway shows the circumference (outer edge) of your kinesphere.

  ○ Transverse Pathway reveals the volume of space within the kinesphere by winding between the center and the outer edge.

- Spatial Pulls act on the body to propel it on a trajectory in space.

- Spatial Intention clarifies the goal of the movement and, therefore, the intention of the body in relation to space.

Space Harmony is a theory that describes the relationships produced by the body as it responds to the *spatial pulls* inherent in nature. Each point in space has a corresponding affinity to **Body**, **Effort**, and **Shape**. As you connect the points through movement, you create a dynamic relationship among the components, much like striking a chord on the piano.

- A Laban Scale is a specific movement sequence that reflects the most efficient and expressive pathway between each point of a platonic solid. The platonic solids that Laban considered are the cube, the octahedron, the icosahedron, and the dodecahedron. Laban's Scales are a means whereby the mover "connects the dots" in space, which in turn allows the mover to capitalize on the possibility of harmonizing internally and externally with the universe.

Relationship is the interplay among **Body**, **Effort**, **Shape**, and **Space**.

Anatomy Illustrations

Front of Body

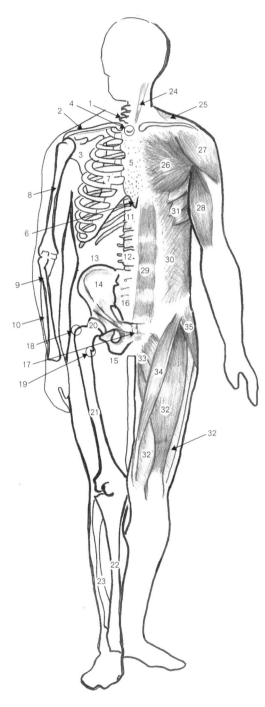

Bones
1. Cervical vertebrae
2. Clavicle
3. Scapula
4. Sternoclavicular notch
5. Sternum
6. Xiphoid process
7. Ribs
8. Humerus
9. Radius
10. Ulna
11. Thoracic vertebrae
12. Lumbar vertebrae
13. Iliac crest
14. Ilium
15. Ischial tuberosity (sits-bone)
16. Sacrum
17. Pubis
18. Greater trochanter
19. Lesser trochanter
20. Femoral joint
21. Femur
22. Tibia
23. Fibia

Muscles
24. Sternocleidomastoideus
25. Trapezius
26. Pectoralis major
27. Deltoids
28. Biceps
29. Rectus abdominis
30. External obliques
31. Serratus anterior
32. Quadriceps
33. Adductor group
34. Sartorius
35. Tensor fasciae latae

Illustration 1

Back of Body

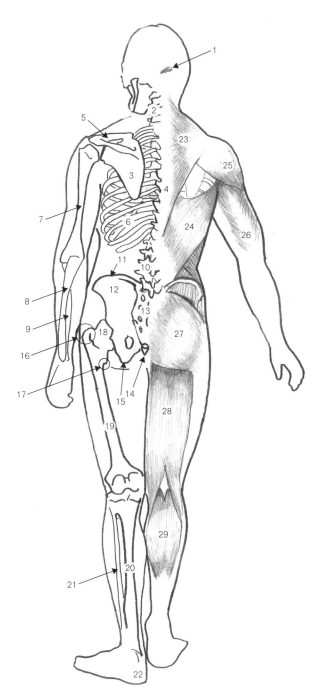

Bones
1. Occipital protuberance (occiput)
2. Cervical vertebrae
3. Scapula
4. Thoracic vertebrae
5. Clavicle
6. Ribs
7. Humerus
8. Ulna
9. Radius
10. Lumbar vertebrae
11. Iliac crest
12. Ilium
13. Sacrum
14. Coccyx
15. Ischial tuberosity (sits-bone)
16. Greater trochanter
17. Lesser trochanter
18. Femoral joint
19. Femur
20. Tibia
21. Fibia
22. Heel

Muscles
23. Trapezius
24. Latissimus dorsi
25. Deltoids
26. Triceps
27. Gluteus maximus
28. Hamstrings
29. Calf muscles

Illustration 2

#3: Spine

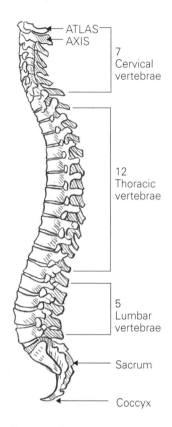

ATLAS
AXIS

7
Cervical
vertebrae

12
Thoracic
vertebrae

5
Lumbar
vertebrae

Sacrum

Coccyx

#4: Pelvic Bowl

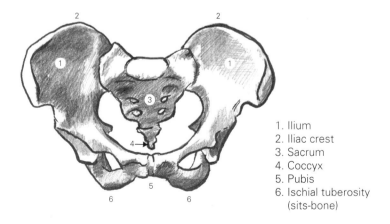

1. Ilium
2. Iliac crest
3. Sacrum
4. Coccyx
5. Pubis
6. Ischial tuberosity
   (sits-bone)

Illustrations 3 and 4

#5

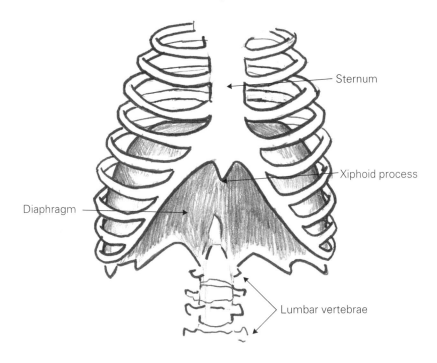

Sternum

Xiphoid process

Diaphragm

Lumbar vertebrae

#6

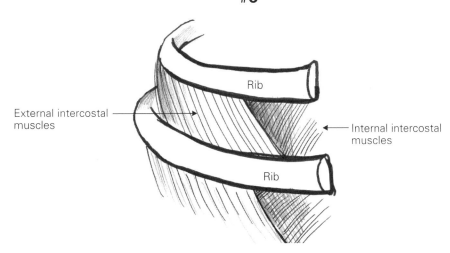

Rib

External intercostal
muscles

Internal intercostal
muscles

Rib

Illustrations 5 and 6

#7-10: Stomach Muscles

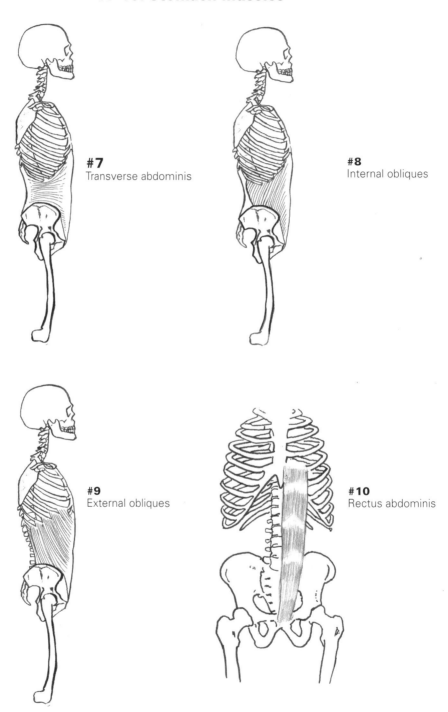

#7
Transverse abdominis

#8
Internal obliques

#9
External obliques

#10
Rectus abdominis

Illustrations 7, 8, 9, and 10

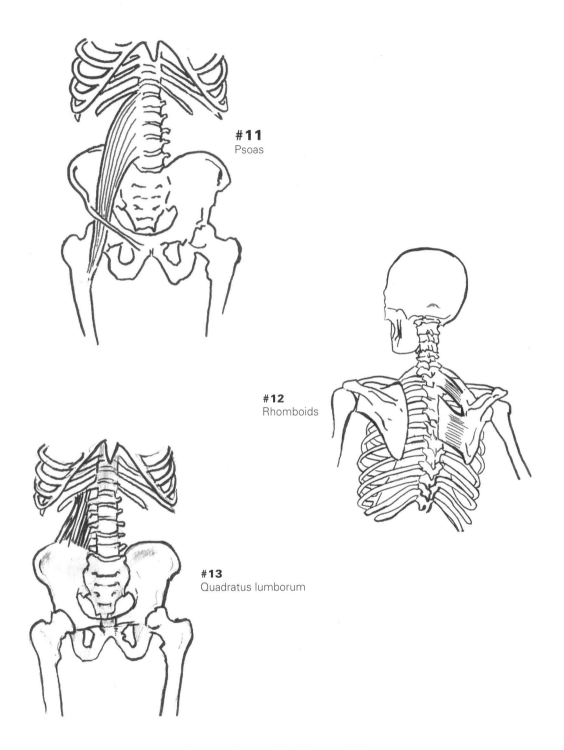

#11
Psoas

#12
Rhomboids

#13
Quadratus lumborum

Illustrations 11, 12, and 13

Head and Neck

#14
1. Temporal bones
2. Temporomandibular joint
3. Superior maxillary bone
4. Inferior maxillary bone (mandible)
5. Hyoid bone
6. Thyroid cartilage (Adam's apple)
7. Occipital bone

#15 and 16
Depiction of muscles that connect the hyoid bone to the thyroid cartilage, head, jaw, chest, and scapula.

#17
Masseter muscle

Illustrations 14, 15, 16, and 17

Anatomy for Speech

1. Lips*
2. Teeth*
3. Alveolar ridge*
4. Hard palate*
5. Nasal passages
6. Soft palate*
7. Uvula
8. Tongue*
9. Epiglottis
10. Vocal folds
11. Trachea
12. Esophagus
13. Spine
14. Mandible*
*Articulators

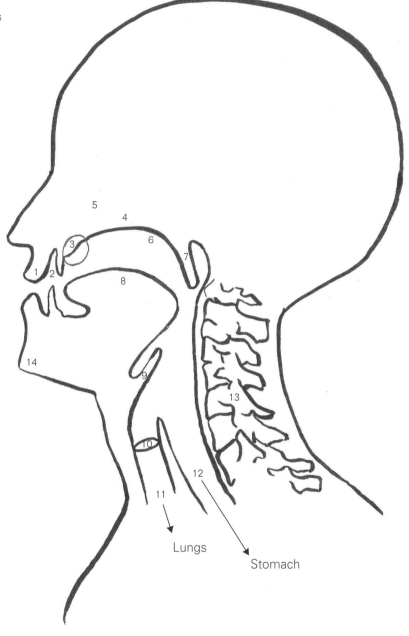

Illustration 18

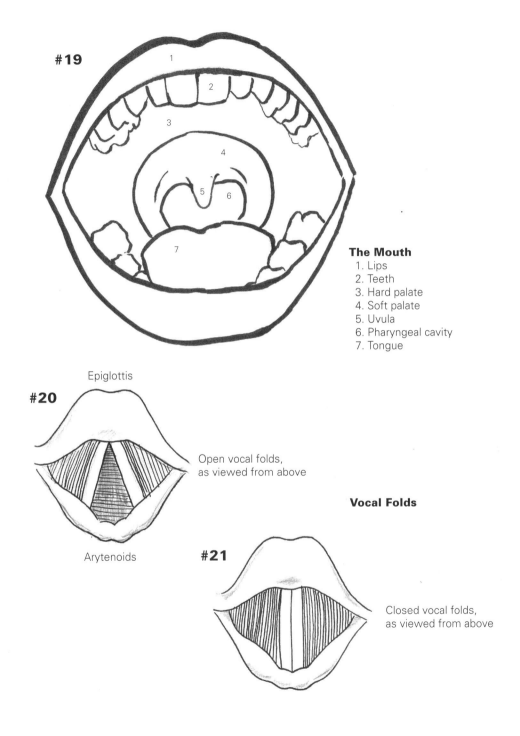

#19

The Mouth
1. Lips
2. Teeth
3. Hard palate
4. Soft palate
5. Uvula
6. Pharyngeal cavity
7. Tongue

#20

Epiglottis

Open vocal folds,
as viewed from above

Arytenoids

Vocal Folds

#21

Closed vocal folds,
as viewed from above

Illustrations 19, 20, and 21

Level One

"Simple movements require little bodily effort and allow great mental control. Large, complicated movements require great physical effort and allow little mental activity."

–Rudolf Laban

CHAPTER ONE

Breath: Inspiration for Creative Activity
Time Frame: Four one-hour sessions

Your journey toward the integration of voice, speech, and movement begins with the breath. The quality of your connection to the breath affects the quality of all that you do and say. Breath connection is the awareness of and the allowance for interplay between the body and the impulse to breathe for both functional and expressive purposes. Breath connection is the underlying current of support without which the creative use of voice, speech, and movement would not be possible.

Sound begins when the pressure of the outgoing breath induces oscillation of the vocal folds, which causes the air to vibrate as it passes through the folds. The vibrations of the outgoing breath then strike the hard surfaces of the mouth and throat (pharyngeal cavity), creating resonance. The resonance vibrates the air outside the body, thus spreading the sound into the environs. Words are formed when the articulators shape the resonance as it passes through the throat and mouth. Likewise, the breath initiates movement of the body, which "speaks" through the articulations of the limbs and trunk. To some degree, this process is purely functional, meaning that the *mechanics* of breathing, speaking, and moving must reflect a harmonious relationship among the muscles responsible for the task. You will not realize your creative potential unless your functional skills can support your expressive impulses. However, the reverse is also true. As you explore the expressive powers of sound and movement, you will also be improving your functionality. To maximize your potential, function and expression must be attended to consciously before they can be restored to their rightful place in your unconscious.

Perhaps it is helpful to think of movement, voice, and speech as siblings who were separated in early childhood and whose mother is breath. Movement is the oldest, with voice close on its heels. The youngest is speech, which developed through the evolution and refinement of the larynx and articulators. This evolutionary process resulted in the most flexible mechanism for making sound among all of Earth's creatures. Of the siblings, it is the middle child, *voice*, that remains the most mysterious because it is the least concrete. For that reason, let's take a look at the properties that give voice its mystique.

The sound of your voice radiates beyond your body's corporeal boundaries. You cannot propel your body, without serious consequences, through walls, off rooftops, or instantaneously up six flights of stairs. But the voice can and does make such leaps. It continues its flight into space, where the corporeal body cannot go. The voice can shrink to travel through the narrowest of passages or expand to fill an amphitheatre of two thousand seats. Once set free from the body, voice is unhindered by joints, bones, ligaments, and muscles and, therefore, has a potential for flexibility that the body can never achieve. While producing sound is as much a muscular action as reaching for a fork, vocal resonance extends beyond the muscular initiation using the oral (mouth) and architectural space (room, theatre, out-of-doors) as sounding boards. The resulting vibrations produce waves of sound that radiate into the environment much like the disturbance that results by throwing a stone into still water or the trace lines of a Fourth of July sparkler waving in the night. And it all begins with the breath and the impulse to breathe.

Along with digestion, the breath is the deepest exchange between our inner and outer environment, and vice versa. And, like digestion, it is not an option. The functional reality is that we must breathe and eat to survive. However, there is also an expressive reality that is encapsulated in the relationship between inspiration and breath. To be inspired is to breathe; to breathe is to be inspired. The breath connection is what keeps us present in the "now," connected in an authentic way to our self and those around us. This connection is essential if the functional and expressive skills of the actor are to be fully developed.

In order to understand how breath connection affects the relationships among movement, voice, and speech, it is necessary to understand a bit of anatomy, beginning with the bony structure. The bones are the least flexible substance in the body and, consequently, they give support and form to our structure, as well as protection for the organs. The bones are connected together by inelastic fibers called ligaments. Muscles move the bones and, in order to do so, they must be attached to the bone in some manner. Tendons fulfill the job of attaching muscles to the bone. Begin to familiarize yourself with the bones and major muscles illustrated in the Anatomy Illustrations. Each of the bones or muscles mentioned in this narrative has a corresponding illustration.

The chief muscle responsible for breathing is the diaphragm, and of secondary importance are the internal and external intercostal muscles that live between the ribs (page 15). The abdominal muscles and the intercostals principally control the release of air from the lungs. The abdominal muscles are composed of the rectus abdominis, internal and external obliques, and the transverse abdominis (page 16).

The appropriate use of the muscles for efficient breathing is a functional consideration. However, there is an interdependency between function and expression. When you are working on improving your functional skills for speaking, singing, or moving, you are also enhancing your expressive potential and vice versa. Breath initiations that support expressive activities, as well as those for purely functional purposes, are born out of *impulses*. It is important to note that one of the hallmarks of an excellent actor is the ability to *act on impulse*. Acting on impulse is the instantaneous whole-body response to a *need*. In life, we constantly have impulses. Some impulses we recognize and act upon and some we don't. We have an itch; we scratch. We feel hungry; we eat. We see an item at the register; suddenly we buy it. Retailers make considerable money on impulse purchases. However, many of our impulses are thwarted or action is delayed because we don't recognize the impulse or, if recognized, we interrupt the impulse with "thinking." Thank goodness! We can't just go around willy-nilly indulging every impulse or we may punch out the next person who crosses us. That said, the skill of acting requires less censorship than real life and, therefore, acting on impulse is desired. To accomplish acting on impulse, the actor needs to quiet the critical-thinking portions of the brain and "just do it." Of course, this is a bit of an exaggeration because the actor must ultimately act within the logic of the character and the given circumstances, and not cause anyone real harm. Acting is, after all, pretend and not real life. On the other hand, whether on stage or in real life, fulfilling the impulse to breathe for the functional purpose of staying alive does not require careful consideration. To breathe or not to breathe; that is not the question. On a practical level, we keep breathing for the obvious reason that we'd rather not die. Even if we hold our breath until we pass out, barring any extenuating circumstances, the body overrides our will and starts us up again. Breathing is organic and spontaneous. We do it without thinking. In order to unite the functional and the expressive impulses of breath together, we will first explore a series of exercises that promote harmony among the muscles responsible for breathing. Functional awareness and activities that emphasize efficiency will help you develop more expressivity.

Through the exercises, you will explore how you may thwart your impulses during expressive activities due to heretofore unnoticed, inefficient functional habits. Dysfunctional habits are body-level inefficiencies whose inceptions can be traced to physical and/or psychological issues. These inefficiencies may cause you not to recognize your impulses or, if recognized, to distrust them. Therefore, to develop recognition and trust of your impulses, you will begin with the breath. You will bring the activity called breathing into your consciousness, examine your personal relationship to the breath, identify habits that may be inefficient, practice new possibilities, and (ultimately) return the process of breathing to its home in the unconscious. This is a big journey and the goal is to recognize, trust, and act on your impulses without judgment. Identifying and fulfilling the impulse to breathe will ultimately support you both functionally and expressively.

The impulse to breathe initiates a contraction of the external intercostal muscles, thus causing the rib cage to widen and lift as the diaphragm contracts downward toward the abdominal cavity. The diaphragm's fervent wish is to return to its resting position as soon as possible. Consequently, the abdominal muscles pull in toward the spine, causing viscera of the abdomen to press up on the diaphragm, which puts pressure on the lungs. Secondarily, as the internal intercostals contract, they pull the rib cage in adding to the pressure on the lungs. These activities cause an exhalation. When there is an impulse to make sound or movement, the abdominal muscles and the intercostals work together to help the diaphragm resist returning to its resting position too quickly, thus allowing for a sustained release of breath. It is on this sustained release that we can phonate and/or produce a phrase of movement. Of course, you can also inhale and exhale purely from a conscious control of the muscles. But if the breath is to serve an expressive purpose, it is crucial that how and when you use the breath is a response to the impulse to express oneself moment to moment through movement and sound. The quality of the breath connection is governed by the functional efficiency of the muscles involved as they respond to the impulse to express oneself.

As you work through the following exercises, pause and use the Anatomy Illustrations section to locate the bony landmarks and muscles as they are mentioned. For some readers, it may be important to understand the anatomy as the exercises are explored; others may prefer to work with images. Keep in mind that imagery based in some "body reality" is often the most potent. While it is not necessary to know the anatomy to get some benefit from the exercises, I do encourage you to "get the lay of your land" by consulting the Anatomy Illustrations.

Breathing through the Still Shape Forms

The basic concepts of Laban Movement Analysis (LMA) are **Body**, **Effort**, **Shape**, and **Space** (BESS). Your journey toward the integration of voice, speech, and movement will begin with **Shape**.

Shape is the link between **Body** and **Space**, because it reflects and projects our inner conditions to the outside world. **Shape** is expressed most simply through the Still Shape Forms, the most basic forms that the body can make in stillness. Therefore, it is fitting that our breath, sound, and movement explorations should begin here. During the following exercises, you will not only explore the effect of the Still Shape Forms on your breath, body, and voice; you will also explore how the body moves toward and away from these Forms. For our purposes, we will explore four Still Shape Forms: Wall, Ball, Pin, and Screw.

Still Shape Forms

  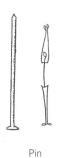 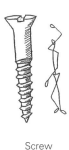

Wall   Ball   Pin   Screw

- Lie on your back in a Wall Shape and feel the bony landmarks in contact with the floor. (In this instance the bony landmarks are heels, sacrum, shoulder blades, and occiput, page 13.)
- As you breathe, notice that the inner architecture of your trunk changes shape with the breath.
- Observe that the body subtly *shrinks* toward and *grows* away from center (navel) with each breath.

The subtle movement of the breath and body *growing* and *shrinking* from center out toward your limbs and from your limbs toward your center is your Shape Flow. Shape Flow is the term that refers to the flexible underlying support for breath, sound, and movement. The action of the breath drawing the limbs toward your navel (*shrinking*) and moving them out again (*growing*) is called Cellular Breathing a term coined by Bonnie Bainbridge Cohen and described in Linda Hartley's book *Wisdom of the Body Moving: An Introduction to Body-Mind Centering*.

- Imagine you are a single cell floating on the water. Feel the inner pulse (Shape Flow of the breath) *shrink* and *grow* your cellular self toward and away from the nucleus.
- Encourage more gross body movement by slowly breathing in as fully as you can without creating tension. Allow the subtle feeling of *growing* to radiate through your limbs, producing a Wall Shape.
- On the exhalation, allow the feeling of *shrinking* to produce a Ball Shape.
- Reverse the process. *Grow* toward a Wall Shape on the exhalation and *shrink* toward a Ball Shape on the inhalation.

The Shape Flow of your breath is now supporting you as you move core→distal and distal→core. However, if this feels awkward or unsupported, it is best to imagine you are inhaling and exhaling toward these Shapes rather than pushing the breath or the body to achieve a perfect Wall or Ball Shape. The important thing is to notice how the breath initiates change within the torso and how this change can radiate into the limbs. With practice, the breath will begin to radiate out further and further and the gross Ball and Wall Shapes will appear.

- Begin with Cellular Breathing and let your body evolve with the breath toward Pin and Screw Shapes.
- Move through all four Shapes: Pin, Ball, Wall, and Screw. The order is not important. Let the Shape change on impulse and be aware of how the body is linking one Shape to the next. Do you have a preference for one Shape Form over another?
- Recuperate by lying in a Wall Shape. Observe your breath interacting with your body. How is it different from when you began? How about the rest of your body? Does it still feel engaged? Are you aware of your Shape Flow and the gentle internal inclination toward Cellular Breathing?
- Repeat all the exercises.

As you repeat the exercises the second time, experiment with the concept: The breath shapes the body, and the body shapes the breath. Do not be strict with yourself about having to achieve concise Pin, Ball, Wall, and Screw Shapes. These designations simply represent four of the basic Still Shape Forms of life, but there are many adjustments and combinations possible on these themes. Be playful. If the breath impulse is strong enough, the body will begin to roll over and even move toward standing. With the picture of your skeletal frame in mind, imagine how the relationships among the bones are in constant flux as you move. For now, it is important not to move longer than a single breath can support; therefore, the duration of each movement will vary according to your breath support. At first, you may find you barely have the support for a fully extended Wall or condensed Ball Shape, much less to roll over or come to a standing position. Keep playing and you will eventually find the breath propelling you toward standing.

From Shape to Sound

Through a careful layering of breathing exercises you will, by the end of this chapter, be sounding through the Still Shape Forms. In order to understand how sound is produced, it is important to have a picture of how the interior of the head and throat contribute to resonance. To orient yourself, take a look at the illustrations of the head, neck, and articulators in the Anatomy Illustrations section, pages 18, 19, and 20.

The air passes from the lungs into the trachea and through the vocal folds that are housed in the thyroid cartilage, also known as the Adam's apple. The breath pressure (also called subglottal pressure) that results from controlling the airflow from the abdominals causes the vocal folds to come together. Pitch is the result of breath pressure. A lot of breath pressure results in higher pitches and less breath pressure in lower pitches. As the air begins its passage through the vocal folds, the folds vibrate (oscillate), causing the airflow to vibrate. This vibration of air strikes the pharyngeal cavity (oral passage), producing resonance as the breath stream leaves the mouth. Articulation occurs when we shape the articulators on the breath stream. Remember, all this is set into motion by the impulse to communicate. The quality of the communication is governed by the efficient use of the muscles that control the breath and the articulators. There are several things that may block an efficient response to stimuli. Such blocks include a lack of functional capability, psychological stressors, or a combination of both. The following exercises are a means toward gaining more functional capabilities while learning to help the body manage any stress that may interfere with responding on impulse.

- Lie on your stomach and rest your head on your arms comfortably. From this posture, feel the bony landmarks (pubis, iliac crest, sternum, page 12) in contact with the floor. Can you feel the gentle to-and-fro of your Shape Flow moving in and out from your core?
- Pant like a puppy and feel the movement of the muscles of the abdomen in relation to the floor. It is not your actual diaphragm you feel against the floor, but rather the muscles of the abdomen that help control the diaphragm.
- As you pant, what is the relationship of your back to the ceiling? How do the right and left sides of your torso relate to the walls in the room?

Notice that the entire trunk of the body is engaged with each inhalation and exhalation of breath. We breathe all the way around, not just from back to front. We also breathe up/down and side/side as well. Awareness of how the breath shapes the body is the starting place to understand the internal three-dimensionality of our body and its relationship to movement. The process of breathing is an excellent teacher and guide to our three-dimensional selves.

In the following exercises, you are asked to "suspend" the breath before exhaling. The word "hold" is not used because it can imply aggressive muscular action involved in the activity. Suspending the breath is about waiting for the impulse to exhale. The same can be true for the inhalation. A moment of suspension takes place just before the body recognizes the impulse to breathe in again. This can and should happen imperceptibly but, at first, you may have to be conscious of pausing and listening internally before initiating the inhalation or exhalation. To that end, I will ask you to suspend the breath for ten counts after the inhalation. Of course, counting to ten is artificial, even antithetical to impulsive breathing. However, suspending the breath on a count of ten is included in these exercises as a way to illustrate what it feels like to keep air in the body and not "spill it" all at once.

Some readers may feel the suspension as normal, and others may find it quite uncomfortable. Your reaction to the suspension is dependent upon your personal breathing habits and is worth taking note of for future reference. Regardless of which reader you are, it is important to eventually find the balance between how much breath is suspended in the body and at what rate it must be released as you phonate to meet the demands of the text. And, most of all, it is important to become acquainted with the impulses to breathe for expressive purposes. Once you have sensed the appropriate amount of breath pressure necessary for the given task, any conscious suspension of the breath before a phonation should be eliminated. From then on, the breath is governed solely by the impulse. The following exercises ask you to drop your jaw from the temporomandibular joint (page 18). How you open the mouth is very important. Follow these steps to achieve the mouth posture that represents a *free and open throat.*

- Drop your jaw from the temporomandibular joint. Feel it swing down and slightly back.
- Let your tongue tip rest behind your lower front teeth.
- Feel the soft palate rise slightly as if about to yawn.

Lie on your stomach and support your head on your arms.

- On impulse, breathe in just enough to smell a flower.
- Suspend the breath for ten counts.
- Relax the muscles of the abdomen as you drop your jaw, thus releasing the breath through a free and open throat.
- Repeat the sequence five times.

- On impulse, breathe in just enough to smell a flower.
- Suspend the breath for ten counts.
- Exhale for ten counts on an "FFFF." It is not necessary to use all the breath by the tenth count.
- Release the remainder of the air on a sigh through a free and open throat by relaxing the muscles of the abdomen.
- Repeat ten times.

During the next set of exercises, you will hum. Picture the hum as a train traveling through the inner architecture of your body on an imaginary railroad track of resonance. Perhaps you can even feel the resonance radiating beyond your body into the floor, the walls, the ceiling. Up/down, side/side, and back/forward, the resonance travels into space. The vibrations are actually moving the air and igniting the space three-dimensionally.

- On impulse, breathe in.
- Suspend the breath for ten counts.
- Hum for ten counts.
- Relax the muscles of the abdomen on the tenth count with a free and open throat.
- Repeat ten times on a different pitch each time.
- Recuperate by noting how your face and chest feel after humming.

The final set of exercises asks you to make open-mouth sounds which are called unstructured sounds. Unstructured sounds are primal vocal sounds that reflect our emotional conditions rather than explicit sense and are produced with the articulators mostly in neutral. The intention of an unstructured sound is usually "to get something off one's chest." It is not just sounding for sounding's sake.

- Return to Cellular Breathing.
- Move through the Still Shape Forms and add unstructured sound.
- Recuperate by coming to rest on your back in active stillness.
- Compare how your body and breath feel now as opposed to the beginning of the chapter.

Over the next few days, make several passes at the exercises in this chapter. This is not for the purpose of "getting them right" but to achieve a feeling of ease and physical understanding. The first several times through will be full of stops and starts and referencing the Anatomy Illustrations. But after several passes, you will begin to find a flow and your body and voice will respond to the work organically. Do the exercises, have an experience, and try not to get caught up with "Is this right?" It is in the *doing* that this question will be answered before it is even asked.

CHAPTER TWO

Bartenieff Fundamentals: Fitness that Supports the Actor
Time Frame: Twenty-one one-hour sessions

In our popular culture, there is a tendency to look at the shape of the surface muscles to determine "fitness." We even have pet names for these "fit" muscles. For instance, "six-pack" refers to the rectus abdominis, and huge, hard biceps are called "guns." "Cuts" refer to the indentations on the surface of the body that delineate the muscles, thus producing a sculptured look. However, ironically, muscles can be overdeveloped and, no matter how visually appealing the total effect may be, overdeveloped muscles hinder flexibility and responsiveness to impulse. Instead of focusing on the outer result, the actor needs to begin with the bony structure and become conscious of the muscles closest to the bones—the muscles we can't see. The actor needs to train literally from the inside→out.

Working from the inside→out is a concept familiar to most actors and references how the actor is affected moment to moment by the character's circumstances emotionally and psychologically. This effect then fuels the action of the scene, giving the play a logical progression based on the psychological underpinnings of the characters. For our purposes, however, I am using the term inside→out concretely: inside of the corporeal body to the surface of the corporeal body. Instead of descriptions like "guns" and "six packs," our language for both fitness and to describe an inside→out process is based in Irmgard Bartenieff's Nine Principles. They are: *Breath Support*, *Core Support*, *Spatial Intent*, *Weight Shift*, *Dynamic Alignment*, *Initiation and Sequencing*, *Developmental Patterning*, *Rotary Factor*, and *Effort Intent*. The Nine Principles serve as the central support for her body re-education system, called Bartenieff Fundamentals. We will be exploring the Fundamentals in detail during this chapter, but let us begin with the "spine" of Bartenieff's work, the Nine Principles. The following descriptions of the Principles have been expanded from their original intent to include how they support voice and speech.

Breath Support: Breath Support is the underpinning for all outcomes of movement and voice.

Core Support: Core Support utilizes the deep structures (bones, muscles, and organs) in the body to promote inner→outer connectivity for movement and voice with flexibility and strength.

Spatial Intent: Our intention relative to space organizes the body and voice to move and sound with clarity. It is easy to think of the body as having a destination, but we don't often apply this concept to the voice. The voice is capable of penetrating space, filling it as a whole or pinpointing a destination for the communication.

Weight Shift: Weight Shift supports the ever-changing relationship of the body to the earth. As the body transports through space, it is in constant negotiation with gravity. *Grounding* is another term used frequently to describe this relationship and, likewise, is often used to describe a connected voice. Without a grounded body, the voice will not be an effective communication tool. Weight Shifts are initiated from the body's *center of gravity*, which is the pelvis.

Dynamic Alignment: The alignment of the body and voice relates to the constantly changing relationships of the parts of the body during movement and stillness, as well as sounding and silence. In this instance, body and voice are truly one. If the body is not engaged in the process of Dynamic Alignment, it will be difficult to produce a voice that is centered. Yet even though some muscles are shared in this endeavor, there are also muscles that specifically support the voice. The muscles responsible for voice are in constant flux, adapting and changing in response to the environment, both inner and outer. If this fluid adaptive process is not present, the body and voice will become fixed and rigid. A rigid result is counterproductive to the goal of staying open, connected, and responsive to the impulses.

Initiation and Sequencing: This is another principle that unites the voice and body as one entity. As the movement or sound is initiated, a sequence of neuromuscular firings begins and kinetic chains of events take place within the body and radiate out into the environment, thus contributing to the outcome of movement and sound.

Developmental Patterning: This principle promotes the awareness of our pattern of development from birth to adulthood. How the body develops from crawling to standing to walking is mirrored in our vocal development, which includes maturing from gurgling, cooing, and crying to more refined and varied vocal production, eventually consummating in precise speech.

Rotary Factor: This principle promotes stability and mobility, resulting in the full range possible for movement and sound. Rotation requires deep articulation of the muscles around the joints to provide stability, from which the voice can benefit. Relative to mobility, through rotation we gain access to three-dimensional space. This principle is perhaps more elusive than the previous ones because the voice is seldom discussed as having a three-dimensional potential. Because we are influenced by the location and shape of the mouth, we tend to think of the voice as only shooting forward into space. By the end of this chapter, however, you will have experienced the voice responding to the Rotary Factor as it twists, turns, and spirals into the environment.

Effort Intent: This is what actors live for: the emotional/psychological connection that motivates the movement and sound moment to moment. Effort Intent can reveal a feeling or mood within an individual or fill an activity with specific intentions relative to **Effort**. In the early chapters, you will explore from the outside→in and discover how movement and sound affect qualitative changes in your emotional conditions and intentions. In later chapters, you will move and sound from an *intention* (inside→out), which affects qualitative changes in your movement and sound.

While these principles give us the marriage contract between body and voice, we still need the practical *fundamental* means by which we bring them into union with one another. However, before we discuss the *how*, let's take a brief look at the *why*. Why is it desirable to begin with the muscles closest to our bony structure? Here is an example. Look at the illustration of the head and neck in the Anatomy Illustrations section and locate the hyoid bone and the thyroid cartilage on page 18. There are several muscles that serve as attachments to and from the hyoid bone. The muscles of the hyoid bone attach into the skull, lower jaw, thyroid cartilage, tongue, clavicle, and underneath the shoulder blades. This tiny floating bone, with its close proximity to the larynx (which houses the vocal folds and includes the thyroid cartilage), carries significant responsibility for supporting a free and open voice. Any excessive tensions in the attaching muscles will certainly result in a constricted sound. Additionally, it is important to recognize that the tongue is a massive articulator and one of the strongest muscles in the body proportional to its size. If it isn't free and flexible, not only will the tone be less open and expressive, but clear articulation will also be hindered. For these same reasons, it is also important that your lower jawbone (mandible) swings down and back with ease. Some of the mechanisms that promote freedom of the tongue and jaw are deep within the neck and not easily palpated by the fingers. Consequently, we need exercises that will "massage" the muscles and ligaments related to the hyoid bone and thyroid cartilage so they can respond without inhibition to the impulse to speak. I have used the hyoid bone and the thyroid cartilage as examples of the necessity to work from the inside→out, but this concept expands to include "massaging" muscles close to your bony structure throughout the entire body.

For the purpose of articulating and training the muscles closest to the bones, as well as building a relationship between the body/voice and the Nine Principles, we will be focusing on the Bartenieff Fundamentals. The exercises will help you identify where you hold excessive tensions and, with practice, these same exercises will educate your body to release these tensions.

There are six basic Fundamentals: Thigh Lift, Pelvic Forward Shift, Pelvic Lateral Shift, Body Half, Diagonal Knee Drop, and Arm Circles. In addition to the Basic Six, what follows are adaptations that expand on them. Before we begin, I recommend that you refer to the Anatomy Illustrations and familiarize yourself with the locations and names of the bones and muscles. Continue to reference the Illustrations, as needed, throughout this chapter.

I suggest that you work through these exercises slowly, over the span of several weeks. Let your familiarity with each Fundamental grow over time, thus honoring your body's attention span. During your formal education, you were groomed toward a high level of mental concentration, absorbing information through your eyes and ears while your body passively sat at a desk. Consequently, unless you are a trained athlete, you probably need to gradually build your body's ability to concentrate on and learn through movement. Because your learning modalities may have been physically passive up to this point, it is possible that the intellectual part of your brain has at least a twelve-year head start on your "body intelligence." Therefore, be patient and kind to yourself while you attempt to close the gap.

In preparation for the first exercise in this series, lie on your back and identify the bony landmarks that are resting on the floor. Feel where the spine touches the floor. Because of the natural curve in the lumbar and cervical vertebrae, they both arch slightly away from the floor. With your fingers, feel where the femoral head of your leg joins the pelvis. This is a ball-and-socket joint that allows for great mobility, including rotation. Initiate movement in the femoral joints and observe any subsequent movement in the rest of the body. Don't be careful about this; enjoy the mobility this joint promotes and let the rest of your body go along for the ride.

Frog Legs
(Aerial View)

FROG LEGS
Principles: Breath Support, Core Support, Initiation and Sequencing, Developmental Patterning, Spatial Intent, Rotary Factor (in the femoral joint), Effort Intent (unstructured sound)

Lie on the floor in a Wall Shape. Imagine that you are lying in warm sand and exhale as you draw a diagonal line in the sand with the outside edge of your left foot and heel toward your sits-bone. The act of moving from straight to bent is called *flexion*. Inhale as the heel initiates lengthening the leg again. The act of moving from bent to straight is called *extension*. Be mindful of the fold that is occurring in the femoral joint while you alternate right foot/left foot and then both together. Keep in mind that the heels are moving toward the sits-bones and *not* each other.

After several repetitions, reverse the breath pattern. For instance, inhale on the flexion and exhale on the extension, or exhale on both the flexion and extension. It is important to vary the breath organization so that you discover your personal preferences and explore other possibilities. What happens if you do not initiate the movement from the heels, but rather from the femoral joint? The key to expanding our expressive potential is becoming "unstuck" from our habitual patterns.

Now add unstructured sound to each flexion and extension. In this chapter, unstructured sound will be our practical means for revealing Effort Intent through the voice. The intention of an unstructured sound is usually "to get something off one's chest." It is not just sounding for sounding's sake. While Frog Legs probably will not produce a strong emotional response, you nevertheless are still a sentient being, even if the emotional connection is subtle.

PELVIC ROCK

Principles: Breath Support, Core Support, Initiation and Sequencing, Developmental Patterning, Effort Intent (unstructured sound)

Young children tend to discover the Pelvic Rock on their own, no instruction needed. Pelvic Rock is a movement that promotes self-comfort because it quiets our inner chaos with a gentle rhythmic undulation of the spine, thereby promoting the release of extraneous tensions throughout the body.

With both heels drawn toward the sits-bones as in Frog Legs, roll your feet from their outside edges until the bottom of your feet are planted on the floor. Make sure your heels are aligned with your sits-bones. Place your arms just below shoulder height and a bit away from the body with your palms up. From now on, we will refer to this as the Starting Position. Keep your feet stable and firmly planted on the floor.

Pelvic Rock
Starting Position
(Aerial View)

The Pelvic Rock can be initiated in two ways: 1) from your feet with a push/pull motion of the bottom of the feet in relation to the floor, or 2) from your hips by rocking on your sacrum and coccyx. Regardless of the approach, the rocking motion travels up the spine through the chest, and into the head. Consequently, your head will nod up and down, as if gesturing "yes." The bony landmarks on which you are rocking are the sacrum, shoulder blades, and occiput. Allow the head to nod as a result of the pelvic rock. Do not *make* your head nod. If your head does not nod spontaneously, then you are short-circuiting the wave from the pelvis into the head somewhere along the way. The first place to check for tension or restriction is the breath. Observe your breath. If you are holding or impeding your breath at any point, the spine will not respond to the rock fluidly.

Once the head is bobbing freely and the breath is not constricted, it is time to add sound. While rocking, let the outgoing breath become an unstructured sound. Adding sound will help you diagnose any additional areas of tension that prevent a free voice. The sounds will bobble up and down with the head and never feel caught or held in the throat. In fact, you will sound like a child enjoying her undulating sounds as she indulges in the rocking motion. On a functional level, the Pelvic Rock helps the release of unrestricted and flexible sounds because it massages the deep muscles in the throat while directing the whole body toward a fuller head-tail connection.

LATERAL PELVIC SHIFT

Principles: Breath Support, Core Support, Spatial Intent, Weight Shift, Rotary Factor (in a minor way and related to the femoral joint), Effort Intent

Lateral Pelvic Shift
(Aerial View)

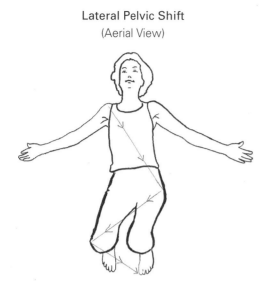

This exercise requires lateral weight shifts and, consequently, is a preparation for walking forward, walking backward, and sidestepping.

Lie on the floor in the Starting Position. Picture your spine and the femoral heads in the socket joints of the pelvis. With your fingers, locate your greater trochanters protruding from the sides of your femurs (pages 12 and 13). Elevate the spine *very slightly* off the floor, keep the pelvis level, exhale, and soften the abdomen as you direct your greater trochanter on your left side toward the wall. This will cause a slight rotation of the femoral heads in the socket joints. Be careful not to twist the spine or hike the hip toward the ribs. Lower your spine down gently and feel the slight diagonal pulls from shoulder to hip, hip to knee, and knee to foot. Shift back to center and rest. Repeat the process on the right.

Imagine that sound can emanate from your greater trochanters and coccyx as you shift. When you are center, imagine the coccyx releasing the sound. When you shift to the right or left, imagine that the sound is emanating from the right or left greater trochanter. How does the image of emanating your voice from these bony landmarks affect your sound? Take the time to rest in each location and feel how the relationships among parts of the bony structure change with each shift.

PELVIC FORWARD SHIFT
Principles: Breath Support, Core Support,
Spatial Intent, Weight Shift, Effort Intent

This exercise teaches you how to initiate advancing and retreating from the pelvis and is a preparation for moving efficiently to a standing position from either sitting or lying down. In this exercise, you are shifting your weight forward and back. The principal players in this move are the hamstrings, abdominal muscles, the pelvic floor, and to some degree the psoas. Review these and the spine in the Anatomy Illustrations section, pages 12, 13, 14, 16, and 17.

Pelvic Forward Shift

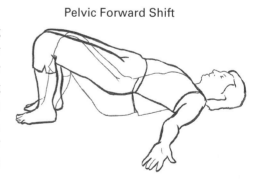

Return to the Starting Position. Picture the length of the spine between the occiput and the coccyx. Visualize your next breath traveling along this length. On your next exhalation, allow your abdominals to relax toward the spine as you press your feet into the floor, and direct your exhalation and pubis to the place where the ceiling and the wall meet. *Word of caution: As your spine rises and your pelvis shifts toward your feet, do not let your knees go past your toes.* If you are connected to your breath and working efficiently, you will feel your hamstrings engage and your femoral joint open as your spine shifts forward and up. Your *spatial intention* (forward and up) helps to shift your weight onto your feet while your shoulders remain on the floor. To return to the Starting Position, reverse the action.

The Forward Pelvic Shift causes the femoral joint to open and fold in the same way needed for advancing and retreating, or moving efficiently from sitting to standing. As you practice, take care not to arch your back or roll the spine to come up or down. To make sure you are shifting and not rolling, place one hand on the sternoclavicular notch and the other hand on your pubis (page 12). Can you keep this distance constant as you move into the forward up position and down again?

When the Forward Pelvic Shift becomes easy, add unstructured sound to each of the shifts. To find support for the Forward Pelvic Shift with sound, put your attention on the femoral joint, the hamstrings, the psoas, the gluteus, and your pelvic floor. To keep the sound open and free, it is crucial that you do not harden the abdominal muscles by pushing them out on the exertion. Although it may be counterintuitive at first, allow the abdominal muscles to relax toward your spine as you exhale and shift. In addition to the abdominal muscles, it is equally important to keep the lumbar region of the spine and the gluteus as relaxed as possible. Because this is an exercise that taxes the hamstrings, limit the number of repetitions to avoid overworking them. Excessive tensions in any of the areas mentioned are counterproductive to developing both efficient movement and clear, unobstructed sound.

SPINAL SEQUENCING
Principle: Breath Support, Core Support, Spatial Intent, Initiation and Sequencing, Weight Shift, Effort Intent

Spinal Sequencing is an excellent recuperation from the Forward Pelvic Shift. It changes the direction of the pelvis from toward the feet to over the head. Unlike the Forward Shift, Spinal Sequencing is a roll-up/roll-down movement, which allows for a shortening of the distance between the pubis and the sternoclavicular notch. This means the rectus abdominis will contract and then lengthen during the exercise and your weight, which is initially distributed along the floor, will shift onto your shoulders.

Lie on the floor in the Starting Posture. Place one hand on the sternoclavicular notch and the other hand on your pubis. As you exhale, begin to roll your spine up from the coccyx one vertebra at a time and direct the pubis toward the wall beyond your head. As you proceed, feel your weight shift toward your shoulders. On your next exhalation, roll down vertebra by vertebra until your back is resting on the floor. As you roll up and down, feel the distance between your hands shorten and lengthen.

Now challenge yourself to vary the breath patterns. By that I mean breathe in rolling up and exhale rolling down. Exhale rolling up and inhale rolling down. Inhale while lying flat and roll up and down on the duration of one exhale. No doubt you will identify breath patterns that feel "right" or "natural" for the activity. But don't let that stop you from mixing it up a bit. There is no "right" pattern. You are identifying your habitual inclinations and making new choices.

Add unstructured sound to these experiments. Throughout the exercise, the voice should remain open and flexible. If not, identify the places where the voice "catches" or becomes trapped. Work gently until the movement and sound are one. This requires that the abdominal muscles do not work any harder than is absolutely necessary to accomplish the move.

Thigh Lift: Pre-Lift

THIGH LIFT: PRE-LIFT
Principles: Breath Support, Core Support, Spatial Intent, Weight Shift, Initiation and Sequencing, Effort Intent

This Fundamental is a preparation for walking and talking simultaneously. It is also a preparation for climbing. At first, it may appear to be very simple, but this is a deception. The challenge is in its subtlety.

Lie on the floor with the legs long, palms up, arms slightly below the shoulders and away from the body. Even with your legs long, the heels should align with your sits-bones. To facilitate this, rotate your thighs slightly inward and rest on the center back of your heels.

Once in the posture, exhale, softening your abdomen as you draw your left heel toward your sits-bone until the foot is firmly planted on the floor with the knee up. As you inhale, initiate lengthening the leg along the floor from the heel. This action will restore the leg to its original position. It may be helpful to imagine that you are lying in warm sand and your heel is drawing a line in the sand to and from your sits-bone.

Here comes the subtle part. Efficiency during this exercise is dependent on the psoas. When you exhale, you are tickling the psoas to contract, which encourages the femoral joint to fold, thus assisting in drawing the heel toward your sits-bone. This is a very subtle feeling and can easily be overridden by any extraneous tensions. Consequently, it takes time and practice to feel the inevitable contraction of the psoas.

For expressive purposes, it is important to experiment with varying the breath pattern. For instance, try an inhalation on the flexion and an exhalation on the extension. Which breath pattern feels the most natural to you? Part of your goal, as with all of the Fundamentals, is to uncover your habitual breathing patterns and vary them on purpose. Now repeat the exercise with unstructured sound. How are the expressive qualities of the sound affected by the body and breath organization?

Let's amend the exercise again by lying in the Starting Position. The relationship of the underside of the stable foot to the floor gives more stability to the body as the mobile heel lengthens the leg away and then toward the sits-bones again. Now try changing the initiator by extending from your femoral joint rather than the heel. Can you feel a qualitative difference between initiating the move from your hip joint as opposed to your heel? Try initiating with your knee. Once again, there is no right or wrong, just different.

Choreographer Oskar Schlemmer said, "Walking is a grave event." And indeed it is. Practicing the Pre-Lift is the beginning of developing a fluid and efficient walk. However, the goodies are not just in being efficient and "correct," but also in exploring myriad possibilities that may be useful for character work. All of this becomes even more interesting when you add sound or words.

Experiment with unstructured sound during each Pre-Lift and vary the initiators. Be aware that once you begin to change up your initiators, you are experimenting with potential character walks. At the end of your practice, try walking from these various initiators and see what happens to both your body and sound. As a result of your experiments, you might find yourself inventing a character or two. While character exploration is important to the actor, it is just as vital to identify your own walk—the walk that everyone, including you, recognizes as *you*. Varying the breath pattern, varying the body-level initiators, and adding sound supports your goal to walk and talk both efficiently and expressively as yourself and as a character.

THIGH LIFT
Principles: Breath Support, Core Support, Spatial Intent, Weight Shift, Initiation and Sequencing, Effort Intent

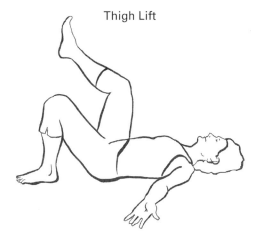

Thigh Lift

This exercise is also preparation for walking as well as crawling, running, stair climbing, and marching.

Begin in the Starting Position. Create stability by pressing the left foot into the floor. Exhale, softening the abdomen toward the spine. As the psoas contracts, a deep femoral flexion will raise the right lower leg toward the ceiling, and the knee toward the sternum. Keep the angle of the knee joint consistent. Let the right foot drop gently back to the floor. Repeat, alternating the legs. Don't forget to keep the underside of the stable foot well connected to the floor.

As the femoral joint folds and the thigh lifts in response to the interaction between the breath and the psoas, add unstructured sound. With practice, you will become sensitive to the moment that the Thigh Lift becomes "inevitable." If the psoas is allowed to do its work, then the muscles needed to support the voice (mainly the abdominal muscles) are free to do their job. If the abdomen hardens or bulges in the effort to walk, run, climb, etc., then your throat will feel tight and the sound will lose flexibility during the activity.

As with the previous exercises, find out what happens if you reverse the breath organization. Inhale on the lift and exhale on the drop. Which organization is more intuitive for you? Remember, we want to keep our expressive choices open.

PREPARATION FOR THIGH ROTATION
Principles: Breath Support, Core Support, Rotary Factor, Weight Shift, Effort Intent

This preparation will help you understand the differences between *rotating* the femoral head in its socket, *adducting/abducting* the leg, and *flexion/extension*. They are all distinct actions.

To explore a pure thigh rotation, do a Thigh Lift and put your hands around your thigh as close as you can to your femoral joint. Turn the thigh as if you are trying to unscrew the femoral head from the pelvis and screw it back in. This will not create a big movement. Your calf and foot will go along for a short ride, but they are not the initiators of the movement. To explore adduction and abduction, put one hand on the outside of the thigh and one on the inside of the thigh and open and close the thigh toward (adduct) and away (abduct) from the spine. Lastly, to explore flexion and extension, put a hand on top of the place where the femoral joint joins the pelvic bowl and fold the joint so the thigh comes toward the chest (flexion) and unfold it so the thigh moves away from the chest (extension).

These are the five actions: rotation, adduction, abduction, flexion, and extension. Practice these actions until the difference is clear.

Thigh Rotation
(Aerial View)

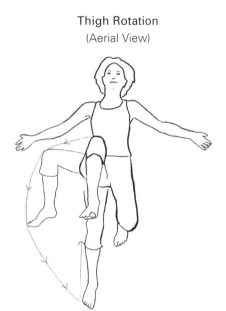

THIGH ROTATION
Principles: Breath Support, Core Support, Rotary Factor, Spatial Intent, Weight Shift, Initiation and Sequencing, Effort Intent

Thigh Rotation assists in twisting and turning. As you execute the following moves, keep one hand on the iliac crest (see page 14) of the right hip to ensure the pelvis does not roll with the motion. In other words, keep the pelvic bowl stable. Imagine you are lying in sand and have a bowl of water, which you do not wish to spill, sitting on your abdomen.

Lie in the Starting Position. Do a Thigh Lift on your right side. As you breathe out again, rotate and abduct the thigh. Let the foot find the "sand" and extend the leg out, drawing a diagonal line in the sand away from your sits-bone. With your heel, begin to draw an arc in the sand until the center back of your heel is aligned with your sits-bone. As you breathe out again, continue with a Pre-Lift, and draw a straight line with your heel toward your sits-bone (flexion) until you return to the Starting Position. Repeat on the left side. Because you are maintaining the stability of the pelvis, the arc shape in the sand will not be large. Do not sacrifice the stability of the pelvic bowl in an effort to make a big arc. That is not the point. The point is to make acquaintance with your femoral joint and its range of motion. You can facilitate the stability of your pelvis further by allowing your left leg to fall open slightly with the knee remaining bent as the mobile leg draws the arc.

Experiment with the breath sequence. When are you inhaling? When are you exhaling? Can you do the reverse of your inclination? As the exercise gets easier, add unstructured sound. Phrase the phonation to match the duration of the exercise from start to finish on one side. If you do not have sufficient breath support for the duration of the exercise, then take as many breaths as necessary. For instance, add sound through the abduction of the thigh; replenish the breath and make sound as you extend the leg on the diagonal; replenish the breath and make sound as you draw an arc with your heel until it is aligned with the sits-bones; replenish your breath and make sound as you draw the heel toward your sits bone (Pre-Lift), returning your leg to its original position.

Once it is easy to keep the pelvic bowl stable, experiment by allowing the pelvis to go along for the ride. Does the mobility or stability of the pelvic bowl affect your sound? Observe—but don't judge—the qualitative and functional differences. Both have potential value to you as an expressive being.

Diagonal Knee Drop with Spoke Arms
(Aerial View)

DIAGONAL KNEE DROP WITH SPOKE ARMS
Principles: Breath Support, Core Support, Spatial Intent, Initiation and Sequencing, Weight Shift, Effort Intent, Rotary Factor

The Diagonal Knee Drop with Spoke Arms deepens the exploration of contralateral pulls, which were introduced in the Lateral Pelvic Shift. The diagonal pulls run from shoulder to hip, hip to knee, and knee to foot. The Spoke Arm movement promotes flexibility in the shoulder girdle and chest, which in turn encourages the release of the head and neck.

Review the muscles of the torso, front and back, and notice which muscles are laid out on the diagonal (pages 12 and 13). During this Fundamental, the gentle rotation in the spine engages the inner and outer obliques and the latissimus dorsi to do what they were meant to do—spiral. Because the obliques connect into the rib cage, there is a danger that they will pull the rib cage down when it is preferable to encourage the ribs to lift and open to support the voice. The expansion and contraction of the rib cage is dependent on the intercostals, but they do not have the strength or the mass of either the obliques or the latissimus dorsi. Diagonal stretches help bring these powerful muscles into balance with the intercostals, allowing the rib cage to remain buoyant and free during the phonation. Additionally, the obliques and the rectus abdominis (which lies vertically on the skeleton) lie over the transverse abdominis. The transverse abdominis has a major responsibility for connecting the viscera with the diaphragm and, therefore, for controlling the exhalation for a free and open sound. Consequently, you must educate the rectus abdominis and the obliques not to overpower the transverse abdominis, which would accelerate the exhalation too quickly for expressive use. Just as important, the Spoke Arm movement creates an inner massage for the larynx, vocal folds, and their attendant attachments that lie deep in the throat.

The word "drop" may suggest to some readers a passive relationship of the knees to the movement. But this is not what is desired. The knees are not "giving up" and consequently "dropping" to the right or left. Instead, they are actively *reaching* to the right or left until the leg closest to the floor meets the floor. If your leg cannot rest on the floor, "raise the floor" with a rolled-up towel placed between your knee and the floor.

Begin in the Starting Position. On an exhalation, drop your knees to the right. Feel the right foot roll to its outside edge and the left foot roll to its inside edge. Do not attempt to put your legs one on top of the other, but let them reach and notice the new relationship of the knees to each other. Also, notice the relationship of your feet and pelvis to the floor. Turn your head to look at the fingers of your left hand. On impulse, inhale, and on the next exhalation, follow the fingertips with your eyes as you skim your arm over your chest in the sequence: hand, lower arm, upper arm, and shoulder. The fingers of the left hand are traveling toward the fingers of the right hand. On the exhalation, keep your eyes on your fingertips and initiate movement from your scapula, which will return your arm to its original position.

Following the fingertips with your eyes causes a mini head roll and thus encourages a relaxed head and neck. After several repetitions, exhale as you soften your abdominals and return to the Starting Position. Repeat the exercise, dropping the knees to the left and mobilizing the right arm. Experiment with keeping the hip stable as you Spoke Arm across the body. This can be accomplished with a *gentle* contralateral pull in the pelvis in the opposite direction from the mobile arm.

When it is easy to stabilize the hip, experiment with allowing the hip to be part of the sequence of movement. The movement of the hip will allow a greater range of motion in the scapula but you will not feel as intense a screw shape or twist through the spine. As always, both approaches have value.

Repeat the exercise with unstructured sound. Organize the length of the sound to be of equal duration to the Spoke Arm movement forward and back. If the sound becomes restricted, work through the tensions slowly until movement of the head, neck, and sound are fluid.

Imagine that sound can emanate from your fingertips and scapula. Imagine that the fingertips and scapula can independently initiate both sound and movement. Does the sound that emanates from the fingertips differ from the sound that emanates from the scapula? Play and, as always, challenge yourself to change the breath/sound patterns and take note of your habitual preferences.

DIAGONAL KNEE DROP WITH CARTWHEEL ARMS
Principles: Breath Support, Core Support, Spatial Intent, Initiation and Sequencing, Weight Shift, Effort Intent, Rotary Factor

This Fundamental is preparation for contralateral use of the limbs, as in normal walking. It also continues your preparation for twisting or spiraling.

Lie on your back in the Starting Position. On the exhalation, Diagonal Knee Drop to the left. As the knees drop, let the left hand reach toward the left knee and the right hand reach along a diagonal line (toward but *not* next to the head). Simultaneously, roll the head to look at the fingers of the right hand. There is now a diagonal line from the fingertips of the right hand to the fingertips of the left hand. Take time to breathe in this position. Feel the movement of your abdomen with each inhalation and exhalation.

Feel the spiral in the spine and the diagonal pulls in the surrounding muscles. To return to the Starting Position, exhale as you soften the abdomen toward the spine, raising the knees back to center. Likewise, your arms return to just below your shoulders. Repeat on the right side.

As you continue to explore the exercise, notice the following relationships: head↔neck, shoulder↔hip, hip↔knee, and knee↔foot. Feel the zigzag of your bony structure. Picture the front and back muscles of the torso spiraling into place. How do the intercostals, the obliques, and the latissimus dorsi respond to breathing in this position? How does your throat feel? Are your head and neck relaxed?

Diagonal Knee Drop with Cartwheel Arms
(Aerial View)

If your throat is open and free as you breathe, augment this Fundamental by adding unstructured sound. Explore unstructured sounds throughout the sequence. Imagine that your voice is traversing your inner architecture by moving along the internal pathways shaped by the position of your body. At its best, the torso is a flexible chamber in which the breath and sound (like water) take on the shape of the container being filled.

ARM CIRCLES
Principles: Breath Support, Core Support, Spatial Intent, Initiation and Sequencing, Weight Shift, Effort Intent, Rotary Factor

Arm Circles promote shaping motions for the use of tools or for expressive movement. Because this Fundamental calls for a complete head roll, it provides release in the head and neck muscles.

Assume the posture for Diagonal Knee Drop with Cartwheel Arms to the left side. Let your eyes focus on the fingers of your right hand and imagine you are lying in sand. On an exhalation, keep your fingertips connected to the "sand" or as close as possible and draw a clockwise circle with your fingertips around your head. Be mindful of the moment when your arm wants to rotate in the humerus joint. The rotation will turn the palm from face up to face down. On another sustained exhalation, soften your elbow and continue to draw the circle around your head, passing your fingertips by your shoulder and down toward your waist. Keep following the fingertips with your eyes. Relax the abdominal muscles toward the spine as your arm, now shaped as if gathering a large bunch of flowers, passes over your stomach. As the journey continues, feel the rotation in the humerus joint, causing the palm to face up as if scattering the flowers. Find the sand again with your fingertips and close the circle. Make an effort to keep the pelvis stable and the abdominal muscles soft and pliable. Repeat

Arm Circles
(Aerial View)

the exercise to the other side. As you repeat the exercise on both sides, reinforce your awareness of the rotation in the humerus joint by placing your hand on the joint to feel the rotation several times, forward and back. Observe the reaction in the rest of the arm and scapula.

Add unstructured sound. Observe if the throat stays open and free as you proceed through the exercise. If not, slow down and work through the places where the voice tightens or catches in the throat. Encourage a slight feeling of a yawn with the tip of the tongue forward and resting behind the lower front teeth.

During the Diagonal Knee Drop with Spoke Arms, you created a mini head roll. In this Fundamental, you are employing a complete head roll on the floor as you follow your fingertips all the way around. This wonderful head roll massages the deep internal vocal muscles and ligaments and diagnoses areas of excessive tension. You will know if you have located areas of tension if the voice tightens or the torso hardens in the activity. Work slowly through these blocks and with practice you will feel a deep relaxation and vocal release.

DIAGONAL KNEE DROP, ARM CIRCLE TO SEATED POSITION
Principles: Breath Support, Core Support, Spatial Intent, Initiation and Sequencing, Weight Shift, Effort Intent, Rotary Factor

The diagonal sit-up is preparation for large spatial circles that can be used for expressive movement or functional activities such as swinging a baseball bat or an axe. This exercise is best practiced in stages to make sure you are not hardening the abdominal muscles or tightening the neck.

First Stage: Begin in the posture for Diagonal Knee Drop with Cartwheel Arms with your knees dropped to the left. On an exhalation, begin to circle your right arm clockwise. As the arm circles toward the torso, hollow the abdominal muscles toward the spine, bringing the upper chest off the floor slightly and returning to the floor as the arm passes beyond your waist. As you did in the previous exercise, track your fingertips with your eyes.

Second Stage: Repeat the Knee Drop, Arm Circle several times. With each repetition, as your arm passes over your belly and you hollow the abdominal muscles toward the spine, bring the upper body off the floor a bit more until you achieve a seated position. Keep in mind that you may be tempted to tighten the abdominal muscles or the neck to give yourself a boost. Elevate only as much as possible without tightening. Likewise, you may be tempted to support yourself on your arm in order to rise.

Instead, be patient and discover the essential body organization and core support needed to accomplish the task. Core support is the key to this exercise. With practice, as the body and breath organize themselves efficiently, you will find yourself spiraling to a seated position.

Diagonal Knee Drop,
Arm Circle to Seated Position

Third Stage: To return to the floor, exhale and, with your eyes, follow the fingertips of your hand as it retraces its pathway back to the floor. Try not to flop down to the floor. Keep your breath and core support fully engaged in the activity until you return to the Diagonal Knee Drop.

Stage Four: When you are able to maintain a free and open connection to the breath, add unstructured sound. Do not "control" the sound. Let it spiral with the body, which means that the pitch and volume of your voice are the aural representations of the movement. For fun, with your body in stillness, create the spiral with just your sound.

DIAGONAL KNEE DROP, THIGH LIFT SCOOP
Principles: Breath Support, Core Support, Spatial Intent,
Initiation and Sequencing, Weight Shift, Rotary Factor

This exercise contributes to the development of your core support. Take a moment to review the illustrations of the abdominal muscles.

Lie in the Starting Position. On an exhalation, Diagonal Knee Drop to the left, leaving the arms just below shoulder height. On another exhalation, soften the abdominal muscles toward the spine as you scoop the knees along the floor toward the chest. Continue to exhale and soften the abdominal muscles as you lift the knees over the center of the chest and then *drop* the feet to the floor. You have

Diagonal Knee Drop, Thigh Lift Scoop
(Aerial View)

now returned to the Starting Position. Repeat to the right.

The transverse abdominis will relax toward the spine as long as the rectus abdominis stays long and easy. The obliques and the latissimus dorsi support the diagonal movement. If your core support is underdeveloped, you will harden your stomach muscles and they will push outward. Instead, the abdominal muscles must work together to find the *least* amount of effort needed for the Thigh Lift Scoop, especially if the throat is to remain open, the jaw relaxed, the neck long, and the breath free.

Most of us struggle with extraneous tensions singly or in combinations. However, like most of the Fundamentals, the Diagonal Knee Drop, Thigh Lift Scoop is both a diagnostic tool as well as a means to learn a new habit. Work slowly and notice the moment any excessive tensions creep in. Stop. Release. Begin again. It doesn't matter if you don't get your knees off the floor right away. Take your time to teach your body to release the abdominal muscles toward the spine, and relax your jaw and neck as you lift the knees over the chest.

As you make headway with this goal, add unstructured sound. At no point should you feel strain in the throat. As your core support strengthens and the abdominals find the right balance between work and release, the voice will become free and unhindered.

Heel Rocks

HEEL ROCKS
Principles: Breath Support, Initiation and Sequencing, Dynamic Alignment, Effort Intent

Heel Rocks are a wonderful recuperation from the exertion required in the previous exercise. As a matter of fact, Heel Rocks promote relaxation for the whole body from any stressor. Because this exercise promotes head-to-heel connectedness, it is basic to developing dynamic alignment. Heel Rocks, like the previous Fundamentals, are a diagnostic tool for identifying physical and vocal tensions. As you rock, you will notice these bony landmarks: heels, sacrum, scapula, and occiput.

Lie on the floor; rotate your legs inward so they rest on the center back of the heels. Keep the back of the knees long (straight legs) and breathe as you "rock" forward and backward on your heels. It helps to be barefoot so your heels can have some friction with the floor. You do not want the heels to *slide* on the floor; they need to *rock*. Likewise, be observant that the head is *not* sliding on the floor but rocking on the occiput as if nodding "yes." Can you feel an undulation rising in this manner: heels→pelvis→torso→neck→crown of the head? Is the breath free and easy or are you clutching or holding your breath? Most of us start out with physical "blocks" and places where the breath disconnects. Work slowly to ease through any blocks until the rock of the heels and the undulation through the spine is continuous with the breath.

Now add unstructured sound. Do not control the sound. Let it undulate with the spine and head. Additionally, as the head bobbles, the lower jaw (mandible) is also going along for the ride. The head is moving away from the mandible as it tilts back and closer to the mandible as it tilts toward the chest. This too affects the sound. At all times, keep a gentle feeling of a yawn in the back of the throat and the tip of the tongue behind the lower front teeth.

UPPER/LOWER BODY HALF (HOMOLOGOUS)

Principles: Breath Support, Core Support, Spatial Intent, Developmental Patterning, Effort Intent

Upper/Lower Body Half (Homologous)
(Aerial View)

The term *homologous* refers to the distinction between the upper and lower body. Our upper/ lower body halves make unique contributions to our personal movement vocabulary. We tend to gesture more from the upper body, which gives us access to the space around us. The upper body accomplishes many finely tuned everyday activities like cooking, eating, brushing teeth, folding laundry. We reach for objects and pull them toward us. We can access and/or change our immediate environment through the upper body. The lower body is what grounds us. It is our connection to the earth. The lower body governs locomotion, change of direction, rotation, and weight shifts. Through twisting and turning, the lower body lets us examine the whole environment. Locomotion allows us to abandon the old environment and travel to a new one. With the lower body, we yield into the earth and push/pull our way toward or away from any given place. The deepest internal muscle that binds together the upper and lower body halves is the psoas.

As discussed previously, the psoas is very sensitive to the breath, and breath support is crucial to functional and expressive movement and voice. We don't want a body and voice that are at odds with each other. We wish to be as one unit whose component parts are in full cooperation with each other. Each muscle must play its specific role and no more. The following Fundamental helps to delineate our upper body from our lower, as well as unite them together.

When we were babies, the unity of the upper and lower body was present on its own. Then life happened and the body forgot its natural upper/lower connectedness. This Fundamental brings us back to the crib to rediscover what the body knew at birth. Before you begin, refer to the Anatomy Illustrations and take a look at the rhomboids (page 17), latissimus dorsi, scapula, femoral joints, and the psoas. Lie on your back in a Wall Shape. The Lower Body Half is simply a repetition of the Frog Legs described earlier. Remember to keep the outside edges of the feet connected to the floor as you draw your heels toward and away from your sits-bones.

Relative to the Upper Body Half, on an exhalation, draw your elbows toward your waist, leaving the back of the arms and hands on the floor (if possible), and then reverse the motion by reaching with the fingertips until the arms are in their original starting position. Can you feel your scapulae move toward and away from your spine? The rhomboids are responsible for adducting the scapulae and assist in moving the scapulae downward. Repeat the upper body movement several times, concentrating on your scapulae.

Repeat again, picturing your latissimus dorsi. This huge muscle, which stabilizes the trunk, assists in the extension and adduction of your arms.

Now move the upper and lower body simultaneously. Exhale as you widen into the Wall Shape and inhale as your elbows and heels move toward your waist and sits-bones, respectively. Reverse the breath organization. Repeat the exercise, alternating your breath initiations, and add unstructured sound.

Imagine that your sound can emanate out your heels, fingertips, and the joints of your arms and legs. Play with initiating the body halves from these various locations. Are the sounds that emanate from the femoral joints qualitatively different from the sounds that emanate from the heels? Elbows? Scapulae? Fingertips? Likewise, how does changing the point of the initiation affect the overall movement? Make this exploration as playful as you can. After all, you are just a babe in the crib making new discoveries.

Right Side/Left Side Body Half
(Homolateral)
(Aerial View)

RIGHT SIDE/LEFT SIDE BODY HALF (HOMOLATERAL)
Principles: Breath Support, Core Support, Spatial Intent, Developmental Patterning, Effort Intent

The term *homolateral* refers to the delineation between our right and left sides. The concepts of "right" and "left" carry both cultural and basic physical meanings. We all tend to favor a particular "side." This is true whether we are referring to a point of view or our favored hand with which to write. It is no secret that for some people, the right hand is dominant, and for others, the left. The favoring of "sides" begins early on in our development and teaches us how to take a stand, to have a point of view. Who hasn't described himself or others as leaning to the "right" (conservative) or "left" (liberal) politically? The separation of right and left is in evidence in many cultures. For instance, in Chinese culture it is believed that the right side of the body governs an individual's masculine attributes and the left side the feminine. These concepts follow some of us even beyond the grave. For instance, the Bible predicts that at the end of the world, the "good" will be assembled on the right-hand side of the Lord and everyone else on the left. In view of all this, the point of the following exercise is to track our connection to our right and left sides without judgment and to attempt to bring them into harmony. This is a tall order for one little Fundamental, but it is a beginning of bringing our right side/left side into cooperation with each other.

Before we start, take a look at the illustration of the quadratus lumborum, page 17. Notice how the fibers of this muscle stretch from the ribs to the iliac crest. Perhaps not as elegant as the psoas, this muscle nevertheless also ties our upper to our lower body. The quadratus lumborum assists in side-bending from the waist, which is a basic element of this exercise.

Lie in a large Wall Shape and imagine that you are a baby searching for your thumb. As you exhale, the knee and elbow on your left side are drawn toward each other, causing a side bend (flexion). Simultaneously, your right side stretches along on the floor (extension). This extension through the right side will help facilitate the flexion in the left side and vice versa.

As you side-bend, allow your head to roll, turning your face toward the thumb of your left hand. As you inhale, re-extend the left arm and leg and let your head roll back to center. Repeat on the right side. After several repetitions, reverse the breath organization and, if things are going well, add unstructured sound. Experiment with initiating the movement alternately from the heels, fingertips, and the joints of the legs and arms. Imagine that sound can emanate from these locations. Is there a qualitative difference in the sound and movement, depending on the initiator?

Now it is time to move some of the articulators responsible for speech! As your elbow and knee travel toward each other, reach your lips toward your thumb, as if you want to suck it. Your lips are now moving from an open circle to a small circle as they reach forward toward your thumb. Allow the lips to relax into the open circle again as you return to the Wall Shape. Repeat the movement and add sound to the movement of the lips. As a result of the movement of the lips, you may identify AH, OO, or OH sounds. Congratulations! You are making precise articulations! Repeat the Right Side/Left Side Body Half sequence while lying on your stomach.

UPPER/LOWER BODY HALF ROLL
Principles: Breath Support, Core Support, Spatial Intent, Weight Shift, Effort Intent, Developmental Patterning

This Fundamental encourages harmony among the upper and lower body halves and the right and left sides. Imagine that you are a baby teaching yourself to roll. Lie on your back in the Upper/Lower Body

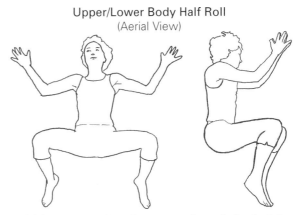

Upper/Lower Body Half Roll
(Aerial View)

Half posture. On an exhalation, initiate a roll by folding your right side on top of your left side. Move your arm and leg at the same rate so that they remain aligned. To return to center, exhale and initiate the roll by reopening the right side until you find yourself balanced on your spine. When balanced on your spine, you may look like a bug that has flipped onto its back, or perhaps like your dog looking for a tummy rub, or a baby with arms and legs in the air. Continue to roll by folding the left side toward the right side until you are lying on your right side. Make sure you keep your head on the floor through out the roll. As an experiment, pause when you are balanced on your spine and, depending on the momentum of your roll, you may rock gently back and forth with the bent arms and legs in the air. Enjoy the motion; it can be very soothing.

At first, initiate each roll back and forth on an exhalation. But as always, it is important to experiment with alternative breath organizations. How many possibilities can you discover? For instance, can you inhale as you roll and exhale as the body comes to stillness? Some of the possibilities will feel natural and others will feel counterintuitive, but all have potentially expressive value. Play like a baby in the crib.

After you have explored the organization of the breath, add unstructured sound. Imagine that the sound is serving as an invisible thread of tensile energy filling the empty space between your hands, knees, and feet. You may stay with unstructured sound or use the basic phonemes (distinct units of speech sounds) discovered in the previous exercise: AH, OO, and OH.

Pure Diagonals
(Finger-Tip Initiation, Aerial View)

PURE DIAGONALS (CONTRALATERAL)*
Principles: Breath Support, Core Support, Spatial Intent, Weight Shift, Initiation and Sequencing, Effort Intent, Developmental Patterning, Rotary Factor

Review the illustrations for the muscles of your torso, front and back. Which muscles are laid on your skeleton on the diagonal? Which muscles are parallel to the spine? Which encircle the skeleton and organs? Your obliques, latissimus dorsi, and the intercostals will be very happy playing in the diagonals because this is how they are built. In fact, many muscles are on the diagonal. Yet twisting and turning tends to be underutilized in our daily life. All day long, our focus is mostly forward. Don't we tend to line ourselves up with the task at hand and attack it straight on? We even *think* forward, as in, "What do I have to do next?"

Diagonal moves are among the most complex the body can do and, because they require rotation, they are the last of the fundamental skills the body attains. In the reverse, as we age, we tend to lose rotation first.

Diagonals train the body to be adaptive in space. Developing contralateral ability also helps the mind to become more flexible. The diagonal promotes inclusiveness, taking in all sides of a question and respect for others' opinions. As an actor, practicing diagonals trains you to be open to all the environment has to offer and to respond on impulse in varied and dynamic ways. Likewise, the voice is challenged to remain open and free as the body spirals. The voice, like our gestures, tends to be directed forward. Yet the voice is perfectly capable of spiraling into space. The following exercises will bring your skeleton and muscles into the most extreme diagonal relationships explored thus far.

There are several possible ways to practice the Pure Diagonals. You can initiate with your fingertips

---

*Also called "cross-lateral" by some LMA practitioners

or you can initiate with your legs. We will first look at fingertip initiation.

Fingertip Initiation: Lie on your back in a large Wall Shape. Look at the fingers of your right arm and on the exhalation, slide your arm over the chest as the left arm moves under your head and, if possible, behind it. You will look and feel a bit like a twisted rubber band. Keep the tensile energy flowing between the fingers and the heels of the feet. Feel the extreme contralateral pull in the body. Don't forget to breathe! Explore unstructured sounds in

Pure Diagonal Leg
(Leg Leading, Aerial View)

this position. On an exhalation, spiral back to your original position by imagining someone is pulling on your right heel. The spine will unwind sequentially until you are back in your original Wall Shape posture. Remember to keep your eyes on the mobile arm's fingertips. This will encourage the head to go for the ride. Repeat the exercise with your left arm.

Now try initiating the pure diagonal with your leg.

Leg Initiation: Lie on your back in the Wall Shape. Exhale and arc your right leg over your left leg. Leave your shoulders and arms on the floor in the original position as much as possible. Feel the contralateral pull (fingers↔toes) through the body. Inhale and exhale in this posture several times. Explore unstructured sound in this position. To return to your original posture, imagine someone is pulling on the fingertips of your right hand and spiral back to your original Wall Shape.

DIAGONAL X ROLLS
Principles: Breath Support, Core Support, Spatial Intent, Weight Shift, Initiation and Sequencing, Effort Intent, Developmental Patterning, Rotary Factor

The Diagonal X Roll can be initiated from the fingertips or from the legs. You can also alternate the initiations as you roll.

Fingertip Initiation: Repeat the Pure Diagonal with fingertip initiation, but this time imagine that someone continues to pull on your fingertips, which spirals your body onto your stomach into a Wall Shape. To return to your back, exhale and arc your right arm over your back and again imagine that someone is pulling on your fingertips, which begins the spiraling sequence. As you are spiraling to your back, the left arm is traveling under the head in order to return easily to its original position. Repeat on the left side. After several passes to the right and left, add unstructured sounds. In order for the voice to remain free, the spiral sequence must be done with ease and efficiency.

Leg Initiation: Repeat the Pure Diagonal initiating with the leg, but imagine someone is pulling on your heel until you roll over onto your stomach. To return to your back, exhale as the right leg arcs over the back of the left leg. Imagine someone is pulling on the right heel, which begins the spinal sequence, which returns the body to its back in the Wall Shape. Repeat to the other side. Repeat the diagonal rolls several times and add unstructured sounds. The sounds will remain free if the head and neck are just along for the ride and are not trying to control the spiraling roll.

SPIRALING UP AND DOWN
Principles: Breath Support, Core Support, Spatial Intent, Weight Shift,
Initiation and Sequencing, Dynamic Alignment,
Effort Intent, Developmental Patterning, Rotary Factor

Spiraling from floor to standing is one of the most complex body organizations that we can attempt. Because the whole body is now spiraling through space, a spark is ignited between the right and left sides of the brain, waking up pathways and synapses that may have heretofore been sleeping or underused. Relative to the use of sound, there are many opportunities during the spiral for the voice to get "caught" or "held." Discovering a free and open sound as you spiral up and down ensures that you are working from an excellent balance of all the muscles involved in the activity. Be patient with this exercise and go slowly. It is important that you identify any excessive tensions. Also, do not attempt this exercise until you are proficient at the Diagonal Knee Drop, Arm Circle to a Seated Position.

In the following paragraphs, I am describing the spiraling sequence from floor to standing in four stages. It is recommended that you spread your explorations over several days, exploring one stage each day. There is no need to be in a hurry to accomplish the whole sequence. Take your time and thoroughly explore each stage.

Stage One: Start with the Diagonal Knee Drop, Arm Circle to the right side and proceed to the Seated Position. Once seated, on an exhalation, arc your bent knees from left to right with the feet remaining on the floor. The outside of your left foot will roll to its inside and the inside of the right foot will roll to its outside as the knees switch sides. Roll the feet back and forth several times, which will arc the knees back and forth as well. You will feel a deep femoral flexion and rotation in the hip socket. End with your knees dropped to the right.

Stage Two: Repeat Stage One and end with the knees dropped to the right. Exhale and swing your left leg around and to the side of your right knee. Firmly plant the bottom of your left foot on the floor. Swing the leg back again and repeat several times. Practice Stages One and Two, alternating the starting side. Finish with the left foot to the side of the right knee.

Stage Three: Repeat Stages One and Two. When the left foot is firmly planted on the floor to the side of the right knee, exhale, pushing your hands (positioned to the outside of the left thigh) into the floor and send your sits-bones toward the ceiling and your head toward the floor. On another exhale, trace your pathway back to lying in Diagonal Knee Drop with Cartwheel Arms. Repeat the sequence from Stages One through Three several times to the right and to the left.

Stage Four: Diagonal Knee Drop to the right and continue through to Stage Three. When your sits-bones are directed toward the ceiling and your head toward the floor, exhale and swivel on the balls of your feet, rising as you twist in the spine. Direct your eyes and right arm toward the high/left/forward corner of the room and your left arm toward the low/right/back corner. Congratulations! You did it! You are now in a screw shape. On an exhalation, see if you can trace your pathway back to the floor until you are in the Knee Drop with Cartwheel Arms again.

As you get more proficient with the spiral, ascertain if you can spiral up on one exhalation, inhale, and spiral down on one exhalation. Is it possible to spiral up *and* down on one exhalation? Add unstructured sound. The voice will take on the shape of the spiraling body. Therefore, do not try to control the pitch or keep the tone steady. Maintain a free and open throat and let the sound go on the journey. The voice may demonstrate pitch and volume changes as you spiral. Don't inhibit any vocal responses.

No doubt you will uncover places in the spiral where you hold your breath, control the move from the head and neck, clench your jaw, and/or hike your shoulders. These tensions are counterproductive to the development of an integrated body and voice. Therefore, seize this opportunity to identify any places of tension and work slowly through them until the breath, sound, and spiraling action are one. Keep in mind that if you can achieve a free and open voice during this challenging body organization, then you can probably maintain it in most circumstances related to acting.

The previous chapter addressed the importance of Breath Support to the outcome of movement and voice. In this chapter, the vital underpinnings for movement and voice outcomes were expanded to include all of the Nine Principles, which were given life through the Bartenieff Fundamentals. Keep in mind that the larger purpose for all that we have explored thus far is to gain an understanding of the crucial link between function and expression. It is perhaps obvious to say that when you focus on function you are enhancing your expressiveness, and when you focus on expressiveness you are enhancing your functionality. The interplay between function and expression is the cornerstone of this book, but that interplay is incomplete without the presence of Laban's other major movement themes: stability/mobility, exertion/recuperation, and inner/outer, which have all been discussed and made actual through the exercises.

At this point, it will be useful to revisit chapter 1. Repeat the exercises and be mindful of Laban's major themes and Bartenieff's Nine Principles, all of which find practical application in the Fundamentals. You will notice that you are moving and sounding with more awareness, ease, and flexibility.

CHAPTER THREE
Detailed Explorations for Breath Support
Time Frame: Fourteen one-hour sessions

In this chapter, we will deepen our understanding of the Principle of Breath Support. There are many possible approaches to breath support, and the "correct" approach is that which best serves the activity in which you wish to engage. Therefore, the exercises described are designed specifically to serve the needs of the actor.

The exercises to follow are divided into three sections. The first section focuses on building the relationship between the intercostal and abdominal muscles. The second section focuses on building strength, stamina, and effortlessness into the intercostal muscles so that they can better assist a controlled exhalation for voice production. The third section focuses on sensitizing you to the movement of your back as you breathe.

Since an expressive sound and body begins with the impulse to breathe, it is very important that you feel the impetus that initiates each inhalation as you practice the exercises. The impetus may stem from the purely functional need to expel the carbon dioxide and replenish your oxygen or from the expressive need to speak and/or move. The impulse to breathe is very subtle and easy to override if you rush. Be patient. Listen to your body and it will tell you when to breathe. This may sound strange because you have been breathing successfully enough to stay alive since you were born. However, the question is, "Are you breathing in the most efficient way possible to maximize your impact as an actor?" Observe the breath patterns of others in everyday life. The array of breathing patterns is huge and no one dies from this variety. But the actor, like the singer, has unique needs, and these often are not addressed by most individuals' habitual breathing patterns.

Because the exercises in the first two sections require almost no gross body movement, be aware of your body's need for relief from this relative stillness. To recuperate, revisit some of the exercises in chapters 1 and 2. Use the Anatomy Illustrations to see the muscles named in the exercises.

Relationship of the Intercostal and Abdominal Muscles to the Breath

A relationship among the intercostal and abdominal muscles is desirable because the abdominal muscles assist in contracting the diaphragm downward on the inhalation and help control the release of the breath on the exhalation. As the *external* intercostal muscles contract, the rib cage lifts and expands to give the lungs the necessary room to inflate. The *internal* intercostals assist in supporting a controlled release of the exhalation by bringing the rib cage downward, thus narrowing the space allotted to the lung expansion.

When you lie on the floor in the Starting Position, determine whether your alignment could benefit from placing a book under your head. If your head rolls back and your chin points toward the ceiling, then you may need to support your head with a book to accommodate your cervical curve and to lengthen your neck muscles. In addition to using a book, the Pelvic Rock and Heel Rock can help you find a neutral position for your head. Alternatively, you may tilt your head back and forth, directing your chin toward the ceiling and then toward your chest several times before resting on your occiput.

During all of the following exercises, take particular notice of the instructions to "sigh" or "sigh-out." These instructions could easily be misunderstood to mean a passive or under-energized action. This is not the intent. Think of sighing out as the vocal action you take when you are getting something off your chest or a "sigh of relief," as coined by Kristin Linklater in *Freeing the Natural Voice*. The sigh manifests as the beginnings of vocal resonance and is the first expression of your emotional connection to the impulse to speak, i.e., unstructured sound. The instruction to "breathe in through your nose" will prevent gasping in the air and ensures that you will not overbreathe. Ultimately, your decisions to breathe in through your nose or mouth will be governed by your functional and expressive needs on a moment-to-moment basis.

- Lie on your back in the Starting Position. On impulse, breathe in through your nose just enough to smell a flower.
- On impulse, release your breath on a sigh through a free and open throat, which is described in on page 29 in chapter 1.
- Repeat the sequence five times.

- With your hands on your lower rib cage, breathe in through your nose just enough to smell a flower. Feel your ribs gently expand. As the ribs are expanding, feel your abdomen hollow toward your spine.
- With a free and open throat, relax your intercostals and release your breath, letting it all out on a sigh.
- Repeat the sequence ten times.

- Place one hand on your lower ribs and the other on your navel. On impulse, breathe in through your nose to expand the lower ribs.
- Keep your rib cage expanded and release your abdomen toward the spine, sighing-out through a free and open throat.
- Release the intercostals on a sigh.
- Repeat the sequence ten times.

When you release the abdomen, there will only be a hint of breath expelled, and therefore a *very tiny* sigh of relief. This is because the abdominal muscles are engaged only marginally at this point. However, when you release the rib cage, the sigh will be more substantial. Remember to maintain the free and open throat as you release the rib cage.

- Place one hand on your lower ribs and the other on your naval. On impulse, breathe in on a count of six: three counts through your nose to expand the rib cage and three counts to expand the abdomen toward the ceiling. The ribs *do not* continue to expand as the abdomen expands.
- Let the rib cage "float" as you release the abdomen toward the spine on a sigh.
- Pause.
- Release the rib cage on a sigh.
- Repeat the sequence ten times.

In this sequence, the sigh from your abdomen will be almost as strong and substantial as the subsequent sigh from your intercostals. When you feel secure about the distinction between the intercostal and abdominal muscles, remove the pause between the exhalations.

Before continuing, take a moment to review the order of the body's response to the breath that can be felt by your hands. Inhalation: a) lower ribs move up and expand, b) the abdomen expands outward. Exhalation: a) abdomen relaxes toward the spine, b) the ribs move toward the spine and down toward the hips. What you cannot feel with your hands is the contraction of the diaphragm downward toward the pelvic bowl on the inhalation. This action displaces the muscles and organs of the lower trunk outward. On the exhalation, the abdominal muscles control the release of the diaphragm and the internal intercostal muscles control the release of the rib cage. Together these actions expel the air out of the body.

- Place one hand on your lower ribs and the other on your naval. On impulse, breathe in through the nose to expand the ribs on three counts and then the abdomen on three counts.
- Sigh out on a count of six, three from the abdomen and three from the rib cage.
- Repeat the exercise ten times, increasing the count of the exhalation each time. Do not exceed what is comfortable. You do not want to squeeze the air out.

The purpose of counting on both the inhalation and exhalation is to slow down your internal process sufficiently enough to become aware of the movement of the rib cage and abdomen. Additionally, counting as you exhale helps you gauge your progress toward increasing the duration of the exhalation. However, do not become goal oriented relative to how long your exhalation must last. The count is in service to the breath; the breath is not striving to achieve a particular count. Practice and be observant, and the rest will take care of itself. As you find your personal rhythm for respiration, your parasympathetic nervous system, which is commonly referred to as the "rest and digest" system, will become engaged and a feeling of relaxation will permeate the exercises.

Intercostal Strength and Ease

To support lengthy and complex phrases, it is important that you learn to keep the ribs gently expanded while the muscles of the abdomen, in cooperation with the diaphragm, do the yeoman's job of supporting the breath for voice. Yet it is also crucial that the ribs do not become rigid; instead, they must stay buoyant, like a balloon filled with helium. To allow the abdominal muscles to support the voice takes both strength and ease in the intercostal muscles. Therefore, the following exercises require that the ribs maintain their expansion. You will focus the action of the breath only in the muscles of the abdomen. That is not to say that you will never use the reserve of breath in your ribs. To the contrary, when you need additional breath to support your activity, you will use the intercostals to control the release of the reserved breath. But, for now, we are building intercostal strength with our attempts to isolate the abdominal muscles from the intercostals.

- Lie in the Starting Position with one hand on your lower ribs and one on your navel.
- On impulse, breathe in through your nose to expand the ribs on three counts followed by the abdomen on three counts. Feel the abdomen grow toward the ceiling.
- Keep the rib cage expanded and sigh out on a count of three through a free and open throat, allowing the abdomen to sink toward the spine.
- On impulse, breathe into the abdomen again just enough to smell a flower.
- Sigh out on six counts.
- Repeat the sequence five times, increasing or decreasing the count of each exhalation while maintaining the expansion of the rib cage.
- At the end of five repetitions, relax the rib cage by sighing out the air it has stored.
- Recuperate and repeat the whole sequence five times.

Reflect on your execution of the exercise. Could your ribs remain expanded throughout the five repetitions of the exercise? Did you have any air left in your ribs when you attempted to relax the intercostal muscles? Keep in mind that there is nothing magical about the number of repetitions suggested. They are meant only to be guidelines. It is more important that you discover your present capabilities and work from your starting point. Therefore, the duration of the exhalation and the number of repetitions of an exercise are governed by the amount of ease you are feeling.

The Role of the Back in Breath Support

The purpose of the following exercises is to sensitize you to the role of the back in breath support. Awareness of your back emphasizes the fact that you are a three-dimensional being. The ribs do not stop at the sides of your torso, but have attachments to the thoracic spine as well as the sternum. Additionally, the diaphragm attaches to the xiphoid process, the inner surface of the lower six ribs, and the lumbar spine (page 15). Supple spine and back muscles are as imperative for a flexible voice, as is the movement of the abdominal muscles and diaphragm.

In the following exercises, the instruction to "expand your back with breath" is synonymous with "expand your rib cage with breath." Awareness of the back breath is often missed because the

Child's Pose

movements of the abdomen and the side ribs are more pronounced than the back's movement, particularly if you are lying prone or standing.

The following positions will help you feel the movement of the back on the inhalation and exhalation. Begin by reviewing the Fundamentals. When you come to the Diagonal X Roll that ends on your stomach, fold into the yoga position called Child's Pose.

If your sits-bones cannot rest on your heels while your forehead is on the floor, place a towel between your sits-bones and heels. Rest in the pose and notice how the breath is affecting your back, then begin the exercises.

- On impulse, breathe in and hum several times. As you hum, you may be able to feel vibrations in your back and, if your chest is resting on your thighs, you may feel vibrations in your legs. Likewise, your forehead may contribute to the vibrations you feel in the floor.
- Repeat the exercise and on each new hum, change the pitch to one that is either higher or lower than the preceding pitch. Be aware of where in your body you feel the vibrations manifest.

Cat-Cow

The relationship of the breath and sound to the supple movements of the spine is crucial to an expressive sound that is connected to the body. An inflexible spine will result in an inflexible voice. Cat-Cow, like Child's Pose, has its origins in yoga and is ideal for highlighting this relationship. The mantra for this exercise is: The breath moves the spine and the spine moves the breath. Move from the Child's Pose onto your hands and knees. If you have sensitive knees, place a towel under them or use a mat.

- On impulse, breathe in and move your pubis and forehead toward each other as your back rounds up toward the ceiling.
- On the exhalation, sway your spine toward the floor as the back of the head and coccyx move toward each other. If you feel pressure in the throat, you have gone too far. Keep the movement as fluid as possible.

- Repeat five times.

- Change the order of the breath organization. (Exhale as the forehead and pubis reach toward each other and inhale as the back of the head and coccyx reach toward each other.) Repeat five times.

- Stay on all fours with a flat back and the head aligned with the spine. Gently pant like a puppy.
- Observe the movement of your abdomen as you pant. Can you feel your abdomen jump toward your spine and the small of your back respond with a light, quick move toward the ceiling? The movement in the small of your back is subtle. It may help to have someone put a hand on your back to facilitate your awareness.
- Remain on all fours. On an exhalation, simultaneously move your head and hips in circular motions and feel the resulting movement throughout your trunk.
- Return to stillness with a flat back and the head aligned with the spine.
- Repeat four times.

The following exercise will help you return to silence regardless of whether you have the breath support to keep phonating. Returning to silence without creating tension is as important as initiating and sustaining sound with ease.

- On impulse, breathe in and hum. Drop your jaw and sustain an "AH" for a *few seconds*. (It should sound like this: "mmmmmmAHHHHH.")
- Relax the abdomen instantaneously. This action will stop the sound and drop new air into the body through the open mouth almost simultaneously.
- Repeat ten times, changing the pitch on each new phonation.

- Repeat the last sequence and vary the durations of the phonations. For instance, some phonations may be ten counts, some three, or twelve, or two.
- Return to silence after each count by relaxing the support of the abdominal muscles instantaneously. Feel the new breath fall into the body through the open mouth in preparation for the next phonation.

The instantaneous relaxation of the abdomen stops the sound without disrupting the free and open throat and prepares the body for the next inhalation. The next inhalation falls into the body instantaneously and without constriction, as the abdomen expands toward the floor.

The Monkey Pose, which is a squat, will further facilitate your awareness of how the breath affects your back. Because of the roundness and stability of the Monkey Pose, you will feel the breath expand your back as well as your side ribs and abdomen. For some individuals, the Monkey Pose may be contraindicated due to issues of the knees. In that case, instead of resting on the balls of your feet, substitute sitting on the edge of a chair and rest your arms on your thighs.

Monkey Pose

If you are going to squat, push back onto the balls of your feet from the Cat position. Relax your arches but stay on the balls of your feet, with your sits-bones directed toward your heels and your knees aligned with your second and third toes. Place your fists close together on the floor, forming a triangle between your fists and feet. Align the crown of your head with your spine and allow your back to round slightly. Make sure your weight is balanced in the center of the triangle that is formed by the position of your feet and fists. Because of the inherent stability of this pose, as well as the slight rounding of the back, you are in the perfect position to feel your back expand on the inhalation. As the diaphragm contracts toward the pelvic bowl, the air is drawn into the body. The Monkey Pose allows you to feel the abdomen move toward the floor while the back and side ribs expand.

During the following exercises, unless you are sitting in a chair, experiment with resting one arm on your knee while leaving the other fist on the floor. If your left fist is on the floor, you will feel the right side of your back move more with the breath and vice versa. Also, be aware that you will need to recuperate by stretching your legs intermittently. This pose is meant to be neither an endurance test nor painful. Listen to your body and recuperate as necessary.

- On impulse, breathe in through your nose, feel your lower back expand with breath, and feel your abdomen move toward the floor.
- Relax your back and abdomen on a sigh with a free and open throat.
- Repeat ten times.

- On impulse, breathe in through your nose. Feel your lower back expand with breath and your abdomen move toward the floor.
- Keep your back ribs expanded, drop your jaw, and pant like a puppy. Feel the movement in your abdomen.
- Relax your back and recuperate.
- Repeat five times.

- On impulse, expand your back with breath and hum for ten counts, keeping your back ribs expanded through the phonation.
- On the tenth count, release your back ribs, expelling the rest of the air through a free and open throat.
- Repeat ten times.

- On impulse, expand your back ribs with breath and hum.
- As you make sound, open and close your jaw from the jaw hinge (temporomandibular joint) for several seconds, finishing on an open "AH."
- Release your ribs, expelling the rest of the air through a free and open throat.
- Repeat five times.

- On impulse, expand your back ribs with breath and hum.
- Drop your jaw from the jaw hinge and explore all the ways your tongue can move, creating nonsense phonations (speech sounds).
- Release your ribs, expelling the rest of the air through a free and open throat.
- Repeat five times.

- On impulse, expand your back ribs with breath and hum.
- Drop your jaw from the jaw hinge and explore all the ways your lips can move, creating nonsense phonations.
- Release your ribs, expelling the rest of the air through a free and open throat.
- Repeat five times.
- Repeat all the exercises, but experiment with changing the pitch on which you phonate. Observe how the various pitches affect your ability to support the phonations while maintaining the expansion of the back ribs.

- On impulse, expand your back ribs and abdomen with breath and hum onto an open "AH."
- Count out loud (1, 2, 3, etc.), intoning the numbers. (*Intoning* is the term used to describe sustained speech, similar to chanting.) Intone the numbers only as far as you can without losing the expansion of your back ribs.
- At the end of the count, release the ribs, sighing out any remaining air.
- Repeat ten times, intoning the numbers on different pitches.

With practice, you will be able to increase how far you can intone with ease and you will understand the effect of pitch on duration. Some individuals may find it easier to sustain pitches that are higher in their range, and some individuals lower. There are no rules about this. Treat the practice as play.

- Repeat all the exercises in the Monkey Pose with the following amendment. When instructed to release the back at the end of the exhalation, release *just the abdominal muscles* instead. Feel the breath fall into the body through a free and open throat while the ribs and back maintain their buoyancy.
- After five repetitions of each exercise, during which you are now keeping the rib cage and back expanded, release the back and ribs.
- Recuperate.

This last sequence describes what is called rib-reserve breathing. On a functional level, maintaining the opening of the ribs facilitates the muscles of the abdomen to support the slow release of the breath according to the phrase or thought. The goal is to let the muscles of the abdomen—in conjunction with the diaphragm—take the major responsibility for controlling of the exhalation while the intercostals play a secondary role. When a phrase is too long to be supported by the abdominal muscles alone, the intercostal muscles slowly release the remaining air to support the rest of the phrase. Consequently, you want not only to build *stamina* in the intercostal muscles, but also *sensitivity* to the moment when you need to use the breath that they can control. Additionally, you never want to harden or squeeze the muscles of the abdomen or the intercostals in an effort to speak. "Buoyant" and "with ease" are the operative words. Child's Pose, Cat-Cow, and Monkey Pose begin to sensitize you to the importance of the back to efficient breath support for voice. Before moving on to the next chapter, fully recuperate with Cellular Breathing, Still Shape Forms, and Bartenieff Fundamentals, and then practice the exercises in this chapter again.

No doubt you have noticed that the approach to breath support in this chapter has been very structured, and at first it may feel prescriptive. This is principally because you are inhibiting your habitual responses to breathing. With practice, this will pass, and new, more efficient habits will take over. In the meantime, if this approach causes you frustration because it is not "natural" to your habitual patterns, be patient. Keep in mind that as an actor, you are called upon to engage in extraordinary activities. Consider this: You are an adult, dressing in clothes that are not your own, saying words you didn't think up, moving in specific, predetermined ways, and attempting to make it all look and sound like "real life" in front of hundreds of people at a time. What is "natural" about any of that? The dialogues written by many of the best playwrights are not "natural" to our everyday speech. Such writers include Shakespeare, George Bernard Shaw, David Hare, August Wilson, Susan Lori Parks, Tom Stoppard, Tony Kushner, Charles Mee, and Edward Albee, to name just a few. Many of the speeches in their plays are equivalent to arias and, depending on the director, the physical acting may challenge the actor to be on par with an athlete. Consequently, both movement and voice require, as Eugenio Barba wrote in *The Paper Canoe*, an "extra-daily technique." Done well, the plays sound and look as though they have a foothold in some sort of reality, no matter how esoteric or abstract the play may be. With the appropriate technique, the actors render the play plausible and effective. Without an "extra-daily technique," the challenges in the play can become insurmountable as the story suffocates in the excessive physical and vocal tensions of the actors. Therefore, the exercises proposed throughout this book are meant to provide a technique that supports the extraordinary requirements of make-believe.

CHAPTER FOUR

Neutral Dynamic Alignment: Radiating Your Physical Presence
Time Frame: Ten one-hour sessions

With every shift of your trunk, change in your feet, head, hands, arms, or tone of voice, you are sending messages to the world about who you are, how you feel, and what you value. As an actor, it is desirable to develop a dynamic alignment that doesn't pigeonhole you as one character into perpetuity, but rather one that says: "I am present. I have stamina. I am a balanced individual. I am ready to transform."

Neutral dynamic alignment is not a descriptive term for "perfect posture." There is no such thing as "perfect posture." Your dynamic alignment is the shape your body assumes when you are *your best self on a very good day*. When you stand in neutral dynamic alignment, connected to the breath, your presence radiates and the observers witness your vital essence. Radiating your essence transcends race, education, and economic background, and precludes attitudes that could say: "I am *this* and this *only*." As witnesses to your essence, we become curious and are compelled to know more about you.

There are, of course, psychological and functional reasons why it may be difficult to reveal your essence. To appear fully present, you need to recognize and release any excessive tensions. With the exercises you have done so far, you have made inroads to identifying and releasing some of your habitual patterns and physical blocks. Your next challenge is to employ the benefits of your previous practice while standing in "active stillness." *Active stillness* is the term used to describe a body in *apparent* stillness. It is apparent and not actual because the body is in constant flux as it adjusts moment to moment to the business of being alive. We are not actually *still* until we are dead. Standing in active stillness is challenging because, once standing, you have the full responsibility for the uprightness of your body. To "lock" or "hold" the body in an effort to maintain uprightness undermines your connection to the breath and is, therefore, counterproductive to expressiveness. Yet as you attempt to relax the abdomen toward the spine on the exhalation, gravity is no longer your friend, as it was when you were lying prone. Gravity pulls the rib cage down even as we endeavor to lift and open it on the inhalation. It is the goal of this chapter to develop the muscular organization and core support needed to accomplish uprightness *with ease* and to simultaneously support a free and expressive voice. Our means for accomplishing this will be to explore how the body can be shaped along the continuum from floor to standing while letting the voice go along for the ride. Traditionally, rolling up vertebra by vertebra is practiced as the pathway toward standing. The following is just such an exercise and it flows out of the sequences described for Child's Pose, Cat-Cow, and Monkey Pose. Review these exercises before proceeding.

ROLLING UP VERTEBRA BY VERTEBRA

From the Monkey Pose, push back onto your heels and hang over. Direct the top of your head toward the floor and your sits-bones toward the ceiling, but keep your knees slightly bent. You can sway from side to side, but do not bounce up and down. If this position puts any strain on your lower back or hamstrings, there are a couple of alternatives: you may rest your hands on your thighs or widen your stance and rest your hands on two books of the same size placed a comfortable distance from your toes.

- In a *restful* forward bending position, expand your back with breath and hum.
- Repeat the hum five times, on a different pitch each time.
- Continue to hum and explore various pitches while you roll up vertebra by vertebra a short distance.
- Pause and replenish your breath.
- Continue the journey toward uprightness as you hum. Pause, as needed, to replenish your breath. It is *not* the goal to rise to standing on one breath.

As you are rising, find the appropriate moments to:
- Open the backs of your knees.
- Center your ribs over the pelvis.
- Roll your trapezium down your back.
- Open across the front chest.
- Allow the neck to roll up, balancing the head on the atlas/axis of the spine.

Once upright:
- Adjust your feet to be parallel under your femoral joints.
- Direct your coccyx toward the place between your heels.
- Check that the ribs are open and lifted.
- Check that the upper chest is wide.
- Check that the shoulders are relaxed and away from the ears.
- Check that the crown of the head is directed toward the ceiling.
- Check that the abdominal muscles are gently moving the abdomen in and out with the breath.

- Stand in active stillness and observe how this alignment feels.
- Alternate between standing in this "new" alignment (neutral dynamic alignment) and your habitual posture. Observe the differences between the two.
- Walk around the room. Alternate between your habitual alignment and your neutral

dynamic alignment. Do not judge one to be more desirable than the other. Instead, focus on observing what is different and what is the same. How is your breath affected?

- Abandon both your habitual and new alignment and invent a variety of possible alignments. That is to say, "reshape" your body and let your imagination be affected by these new possibilities.
- Explore your invented alignments with locomotion (walk, run, crawl, etc.) What "stories" do your body-shapes tell? Are there elements of the Still Shape Forms (chapter 1) emphasized through these alignments?
- Return to the neutral dynamic alignment you discovered from rolling up vertebra by vertebra and stand in active stillness.
- Shift back and forth between your neutral dynamic alignment and your habitual posture.

If initially your neutral dynamic alignment felt awkward, perhaps now it feels like just another choice. The most important consideration relative to alignment is not to judge one alignment as superior to another. All body shapes can have expressive purposes. If the alignment of your body is suiting your purpose, then that alignment is "correct." "Wrong" is to be stuck in one alignment, thus limiting your creative possibilities. In addition to identifying your neutral dynamic alignment, it is also your goal to be able to access the alignment that best reveals the character you are portraying.

THE WALL

Standing often causes an individual to overengage the abdominal muscles in an effort to maintain balance and uprightness. The excessive abdominal tensions leave the breath support weakened because the abdominal muscles cannot relax enough for the breath to fall into the body. Using the wall for support will help you find the balance needed in the abdominal muscles for both uprightness and breath support.

The following exercise requires strong thighs and core support. If you fatigue quickly, you need to practice this position frequently to strengthen your core, or uprightness may rob you of the necessary breath support for voice. Because this position can be taxing, when you get tired or feel tension in the thighs, buttocks, or back, recuperate by coming away from the wall and rolling down and up vertebra by vertebra several times.

- Position your feet parallel to each other and your heels about two inches away from the wall. The distance between your knees should be slightly narrower than the width of your shoulders.
- Place your back against the wall and leave your head free. The head should *not* be resting against the wall. The space between your occiput and the wall accommodates the necessary cervical curve, similarly to lying with a book under your head when prone. Which bony landmarks are touching the wall?
- Feel how much space there is between the wall and the small of your back.
- Draw your knees forward into the center of the room until they are flexed and positioned

over, *but not beyond*, your toes. Is the small of your back closer to the wall? Can you feel the relationship between this posture and the Starting Position on the floor?

- With knees bent and your back against the wall, open your ribs with breath and sustain the opening as the abdominal muscles move in on the exhalation and out on the inhalation. Feel the changing relationship between your back and the wall.
- Add unstructured sound.
- On an exhalation with a free and open throat, keep the rib cage expanded as you open the backs of your knees until you are fully upright again. Is the relationship between your lower lumbar and the wall different from when you began? Keeping the rib cage expanded, breathe and feel the resulting movement of the abdominal muscles.
- Continue to stand fully upright, supported by the wall, and add unstructured sound.
- On an exhalation, move away from the wall and take a walk around the room as you maintain this alignment.
- Alternate between your habitual alignment and your "new" alignment. What has changed? Perhaps the distinction between your habitual alignment and your neutral dynamic alignment is blurring?

The support of the wall helps the body organize itself with sufficient breath and core support around three essential activities: standing, walking, and talking. As these activities become fully supported, the body can respond with ease to impulses that require all manner of locomotion and vocal choices.

SHAPING YOUR BODY AND SOUND THROUGH LEVELS FROM ONE TO TEN

The Still Shape Forms offer another approach to gain the necessary balance in the abdominal muscles for both uprightness and breath support for voice production. Now is a good time to return to the exercises in chapter 1, which include moving on impulse through the Still Shape Forms: Pin, Ball, Wall, and Screw. For our purposes, the Still Shape Forms are approximations and not attempts to produce perfect Forms. Rather, they are reminders of the basic shapes the body can make in movement and stillness.

Other than a loose approach to the Still Shape Forms, the only other structures for these exercises are levels. Imagine that there are ten levels from floor to standing. Level One is on the floor, Level Five is halfway to standing, and Level Ten is represented when you are balanced on the balls of your feet or, for an added challenge, balanced on one foot! You have achieved a level change *only* if your head has risen to the next level. A head level change means that the head is rising incrementally and the body is supporting the rise through *Breath Support, Core Support, Initiation and Sequencing, Spatial Intent, Rotary Factor,* your ever-changing *Dynamic Alignment,* and *Effort Intent* (to be discussed in detail later in this book). With the inclusion of unstructured sound, we will call the integrated dynamic shapes and sounds that link the levels together "body/sound-shapes." Without the body/sound-shapes to serve as the string, the levels would have no relationship to each other. There would be no story—just isolated events.

- Lie on the floor in any shape you want and breathe.
- Initiate a body/sound-shape rising to Level Two.
- On another body/sound-shape, return to Level One.
- Choose a new shape on the floor and build from Level One to Level Two to Level Three with the evolving body/sound-shapes linking the levels together.
- Continue in this manner until you have built numerous pathways with sound from Level One to Level Ten and from Level Ten to Level One. Take note that you are not trying to sustain the sound on one breath through multiple levels. Breathe as needed for both functional and expressive purposes.
- Explore body/sound-shapes through the levels but not in numerical order. For instance, without pausing at the intermediary levels, rise from Level One to Level Three, from Level Three to Level Seven, and back to Level Two, etc. Encourage your body and voice to shape their way to the subsequent levels as opposed to going there directly. Think of these pathways as the "scenic routes" toward your neutral dynamic alignment.
- After several passes up and down, stand in your neutral dynamic alignment and do a personal inventory. How does your alignment feel now?

Obviously, you are not looking for *the* dynamic alignment, but rather, exploring the possibilities. During your journey from Level One to Level Ten, you are moving through various dynamic alignments and sounds. If you repeatedly sound on the same pitch, with the same intensity, volume, and rate regardless of the level change, slow down and sense every moment of the journey. Challenge yourself to keep shaping your body and sound in new and perhaps unexpected ways. As your imagination catches fire, you will connect the dots until each journey between the levels is rich and full. Imagination! It is always important to invite your imagination into these experiments.

Dynamic alignment is not a place or a position, but rather a reflection of the ever-changing relationships among the component parts of your body's inner architecture during movement or stillness. With each breath and heartbeat, a change occurs. The observer perceives "apparent stillness." You look still but you are not. You are a living organism constantly adjusting your inner life (inside the body) to the external surroundings (the room, bus, theatre, apartment, etc.).

Keep in mind that your neutral dynamic alignment is just *one* choice. Embracing the subtleties of active stillness allows you to inhabit this alignment without becoming fixed or rigid. Instead, you are dynamically balanced as if on the head of a pin, ready to go in any direction your imagination leads you.

CHAPTER FIVE

Resonance and Center Pitch: Revealing Your Vocal Presence
Time Frame: Five one-hour sessions

The term "resonance," when applied to voice, refers to the quality of the sound. The particulars of an individual's resonance often govern whether we deem that voice to be soothing, captivating, irritating, seductive, or harsh, to name a few of the possible descriptions. Therefore, it is important that you examine resonance relative to how and where it is produced in the body and what your personal inclinations are relative to your own vocal resonance. Just as you may have unconscious habitual postural patterns that block you from revealing the full range of your expressiveness, you may also have unconscious vocal habits that are just as inhibiting. Resonance is one of the key areas of habituated vocal behavior. While our habits certainly make us feel like ourselves, they can also block our expressive potential and serve as a cover for who we really are. Therefore, it is in your best interest to become conscious of habitual behavior, and assess its efficacy in revealing your true dynamic self and expanding your creative choices. But before you identify and assess your favored area of vocal resonance and attempt to expand it, let's start with how resonance is produced on a physical level.

On an exhalation, your breath vibrates as it passes through the oscillating vocal folds. The vibrating breath then strikes hard surfaces that can vibrate at a frequency adequate to produce sound. Such surfaces are the throat, mouth, hard palate, and nasal cavities. The vibrations produced by those hard surfaces can produce sympathetic vibrations in the head and chest, which also contribute to the resonant tone. As the vibration of the air strikes the hard surfaces (also called "areas of resonance"), sound is produced. There are varying opinions on how many areas of resonance there are in the body. Some specialists say there are as many as twelve areas of resonance. For our purpose, we will be focusing on four: chest, mouth, face (nasal cavities), and the top of the head.

While resonance and pitch are not the same things, they are linked. Your lower pitches will tend to ignite the chest resonators, your middle pitches the mouth, and your higher pitches the face and head. Likewise, particular phonemes (distinct units of speech sounds) also tend to resonate more readily in specific areas. "AH" (as in f_a_ther) tends to vibrate the chest, "ER" (as in h_er_ the way the British pronounce it, with almost no "r" sound) the mouth, "AY" (as in f_a_ke) the face, and "EE" (as in sw_ee_t) the top of the head. The following exercises will help you isolate the four areas of resonance. Make sure to apply what you learned in chapter 3 about breath support as you work through these exercises.

- Lie on your back in the Starting Position or sit in a chair. Put your thumb in your mouth, curled up toward but not touching the hard palate, and phonate an "ER." Can you feel the vibration between your thumb and hard palate? If not, keep adjusting the pitch until you feel some vibration (mouth resonance).
- Repeat the process as you phonate "AH" with your palm lightly resting on your chest (chest resonance).
- Repeat the process phonating "AY" with your fingertips touching the sides of your cheeks close to your nose (face resonance).
- Repeat the process phonating "EE" with your fingertips touching the crown of your head (head resonance).

There are relationships among the pitches, the phonemes produced, and the areas of resonance. Certain pitches and phonemes will contribute to bringing the resonators we are considering into prominence. However, producing a particular note or phoneme doesn't necessarily mean the corresponding resonator has been "turned on." The coordination of the muscles responsible for breath support, the free and open throat, and precision of the articulators producing the phoneme all bear some responsibility for the resonance. The phonations and pitches suggested here are those that are most likely to sensitize you to the resonant areas. However, once you have felt the resonators in action, vary your phonations and pitches at will and notice the effect on your resonance. Keep in mind that *the presence of optimum resonance is dependent on the absence of extraneous physical tensions.* This can only be achieved if the muscles that support the body and those that support the voice act in harmony with one another.

As you explore this chapter, one of your goals is to find the pitches that encourage the best balance of vibrations among all your resonators. The area of your vocal range that reflects this harmonious balance among the resonators is called *optimum bone resonance* or *center pitch.* Center pitch is a term that was commonly used prior to the 1960s to describe what is referred to today as "being on voice." However, "being on voice" is somewhat subjective, whereas center pitch is more concrete, and therefore more readily attained. Center pitch describes the pitch where the resonance feels balanced (equally distributed) among the principal resonators. It is interesting to note that *center pitch is to the voice what neutral dynamic alignment is to the body.* Both your center pitch and neutral dynamic alignment reveal your personal essence. As stated earlier, sometimes our habitual patterns act as a disguise, and therefore fail to reveal our intrinsic value to others and undermine our attempts at character work. If we do not know who we are, how can we play a character? How will we know where the specific traits of the character merge with us, and which are separate and need to be developed for a truthful portrayal? Remember, the goal is not to change *who* you are but rather to know and accept your true dynamic self, as well as to embrace and access all of your vocal and physical potential.

Expanding Your Vocal Range

To assist you during the following exercises, I recommend using a pitch pipe to ensure that you are indeed changing pitch and challenging your range. Otherwise, you are likely to repeatedly gravitate to the same three or four pitches, which may be habitual and will not necessarily promote your optimum bone resonance. If you are an actor who suffers from "pitch anxiety," don't worry. This is not an exercise about hitting a pitch dead on, as it would be in singing; rather, it is an encouragement into new areas of your voice. Additionally, a pitch pipe is a wonderful way to begin to train your ear, which is an essential component of dialect acquisition. If exploring pitches is new to you, I encourage you to invest in an A-440 pitch pipe, which names every pitch for you.

- Lie on your stomach and rest your head on your arms. Breathe in and hum several times, on a different pitch each time. Observe where you feel the vibrations in your body. Note how pitch alters your awareness of the vibrations.
- Guided by the pitch pipe, hum on middle C for ten counts.
- Hum on pitches going up the scale by half steps and then down the scale by half steps. The pitch pipe will clearly delineate the half steps. Only go as high or low as you can without straining.
- After each hum, write down the pitch and where in your body you were most aware of the vibrations.
- Repeat the whole sequence up and down the scale four or five times in a row. The goal is to notice which pitches repeat themselves relative to specific areas of resonance, as well as those that seem to produce optimum bone resonance.

- Lie on your back in the Starting Position. Breathe into the ribs on three counts, followed by the abdomen on three counts. Hum. Drop your jaw from the hinge and intone an "AH" (mmmmmmAHHHHH). Sustain the phonation as long as you can while maintaining an expanded rib cage with *ease*, then release the ribs.
- Repeat, substituting ER, AY, and EE.
- Guided by a pitch pipe, hum onto each phoneme going up and down the scale. Which pitches are produced with the most ease? On which pitches do you feel the best balance among your resonators? How does changing the phoneme affect your resonance and relationship to pitch?

If it is difficult for you to feel the areas of resonance while you lie on your back, then come to a seated position or stand. You may become more aware of your chest resonance if you phonate an "AH" with your head dropped back slightly as you lengthen the crown. (You will be looking at the place where the ceiling and wall meet. Do not scrunch the back of the neck in the attempt to look up.) You may find better access to your mouth resonance (ER) with your head level. Your face resonance (AY) may intensify if you look at the floor as you phonate. You may further enliven the resonators if you massage the sinus area of the face on "AY" and "EE" and tap gently on your chest on "AH." Do not underestimate the importance of breath support and a free and open throat to this endeavor.

It will take many passes at this before the relationship among pitch, resonance, and phonation becomes clear. As you did previously, jot down the pitches that tend to affect specific resonators. For instance, perhaps you observe that you feel a balance of vibrations in your mouth and chest when you phonate "AH" on middle C, but only in your face when phonating "EE" on the note F above middle C. Eventually, you will recognize the pitches and phonemes that produce *your* optimum bone resonance. However, be forewarned that as you mature and age, the pitch that you identify as your center will change. Hormone levels, as well as your general health and well-being, will have a strong impact on what you identify as your center pitch. It is also important to consider that environment plays a role. For instance, do you suffer from seasonal allergies? Do you live in a dry or humid climate? What pollutants are present in your environment? Understand that what you eat, drink, and smoke also affects voice production. Therefore, your exploration of center pitch must be a lifelong, if not daily, endeavor, and is not something to be considered a "done deal" at any age.

Expressive Use of Resonance and Center Pitch

Having a rich, resonant voice is insufficient by itself to be considered expressive. You must temper your practice with opportunities to explore center pitch and areas of resonance through exercises that emphasize your imagination. We are all familiar with the voice that initially strikes our ear with captivating resonances, but we soon might realize that it doesn't actually communicate to us at all. We can appreciate the technical ability of a speaker, but the tone (though initially impressive) ultimately can be unaffecting, causing us to lose interest. Actors who suffer from this are accused of "playing the voice" rather than revealing the character, circumstances, and objectives of the story. They are *producing* voice, rather than vocally *responding* on impulse to stimuli. Therefore, a lively responsive imagination is key to the value of this work. Never deny your imagination its life. For instance, perhaps today when you speak primarily with your mouth resonance, you feel authoritative and imagine that you are delivering your last crucial election speech as a candidate running for office. When your imagination is stimulated, act on that impulse all the way to its conclusion without censure or judgment. Don't worry about right or wrong. Give your imagination its head and follow its lead.

The following exercises are designed to help you understand how the areas of resonance promote expressivity.

- Emotional: Express your voice through a specific resonator and respond to how this makes you feel. For instance, engage just your face resonance. How does a preponderance of face resonance make you feel? Can your voice reflect that feeling? Play with each area of resonance in turn.
- Circumstances: Explore how the areas of resonance can initiate imaginative situations through which you can journey physically and vocally.
- Characters: Consider the possibility that as you stretch your vocal range, your imagination may respond to the stimuli by creating characters through your body and voice.
- Finish your practice by returning "home" to the center pitch of *your* voice and to *your* neutral dynamic alignment. How is your voice and body different now from how it was at the beginning of your practice today?

As you practice harmony among your voice, speech, and movement, the effects on your imagination will become amplified. I use the word "harmony" because resonance, pitch, articulation, and movement take place simultaneously, just like a chord of music. However, "resonance" is not a word to be applied only to voice. Just as the voice resonates into space, so does the body. In subsequent chapters, we will explore Laban's theory of Space Harmony, which describes how the body radiates energy beyond its corporeal self, illuminating and revealing the space around it. Laban's theory is predicated on his belief that just as there are sound harmonies that permeate space, there are "space harmonies" that the body produces when moving. Instead of various pitches struck or sung simultaneously, the component parts that make up Space Harmony are the adaptive shapes the body makes in response to the environment, the intention of the movement, and its direction in space (up/down, right/ left, forward/back). These components radiate out and permeate space much like the vibrations of a chord. At present, you are poised at this theoretical doorway, and though only at the threshold, you already bring the resonances of body and voice into harmony with each other. As you deepen your practice, movement and voice will produce an endless array of "chords" that will feed your imagination and thus expand your artistry.

CHAPTER SIX

Speech Shape: Fitness for the Actor's Articulators
Time Frame: Ten one-hour sessions

The articulators are responsible for shaping unstructured sound into structured sound as the exhalation passes through the mouth. The unstructured sound reveals how we feel and the structured sound imbues those feelings with specific meaning. For instance, you may sound gleeful, but it is not until the specificity of your articulation reveals that you are going on a great vacation that we understand the context of your gleefulness.

Sadly, in recent times, the study of articulation has been given a bad rap, weighted down by political and socioeconomic considerations. The inevitable questions are: "Who's to say this group's pronunciation is superior to another group's?" "Why should we have standardized speech?" "Will not standardization contribute to the extinction of many rich and varied cultural approaches to language?" These are multicultural times and the need to act sensitively cannot be overstated. Any perceived conflict with training the articulators can be solved with an examination of the *intention* of the training. It is a false assumption that the practice of articulation is for the purpose of standardizing speech. On the contrary, the intention is to enhance the actor's skill set so that he can reveal—not extinguish—multicultural approaches to speech. The goal is not to standardize speech but the opposite—to globalize it. Therefore, the efficacy of rigorous training in articulation is transparent. How can you give an honest representation of a variety of characters from a host of backgrounds if you can speak only with your own speech habits and regional dialect? As an actor, you are preparing for challenges that exceed everyday expectations. Therefore, you need to pursue an "extra-daily technique" if you are going to be able to reflect the truth of a character's condition. Your goal is not to attain *the* standard of speech, but *myriad* standards that give depth, reality, and integrity to your character. This requires that you develop an incredible amount of flexibility and control over the articulators and sensitize your ear to the nuances of pitch and rhythm. Additionally, when you step into your character's skin, you must do so without prejudice or judgment. Tune your ear to the world around you and take note of how various modes of speaking affect *you*. What assumptions do you make based on how an individual speaks? Unless you are very honest with yourself and identify your hidden preconceived notions, it will be difficult not to ill-judge a character whose speech you may unconsciously believe to be substandard, or the reverse, hoity-toity. This knife cuts both ways. Be aware that an actor who unconsciously judges the character he is portraying is not likely to craft a performance that is an honest reflection of the human condition.

Although the "mouth-shapes" (precise articulation) described are based on the dialect called, variously, Standard Stage, modified Mid-Atlantic, or Classical American speech, this training is not focused on "right" or "wrong" relative to standardizing pronunciation, but on flexibility, strength, stamina, and full-body connectedness. As you proceed through the exercises, you will identify your habitual patterns and challenge your articulators to move in new ways. Overcoming your habitual patterns can sometimes make you feel like you are not yourself. Keep in mind: The purpose is *not to subtract from* but *to add to* your skill level and thereby *heighten* your sense of yourself as an artist. As always, your goal is to expand your expressive choices that would otherwise be limited by your habits. Let's examine where your speech habits were born.

The development of your speech skills and habits began at birth. Even as a baby, you could distinguish your primary caregiver's voice from others. As you were spoken to, your soft palate made subtle adjustments, already finding the shape of your local dialect. You were adopting smart habits to ensure your survival. When you discovered your tongue and lips, you explored them without censure. As your limbs began to reach into your environment, so did your lips and tongue. The development of your motor skills was an essential step toward the development of articulation. Since motor skills and articulation share a common cognitive process, it is difficult to refine articulation without also honing your motor skills. Consequently, speech habits have a foothold in both the movements of the articulators and the gesture life of the limbs. Therefore, it is essential that we free our perception of speech from an intellectual activity to one that is viscerally connected to the body. In other words, let's embrace the concepts: *Speech is movement* and *gesture is speech*.

Before we continue, refer to the Anatomy Illustrations to see the articulators, pages 19 and 20. The moveable articulators are the lips, tongue, mandible (lower jaw), and soft palate. They work in relationship to the immoveable articulators, which are the teeth, alveolar ridge (gum ridge), and hard palate. As the articulators move, they change the shape of the vocal tract, creating speech sounds. As we refine the relationships among the moveable and immovable articulators, we develop the ability to communicate specific information. In chapter 2, during the Right/Left Body Half Fundamental, you stretched your lips toward the thumb, rounding them into an "OO" or "OH" sound. Through reenacting this developmental stage, you began to discover individual speech sounds called *phonemes*. As a baby, you discovered that as your tongue, lips, and jaw moved, your sound was altered enough to elicit a variety of responses from the adults upon whom you depended. Certain sounds and movements compelled your caregiver to bring food, change your diaper, or give a cuddle. Not a recognizable word was spoken, and yet your needs were usually understood. Regardless of your success, this form of communication was obviously limiting. Therefore, it was in your best interest to imitate the speakers around you and learn to articulate your needs.

In chapters 1 and 2, other than exploring with "OO" and "OH," you were mostly engaged in unstructured sound. In chapter 5, you added AH, ER, AY, and EE to your sound bank. In this chapter, you will continue to explore unstructured sounds and the muscular activity of the articulators by refining the mouth-shapes for the sounds OO, OH, AW, AH, ER, AY, and EE. However, it is possible that when instructed to move your articulators randomly, you may trick yourself into additional recognizable phonemes. This is good! That's how we learned to speak.

As we venture further into articulation, it is important to note that the vagaries of the English language render it unreliable relative to the use of spelling as a clue for even basic pronunciation. For instance, the letters "ou" in the word "th*ou*gh" sound like "thr*ow*" and "s*ew*," but in "r*ou*gh" the same two letters sound like the "u" in "b*u*t." Of course, you couldn't help but notice that the "ou" in "s*ou*nd" is yet another sOUnd! English is rife with such examples. Consequently, we need a way of describing sounds in writing that is not related to spelling. One of the most efficient ways to recognize the full range of pronunciations is to learn the International Phonetic Alphabet (IPA). The IPA is a set of symbols that represents the sounds of the world's languages. The operative word is "sound" not spelling. For our purposes, however, we will use phonological symbols to describe sound. Though not as thorough as the IPA, phonological symbols are more quickly understood by most readers. You already recognize the phonological symbols OO, OH, AW, AH, AY, and EE and relate them to sound with no trouble. However, it would be very useful for you to invest in a book of lexical sets that includes the IPA, such as Edith Skinner's *Speak with Distinction*, or *Classically Speaking* by Patricia Fletcher. Both are listed in the bibliography. If you choose to learn IPA, then a good reinforcement is to transcribe the muscular activity exercises for the articulators into the appropriate phonetic symbols.

Vowels and Diphthongs

Vowels and diphthongs are always voiced through a free and open throat with the tip of the tongue resting behind the lower front teeth. OO, AW, AH, ER, and EE are considered pure vowels because the lips do not move once the mouth-shape is attained, whereas "OH" and "AY" are diphthongs. A *diphthong* is comprised of two pure vowel sounds that are so closely blended together, they seem like one. During the phonation of a diphthong, the articulators move during the phonation from one mouth-shape to another.

The particular vowel and diphthong sounds listed in the previous paragraph form the basis for the mouth-shapes that we will build upon in subsequent chapters. As you practice the mouth-shapes, they may feel exaggerated and strange to you. That is fine; in fact, that is good because the sensation of "exaggeration" is a sign that you are building the muscle tone in your articulators necessary to acquire an "extra-daily technique." Therefore, keep in mind that the purpose of the mouth-shapes is to condition the articulators to be able to produce a cornucopia of possibilities. Where and when you ultimately apply them will be dictated by the character and dialect, as well as the venue (stage, film, or television) in which you are performing.

Mouth-Shapes: Muscular Activity for the Articulators

During the following practice, stand in front of a mirror. Take advantage of the feedback the mirror can give you about the accuracy of your mouth-shapes, as well as any signs of extraneous tensions in the face.

SHAPING THE LIPS

- **"OO" Shape** (c<u>oo</u>l):
    - Drop your jaw from your temporomandibular joint (jaw hinge) with a free and open throat.
    - Keep the tip of your tongue behind your lower front teeth and turn your lips out like a fish, encircling the tip of your little finger tightly. The distance between your teeth will resolve to the size of your little finger.
    - "Mime-through" ten times: AH→OO. (A *mime-through* is a *silent* exploration of a mouth-shape for a specific phoneme; it can be applied to phrases of speech as well.)

- **"OH" Shape** (s<u>ou</u>l): The diphthong "OH" is composed of the short vowel sound in "<u>o</u>paque" blended with the short vowel sound in "b<u>oo</u>k." The stress is on the first phoneme.
    - Drop your jaw from your temporomandibular joint with a free and open throat.
    - Keep the tip of your tongue behind your lower front teeth and turn your lips out like a fish, encircling the tip of your thumb. The distance between your teeth will now approximate your thumb's width.
    - Remove your thumb and allow the lips to resolve to the "b<u>oo</u>k" sound.
    - Mime-through ten times: AH→OH.

- **"AW" Shape** (s<u>aw</u>):
    - Drop your jaw from your temporomandibular joint with a free and open throat.
    - Keep the tip of your tongue behind your lower front teeth and turn your lips out to form a rectangle.
    - The distance between your teeth should be slightly smaller than the width of your index and third finger together.
    - Mime-through ten times: AH→AW.

NEUTRAL LIPS AND TONGUE

- **"AH" Shape** (f<u>a</u>ther):
    - Drop your jaw from your temporomandibular joint with a free and open throat.
    - The tongue and lips remain neutral.
    - The distance between your teeth will be approximately the width of the tips of your index and third fingers together.
    - Mime-through ten times.

SHAPING THE TONGUE

The parts of your tongue with which you need to be familiar are the "tip," the sides of the tongue, called the "blades," and the "body" of the tongue, which lives between the blades.

- **"ER" Shape** (h*er*): The "r" is not treated as a consonant in this instance, but as part of the vowel, minimizing the sound of "r" to an "r" coloring.
  - o Drop your jaw from your temporomandibular joint with a free and open throat and keep the lips neutral.
  - o With the tip of the tongue remaining behind the lower front teeth, slightly raise the body of the tongue toward the place where the hard and soft palates meet. The distance between your teeth will measure *approximately* the width of the tips of your index and third fingers together. Can you see the very subtle arch upward in the body of the tongue as you mime from "AH" to "ER"?
  - o Mime-through ten times: AH→ER.

As you produce "AY" and "EE," I will ask you to keep the lips neutral. In some training programs, the lips are slightly spread on these sounds. The "smile" will increase face resonance. If you tend to lack sufficient nasal resonance, then you may want to experiment with a slight smile, or lift of the cheek muscles, on "AY" and "EE." Likewise, if you tend to have an overabundance of nasal resonance or a "thin" voice, you can mitigate that with relaxed lips.

- **"AY" Shape** (f*a*ke): The diphthong "AY" is composed of the short vowel sound in "p*e*t" blended with the short vowel sound in "p*i*t." The stress is on the first phoneme.
  - o Drop your jaw from your temporomandibular joint with a free and open throat and keep the lips neutral.
  - o With the tip of the tongue remaining behind the lower front teeth, the body of the tongue will arch toward the alveolar ridge. Can you see the body of your tongue moving from the neutral position on "AH" to arching forward and up on "AY"?
  - o Mime-through ten times: AH→AY.
- **"EE" Shape** (sw*ee*t):
  - o Drop your jaw from your temporomandibular joint with a free and open throat and keep your lips neutral.
  - o With the tip of the tongue remaining behind the lower front teeth, the body of the tongue will arch higher than it did for "AY." Can you see the action the body of your tongue is taking as it moves from "AH" to "EE"?
  - o Mime-through ten times: AH→EE.

RECUPERATION

- Shake Out the Jaw: Drop your jaw, clasp your hands together, and vigorously shake them back and forth, a motion to which your jaw will respond by also shaking back and forth.
- Massage the Masseter Muscle (page 18): Drop your jaw, then massage your masseter muscles with the heel of your palm and/or slide the heel of your palm down the length of this muscle.
- Tongue Waggle: Roll your head down and hang your tongue out of your mouth. Shake your head, letting the tongue waggle.
- Buzz out your lips on an exhalation. You will sound a bit like a horse.

BREATHE-THROUGH

Another name for the "sighing out" is "breathe-through." The faint, whispery sounds of the breathe-through are the first stirrings of resonance as the air passes through the specific mouth-shapes. As you breathe-through each vowel and diphthong sound, make sure you are applying what you learned about supporting the breath from your intercostal, abdominal, and back muscles.

- Repeat all of the previous exercises on a breathe-through. For example: On impulse, breathe in three counts to the ribs and three counts to the abdomen, then drop your jaw, sighing out on a count of four—two counts are allotted for "AH" and two counts for "OO."
- Breathe-through AH→OO.
- Relax the abdomen and repeat ten times.
- Substitute the vowel/diphthong sounds OH, AW, ER, AY, and EE for "OO" and breathe-through each one as you did for "OO."
- Recuperate.

ADDING SOUND

The following exercises marry the breath-support practices from chapter 5 with articulation. Your goal is to keep your ribs expanded through the phonation without hardening the abdomen. Try to postpone the release of the rib cage for as long as possible without creating tension.

- Lie in the Starting Position with one hand on your lower ribs and the other on your abdomen. On impulse, breathe in through the nose on six counts: three counts to the ribs, followed by three counts to the abdomen.
- Hum on your center pitch and gently chew as if eating something delicious for six counts. As you are "chewing" your hum for six counts, keep your rib cage expanded while the abdomen releases slowly toward the spine. On the sixth count, relax your abdomen, sighing out the rest of the air, if there is any.
- When you feel the impulse to breathe in, expand the abdomen with breath (your ribs are still expanded), then hum and chew again.

- Repeat five times and *then* release the ribs on a sigh with a free and open throat.
- Recuperate with Bartenieff Fundamentals.
- Repeat the previous sequence, but this time "chew the hum" on pitches above and below your center pitch. If needed, use the pitch pipe to guide you. *Caution: Never hum on pitches so high or so low that you feel like you are straining or hurting your throat.*

- On impulse, breathe in through the nose on six counts: three counts to the ribs, followed by three counts to the abdomen.
- Produce an "AH" on your center pitch and open and close your lower jaw from the temporomandibular joint several times during the phonation. It is best to keep the duration of the sound short so you can control the exhalation from the abdomen while the ribs remain floating.
- Repeat five times, exploring pitches above and below your center pitch, and then release the ribs on a sigh.
- Recuperate.

- On impulse, breathe in through the nose on six counts: three counts to the ribs, followed by three counts to the abdomen. Keep the rib cage floating as the abdomen releases toward the spine, supporting a sustained "AH" on your center pitch.
- As you sustain the sound, explore all the ways the tongue and lips can move. At this point, it doesn't matter that the phonations are not recognizable speech sounds.
- Repeat five times, on a different pitch each time, then release the rib cage on a sigh.
- Recuperate.
- Repeat the whole sequence.

- On impulse, breathe in through the nose on six counts: three counts to the ribs, followed by three counts to the abdomen. Keep the rib cage floating as the abdomen releases toward the spine, supporting a sustained "AH" on your center pitch.
- Sustain "AH" for two counts, then glide your lips to "OO." Sustain "OO" for two counts as your abdomen continues to release toward the spine (AAAH→OOO).
- Release your rib cage.
- Repeat ten times.
- Repeat the sequence and substitute OH, AW, ER, AY, and EE for "OO." In the instance of ER, AY, and EE, you will be gliding your tongue from neutral to the arched position appropriate for the vowel/diphthong sound. The lips will remain neutral.
- Recuperate.

Can you feel and see the difference in your lips between OO, OH and AW? Can you feel and see the difference in the shape of your tongue as you phonate the sounds ER, AY, and EE? What is your experience of moving the lips and tongue with precision?

In the previous exercises, you were directed to keep the ribs floating while the abdominal muscles did the work of controlling the exhalation. In the next exercise, you will follow the release of the abdomen with a controlled release of the rib cage to sustain the sound. *Caution: Do not squeeze the breath out from either the abdominal muscles or the intercostals. Keep the flow easy.*

- On impulse, breathe in through the nose on six counts: three counts to the ribs, followed by three counts to the abdomen. Drop your jaw and sustain "AH" on your center pitch, supported from the abdomen, for as long as is comfortable.
- When you have phonated as long as you can *with ease*, supported by the abdominal muscles, *then* the intercostals will slowly bring the ribs downward as you continue the sound.
- Relax and wait for the next impulse to expand your ribs and abdomen with breath.
- Repeat the first two steps five times, then recuperate.
- Repeat the sequence and substitute the other vowels and diphthongs for "AH."

You now have two applications of breath support for speech. The first application requires supporting the sound with the abdominal muscles, while the intercostal muscles maintain a reserve of breath in the ribs. The second application allows for a release of the ribs during the phonation. Besides the duration of the exhalation, what are the qualitative differences between the two applications of breath support?

Ultimately, you have choices relative to how you will impulsively support the voice with breath. The choice will depend, at least in part, on the length of the phrase and the difficulty of the articulation. Eventually the body will be so well practiced at the possibilities that the breath will respond to the needs of the communication on impulse. The word "choice" is not to suggest that the process is "thoughtful," but to acknowledge that more than one impulse can surface at a time and that the body can make instantaneous choices based on both the functional and expressive needs of the moment. If you are truly responding to your impulses, then choices will be made before you even realize there was a choice to be made. With practice, you will to learn to trust your body's wisdom.

Sound-Shapes

You are engaged in a process that makes what was unknown known, relative to how the breath mechanism works. In other words, you have been exploring a structured, functional process. Likewise, our approach to articulation has been very structured. Now you need to recuperate from all this structure by balancing function with expression. During the next exercises, you will explore sounds that are motivated from an expressive need. For this purpose, you will return to an exploration of unstructured sounds and allow them to develop into "sound-shapes." Unstructured sound and sound-shapes are similar in that they may be motivated from a thought, a light breeze on your face, a sudden noise in the room, your cat walking on your stomach, or a memory. It is amazing how many influences, both internal and external, there are to motivate sound. An unstructured sound is expressed with the articulators mostly in neutral, while sound-shapes employ general movements of the articulators motivated from a need to be understood. Sound-shapes form a bridge between our primal unstructured sound and precise mouth-shapes that make our meaning explicit. Sound-shapes bring you to the threshold of precise articulation and explicit sense by promoting movement of the articulators motivated from the need to communicate. You began to examine specific mouth-shapes in chapter 5, and you will continue to develop the muscular activity of the articulators toward many more precise mouth-shapes throughout Levels Two and Three.

As you explore the following exercises, do not feel pressure to name your emotional conditions before you make sound. By the time you think of the name, the impulse has long passed and six more may have taken its place. Nor are you trying to sound "frustrated" or "happy," etc. It is very important to understand the distinction between trying to *sound* "happy" as opposed to allowing your happy feelings to *shape the sound* that emerges. The intention of these exercises is to explore the latter, not the former.

- Lie on the floor in any manner that is comfortable for you.
- Heighten your awareness of how you are feeling, which includes physically and emotionally.
- Allow your moment-to-moment personal conditions to give your sound shape. Perhaps you are feeling frustrated? Give frustration a sound. Or perhaps you feel tightness in your shoulders? Give *that* a sound. Elated? Humorous? Let those emotional or physical conditions shape your sound.
- Continue to explore your conditions moment to moment and allow the sound-shapes to change the shape of your body. For example, if the sound has enough inspiration, it may roll you over or make you sit up. Your sound-shapes may motivate the Still Shape Forms. You may even find yourself standing, crawling, running, walking, twisting, or leaping.
- Build on the previous exercise by shaping your articulators more and more precisely and allow your body to respond with movement. Your articulators are creating "gibberish."

It is almost impossible to do these exercises "wrong." The exception would be to judge yourself or to get "social" or "clever" in any way—especially if you are practicing with others. Let the phonations be potent "nonsense" for now: a moment-to-moment baseline of your sound/feeling. Clarity in your articulations will grow from your *need to be understood*. The mouth-shapes for the vowel and diphthong sounds may become inevitable as you continue to express yourself moment to moment.

While all precise articulations of the vowels and consonants contribute to "sense" and can reveal our emotional state of being, it is the vowels and diphthongs that carry most of the responsibility for reflecting our emotional conditions. The consonants, by putting limits on the vowels or diphthongs, reveal explicit meaning. For instance, "OH" can be sustained for quite a long time and filled with emotion, but until an "s" is articulated in front of it and an "l" at the end of it, the listener does not have the explicit sense of the communication, which is the word "soul."

Together, the precise mouth-shapes for the vowels and consonants bridge our inner life to the outer world with *explicit sense*. We will explore explicit sense in future chapters. For now, pretend that you are a child in a playpen and your toys are the sounds to which your body responds. Let your sound pour out moment to moment without judgment. Having said that, do not put pressure on yourself to make sound all the time. Similarly to movement and stillness, the impulse to make sound is balanced by the impulse to be silent and vice versa. Be aware of the power of silence and its effect on your body.

To find the balance between function and expression, consciously choose to work on one and then the other. The more you alternate between the two, the more they will become one. Clear, precise articulation requires a high level of functional skill, which includes the organization of the body and breath. But a high skill level alone is not enough to make your voice and speech truly expressive. Likewise, without skillful articulators, your expressiveness may remain that of a babe in the crib, desperate to communicate the specifics of your needs.

Level Two

"Every phase of movement, every small transference of weight, every single gesture of any part of the body reveals some feature of... inner life."

–Rudolf Laban

CHAPTER SEVEN
The Actor Revealed through Modes of Shape Change
Time Frame: Seven one-hour sessions

In chapter 1 and again in the subsequent chapters, we explored the concept of **Shape** through the Still Shape Forms: Pin, Ball, Wall, and Screw. We will now expand our exploration of **Shape** to include a category called the Modes of Shape Change. The Modes of Shape Change are: Shape Flow, Arc-like Directional, Spoke-like Directional, and Carving. The Modes of Shape Change reveal one's inner attitudes toward the surroundings and creates a relationship between oneself and the environs. The Shape Change may be motivated from the inside→out (emotional/psychological) or the outside→in (environment/given circumstances).

Shape Flow is all about you! Your mantra in Shape Flow is, "Me! Me! Me!" As described in chapter 1, Shape Flow serves as the underlying support for sound and movement, while Arc-like and Spoke-like Directional movements form a bridge between yourself and the environment. For example, reaching directly for an object or pushing an object away is a Spoke-like movement. Sweeping your arm in an arc, perhaps to indicate, "All this is mine," constitutes an Arc-like movement. The Arc-like and Spoke-like movements are goal-oriented toward some aspect of the environment. Abstractly, Arc-like and Spoke-like can also refer to fixed ideas or black-and-white points of view. Carving is the most complex of the Modes of Shape Change because it is process-oriented rather than self-centered or goal oriented. Carving produces an interactive, cooperative relationship between the environment and self. In the Carving Mode, you are adapting to and integrating yourself into the environs. An example of the Carving Mode is the negotiation between yourself and others as you advance along a crowded city street. On an abstract level, the Carving Mode can represent taking in divergent ideas, processing them, and returning them to the environment in a new form.

Relative to Bartenieff's Nine Principles, the Modes of Shape Change have a strong foothold in Developmental Patterning. Shape Flow represents the self-involvement of infancy. The Arc-like and Spoke-like Directional Modes represent the "I want" and "I don't want" aspects of childhood. The Carving Mode represents the adaptive qualities of adulthood. These simplifications are meant to describe when each Mode is present but are not necessarily exclusive. In fact, as adults, we hopefully employ all of the Modes of Shape Change in a balanced way to serve our needs until aging reverses the process. Slowly we lose our ability to Carve or adapt, then our ability to Arc or Spoke into the environment, and finally, Shape Flow becomes dominant again as we slip into the final stage of life.

Exercises for Shape Flow, Spoke-like Directional, Arc-like Directional, and Carving

The following exercises explore the gestures of the body and the muscular activity of the articulators through the Modes of Shape Change. Relative to speech, some of the exercises principally serve a functional purpose because they examine how one shapes the lips and tongue to create the specific phonemes of spoken English. However, other exercises emphasize an application of Shape Change to develop a more expressive voice. This means that you will use the Modes as images for your sound as it penetrates space. In this instance, the word "image" means visualizing your sound-shape. For example, you will examine the qualitative differences that occur in your voice if you use the Spoke-like Mode as an image as opposed to the Carving Mode. In chapter 1, the Shape Flow qualities during Cellular Breathing are described as *growing* and *shrinking*. These words capture the general quality of Shape Flow and describe a very early developmental stage—infancy. The following descriptive words for Shape Flow provide more specificity and reflect a more mature developmental stage.

SHAPE FLOW
(lengthening/shortening, narrowing/widening, hollowing/bulging)

Return to the section called **Breathing through the Still Shape Forms** in chapter 1. Review the description of Shape Flow and then continue with the following exercises.

- Lie on your back and as you breathe, gently feel your limbs move slightly in and out from your center (Cellular Breathing, chapter 1).
- Let your sound travel with your body.

- Stand in active stillness with your eyes closed and feel your spine *lengthen* and *shorten* as you breathe and sound. Your head and coccyx will subtly move toward and away from your belly button.
- Repeat the previous exercise, substituting *narrowing* and *widening* the chest. As you *narrow*, your torso condenses, moving closer to the centerline of your body. As you *widen*, your torso expands, moving away from centerline of your body.
- Repeat by substituting *hollowing* (sternum moves slightly toward your thoracic vertebrae) and *bulging* (sternum moves slightly away from the thoracic vertebrae).

SPOKE-LIKE DIRECTIONAL
(upward/downward, side-across/side-open, backward/forward)

A Spoke-like Directional Shape Change is accomplished when you move a limb from the centerline of the body outward into the environment in an effort to reach toward an object or person, or to pull that object or person toward your center. You can achieve a Spoke-like Directional movement with almost any body part, including the lips and tongue. On an imagistic level, the intention of the sound, whether structured or unstructured, is exactly the same as the intention of your movement. When influenced by the Spoke-like Mode, you are forming a bridge with your voice and body toward a specific object or person in the environment. Keep in mind: that bridge goes in both directions. This means that the movement and sound can emanate from your center outward toward a specific object, or "pull" that object in toward your center. For instance, if you are sending the phoneme "AY" on a Spoke-like trajectory *upward*, out the top of your head, you need to know what your voice is "reaching" for in the heavens. Likewise, if "AY" forms a trajectory *downward* from the heavens, you need to imagine what is coming into your center.

In the following exercises, you are limited to Spoke-like sounds and movement. If you send "OH" to a specific person, know that the Spoke-like Directional sound-shape of "OH" can penetrate and affect your partner. Also know that your partner will respond by sending a Spoke-like Directional movement and sound-shape back to you. The severe limitation of using only Spoke-like shapes can be both frustrating and liberating creatively. It is frustrating because all your impulses must be filtered through Spoke-like vocal and physical shapes. But the limitations can also be liberating because your *imagination* will respond in unexpected ways. Frustrating or not, it is important for the actor to learn to create within tight parameters. Allow your imagination to be affected. Your response to your imagination is critical to gaining benefit from the exercises. Because an actor is seldom on stage alone, the introduction of partner work is crucial to your development. Therefore, for some of the following exercises you will need a partner.

- Take a few moments to stand in your neutral dynamic alignment, connected to your breath.
- Observe how you feel *today*.

- Work alone. Initiating from the breath, move various body parts with Spoke-like Directional Shape Changes to form relationships with your environs.

- Improvise with a scene partner. Stand facing one another and respond to each other as if in a scene. Your "dialogue" is comprised of sound-shapes and Spoke-like Directional moves with various body parts (fingers, toes, knees, shoulders, sternum, hips, etc.) All the body parts won't conform to perfect Spoke-like shapes, but it is important that your *intention* is to form a bridge between yourself and something/one in the environment.
- When you and your partner intuit the end of the improvisation, return to your neutral dynamic alignment and stand in active stillness.
- Share your experiences with your partner.

- Stand alone in active stillness in your neutral dynamic alignment.
- On a breathe-through, *move just your tongue* in Spoke-like Directional shapes.
- On a breathe-through, *move just your lips* in Spoke-like Directional shapes.

- Improvise with a partner. Your "script" consists of the phonemes OO, OH, AW, AH, ER, AY, and EE as produced through the specific mouth-shapes and Spoke-like Directional movements of the body.
- When you intuit the end of the improvisation, return to neutral dynamic alignment in active stillness. Stand in silence for several minutes and observe how your body feels.
- Share your experiences with your partner.

ARC-LIKE DIRECTIONAL
(*upward/downward, side-across/side-open, backward/forward*)

Just as the title suggests, the body parts move in Arc-like Directional shapes. Rather than piercing the environment directly, an Arc-like Directional shape represents an elliptical tour toward the object or person. Repeat the exercises described in the Spoke-like Directional section, substituting Arc-like Directional Shape Changes. When you have completed those exercises, continue with the following.

- Work alone or with a scene partner. On impulse, move and sound with Spoke-like *and* Arc-like Directional Shape Changes. If working alone, the Shape Changes become your physical "monologue." If working with a partner, the Shape Changes are your physical "dialogue."
- Recuperate by standing silently in active stillness. Observe how your body and breath feel.

- Alone or with a partner, stand in neutral dynamic alignment in active stillness. With unstructured and structured sounds, speak reflecting both Spoke-like and Arc-like Directional Modes of Shape Change with just your voice and speech. Is there a qualitative difference between Spoke-like and Arc-like Directional sounds? For instance, can the sound of an "OO" resonate in a Spoke-like Directional shape? In an Arc-like Directional shape?

During these experiments, you are imagining which Mode of Shape Change the phoneme travels on once it leaves your lips. This skill is a bit like throwing a curveball because, once thrown, the ball travels between the pitcher and the batter on a particular pathway. How the ball moves through the space is what the batter is responding to with the swing of the bat. So it is with Modes of Shape Change and voice. Your partner is responding to how your voice, shaped by your articulators, is describing the space between the two of you. You are the "pitcher" of your voice. As such, your intention, married to your technical skill, allows your voice to travel through space on a particular trajectory. The trajectory will be interpreted expressively and responded to on impulse by the "catcher"—your scene partner. This is not just true for Spoke-like and Arc-like Modes, but for the Carving Mode as well.

CARVING MODE OF SHAPE CHANGE
(*ascending/descending*, enclosing/spreading, retreating/advancing*)

---

*Also referred to as rising/sinking by Laban practitioners.

The Carving Mode of Shape Change emphasizes a three-dimensional adaptation to space and all it contains through *ascending/descending*, *enclosing/spreading*, and *retreating/advancing*. The Carving Mode, relative to voice, is an imagistic tool to expand the vocal choices that can reveal the state of your character. As you explore the following exercises with your body, perhaps you will notice that Arc-like and Spoke-like Directional Modes tend to emphasize the distal parts of the body, while the Carving Mode tends to relate more to the trunk. The first set of exercises does not require a partner.

- Explore the Carving Mode with your full body. You are Carving when you adapt or mold your body to whatever or whoever is present in the environs. Here is a very literal example. Sit in a chair and let your body mold itself into the chair. Turn the chair over and mold your body into this new "chair." Turn it on its side and adapt your body to this chair.
- Stand in active stillness and improvise with your tongue and lips by moving them through the component parts of Carving: *ascending/descending*, *enclosing/spreading*, and *retreating/advancing*.
- Add sound and enjoy all sorts of strange gibberish (sound-shapes).
- Continue to stand in active stillness and explore the Carving Mode with just your voice, keeping your articulators neutral.
- Explore the Carving Mode in both body and voice.
- In silence, continue to shape your body around objects or people sharing the space with you.

The following exercises require a scene partner.

- In silence, improvise in the Carving Mode. Your improvisation may be abstract or realistic. This is an example of a realistic improvisation: Perhaps with an inner attitude of kindness, you approach your partner, who is sitting in a chair. Your attitude motivates you to *enclose* your body around your partner in an embrace. Your partner's inner attitude is affected and as a result, he *spreads* his arms and *encloses* you in an embrace as well.
- In silence, improvise and access the Modes of Shape Change on impulse. Again, your improvisation may be abstract or realistic. For instance, building on the previous realistic example, perhaps during your embrace with your partner, his inner attitude changes to repulsion. Consequently, with a Spoke-like Directional Shape Change he pushes you away. Fearful, you *retreat* (Carving), and then with another shift of attitude, your fist moves in a Spoke-like threatening manner.
- Add sound to the previous exercise. The sounds you make may be structured or unstructured.
- When you and your partner have intuited the end of the improvisation, share your experiences with each other.

- Stand opposite your partner and *remain in active stillness* for this exercise. On impulse, begin a sound-shape improvisation with the four Modes of Shape Change as your dialogue. All your vocal impulses will be filtered through the images of Shape Flow, Spoke-like/Arc-like Directional, and Carving Modes of Shape Change. Can the sounds emanating from your partner change your inner attitude moment to moment, and can you reveal those changes through your sound-shapes?

- Add movement to the previous exercise. All your impulses to move and speak will be filtered through the Modes of Shape Change. Stay alert to how your imagination is affected and respond to it.

- When you and your partner have intuited the end of the improvisation, share your experiences with each other.

Floor Patterns

"Floor Patterns" is the term used to describe the pathways we take to move across the floor. It is important and clarifying to note that correlations exist between the Modes of Shape Change and Floor Patterns. Imagine that you are traveling in wet sand and, when you look back at the trail, you see *straight lines*. This is mimicking the Spoke-like Mode of Shape Change. If your feet left a trail that *arcs*, its correlative would obviously be the Arc-like Mode. Likewise, if your feet left a *winding* pathway, this Pattern would be a correlative to the Carving Mode of Shape Change. Although locomotion with your feet is referenced, keep in mind that traveling doesn't always happen on your feet. Crawling, rolling, slithering, and walking on your hands also represent "traveling." Some of the following exercises alternate between improvising with a scene partner and working alone.

- Work alone. Improvise moving your body on *straight*, *arced*, and *winding* Floor Patterns on impulse.

- With several partners watching, motivate three entrances into the studio playing area or stage. The first entrance will be on a *straight* Floor Pattern, the second on an *arced* Pattern, and the third *winding*.

- Report your experience to the observers and get feedback on what they observed.

- Work with a partner. In silence, improvise moving on the Floor Patterns. Can you shift easily among the Floor Patterns in response to how you are affected by your scene partner?

- When you and your partner have intuited the end of the improvisation, share your experiences with each other.

- Work alone. Experiment with moving on a particular Floor Pattern and gesturing with its correlative. For instance, move on a *straight line* and gesture in a Spoke-like manner.

- Work alone. Experiment with moving on a particular Floor Pattern and *do not* gesture with its correlative. For instance, move on a *straight line* and gesture in the Carving Mode.

- Work with a partner. In silence, improvise with movement. Allow the Floor Patterns and the Shape Changes that emerge to be born out of your impulses.
- When you and your partner have intuited the end of the improvisation, share your experiences with each other.

- Work alone. Travel on one Floor Pattern but vary the Shape Change of your *sound*. For instance, can you travel on an *arced* Floor Pattern while sounding in the Carving Mode? Allow there to be interplay among structured and unstructured sounds.

- Work with a partner. Improvise with sound and movement, using the Floor Patterns and the Modes of Shape Change on impulse as your "script."
- When you and your partner have intuited the end of the improvisation, share your experiences with each other.

The changes in your attitudes or moment-to-moment feelings are revealed to the outside world through the corresponding shape shifts of your body and voice. These shape shifts initiate in your core and radiate out to become the physical manifestations of your attitudes. It is important to sensitize yourself to these internal physical shifts. Each Shape Change has the potential to enrich the story of your character. You have probably noticed that, as your voice shifts shape, the pitch, volume, and rate of phonation vary as well. Vocal variety that is initiated from your inner attitudes and is closely connected to the movements of body will not appear arbitrary. The body/voice connection radiates your dynamic, expressive self into the environment for all to witness. The principal work of the actor is to reveal—to make what was hidden appear—and your chief tool in this endeavor is **Shape**.

CHAPTER EIGHT

Filling Space: Exploring Your Physical and Vocal Kinesphere
Time Frame: Ten one-hour sessions

We briefly touched on Laban's theory of Space Harmony in chapter 5. Now, with the introduction of Modes of Shape Change, you are ready to dive a little deeper into this theory.

Laban did not believe in "empty space." In fact, his theory of Space Harmony is predicated on the belief that **Space** has life, and that life is movement. To make the life of **Space** visible, Laban created a series of movement sequences called Scales, which are based in the martial arts and will be discussed later in the book. For now, we only need to consider that **Space** contains "pulls" on which one can ride—like surfing a wave in the ocean—if it can be caught just right. No doubt, at some point, you have said, "I don't know why I went there. I felt pulled in that direction." Or, "I was pulled toward you." Or, a director said, "Go where you are pulled and let's see what happens." Your relationship to the pulls inherent in **Space** may be mysterious but not uncommon. Your exploration of **Space** and "surfing" the pulls begins in your kinesphere.

The furthest reach of your limbs around your body while stationary designates your personal kinesphere. And when you walk, run, crawl, etc., your kinesphere travels with you like a bubble in which you occupy the center. This personal space can be further illuminated by the exploration of *far*, *intermediate*, and *near reach*. *Far reach* touches the outer edge of your kinesphere, *intermediate reach* describes the middle distance between your body and the edge of your kinesphere, and *near reach* is the furthest distance from the edge of your kinesphere and is that which is closest to your body. For instance, you brush your teeth in *near reach*, write on a blackboard in *intermediate reach*, and release a Frisbee in *far reach*.

To explore your kinesphere is to become familiar with how you possess and fill your personal space. As an experiment, pick someone to whom you will wave good-bye. Stand in active stillness and wave your farewell three times, once in *far reach*, second in *intermediate reach*, and third in *near reach*. The objective, to wave to a specific person, creates intention in relation to space. Choosing *far*, *intermediate*, or *near reach* alters the quality of that intention. How did the quality of the intention change due to altering your reach space? The following exercises give you more opportunities to play in your personal kinesphere.

- With at least one foot firmly planted so that you do not travel, explore your personal kinesphere around the entire circumference of your body (*far reach*). Start with your arms but make sure you explore the *reach space* of your other body parts as well.

- Now explore the space *between* your body and the edge of your kinesphere (*intermediate* and *near reach*).

- Explore everyday activities and observe your use of *reach space*.

- Try to do an activity with a *reach space* that is illogical given the activity, such as brushing your hair in *far reach*, or reading a book in *near reach*. Of course, your hair will remain unbrushed and the book will be blurry. But the *intention* to brush your hair or read, regardless of the inappropriate *reach space*, may spark your imagination in some way. Experiment and have fun!

Central, Peripheral, and Transverse Pathways (CPT)

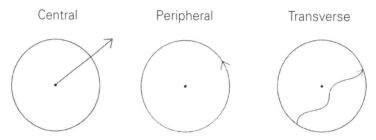

Central   Peripheral   Transverse

Revealing your personal space is further governed by the pathway your movement travels on between your center and the edge of your kinesphere. The pathways of movement are described as Central, Peripheral, or Transverse Pathways (CPT Pathways). A Central Pathway radiates in and out from center. A Peripheral Pathway describes the edge of your kinesphere, and a Transverse Pathway makes visible the volume of space within your kinesphere by winding between the center and the edge. Additionally, these Pathways can manifest in *near*, *intermediate*, or *far reach* depending on the activity and the intention of the mover.

By definition, CPT Pathways infer the presence of *spatial pulls* and *spatial intent*. A *spatial pull* is literally **Space** actively pulling on the body, which creates *spatial intent*. *Spatial intent* answers the question, "Where am I going?" It is important to note that the clearer the goal or intention, the more likely it is that the neuromuscular system will respond with ease to the impulse to move. And when the *spatial pulls* and resulting *spatial intents* are acted upon, your body reveals its kinesphere through CPT.

Perhaps you can tell from the description of CPT Pathways that there is a correlation between CPT and the Modes of Shape Change. The correlatives to Central, Peripheral, and Transverse Pathways are Spoke-like Directional, Arc-like Directional, and Carving Modes of Shape Change, respectively. You also may notice that the Floor Patterns have an obvious correlation to CPT Pathways, namely: *straight* (Central), *arced* (Peripheral), and *winding* (Transverse). So what is the difference between Floor Patterns, Modes of Shape Change, and CPT? Floor Patterns involve locomotion, CPT enlivens our personal kinesphere, and Modes of Shape Change are designed to bring us into the environment.

Therefore, when you explore CPT you may feel the movement is more personal because CPT reveals your personal space. When you emphasize the Modes of Shape Change, you move to form relationships with the environs and all it holds. Floor Patterns allow you to explore the environment through locomotion.

That is all well and good for the body, but what about the voice? Just as the body has a personal kinesphere, so does your voice. Your *vocal kinesphere* can be defined as the space that is revealed through the resonance of your voice when your body is in active stillness. It is easy to mark the edge of your physical kinesphere. But where is the edge of your vocal kinesphere? The furthest edge of your vocal kinesphere is at the limits of your vocal reach, which is beyond your limbs' furthest reach. The questions then become: "What space can my voice fill with ease? What is revealed about this space through my voice? What happens to the body as the voice moves in its vocal kinesphere?"

If the body is to follow the voice, one of the possibilities is that the body will be compelled toward locomotion, perhaps engaged in a losing game of tag with the voice. It is a losing game because the voice can travel where the body is prohibited to go due to its corporeal limitations. As stated in chapter 1, the voice can penetrate walls, fly up and down steps in nothing flat, shrink to pass through a small crevice, or grow to fill a large theatre.

Just as the body responds to *spatial intent*, so does the voice. The voice responds to the intent and rides on Central, Peripheral, or Transverse Pathways, thus enlivening your personal space. The vocal Pathways are heard as distinct from one another because they encourage vocal variety, such as variations of pitch, volume, rate, and shifts of vocal resonance. The variety of expressive sounds born out of the speaker's *spatial intent* and revealed through CPT Pathways help the actor tell the story of the play in dynamic ways. And, in turn, this process *pulls* the audience members into the story, causing their *spatial intent* to become fixed on the actors.

But how do you sensitize yourself to the *spatial pulls* and *spatial intents* that reveal your vocal kinesphere? In order to experience *spatial pulls* and respond with clear *spatial intent*, it is crucial that you are motivated from your imagination. It is understood that the actor's relationship to imagination is somewhat individualized. Some actors will explore prescribed concepts, such as CPT Pathways, and their imaginations will ignite and find the answers to questions such as: "Who am I? Where am I? What am I doing? Where am I going?" Other actors will stimulate the movement by first imagining the details of a story whose component parts are the given circumstances, actions/objectives, and character. The question they ask is: "If I imagine a specific circumstance, action/objective, or character, how will my voice and body respond?" Regardless of the question, the answer is discovered in the *doing*, not through intellectual analysis. This is true whether tickling the imagination through prescribed movements and discovering logical justifications for the physical and vocal behaviors, or exploring how the body and voice are affected by imagining the story. Regardless of the tactic, in order for the exercises to have value, an active and responsive imagination is key.

To release your imagination, it is crucial that you do not worry about the terminology or "getting it right." Frankly, there is no "right." There is only play. As you explore, you will no doubt notice that the Pathways, Modes, and Floor Patterns are so closely interrelated that when you are truly working moment to moment they may lose their individual distinctions, but not their influence on you. Trust that after you feed yourself a stimulus such as, "Make sound on a Central Pathway," you can let go and experiment. Don't try to monitor yourself. The instructions you give yourself will inform your movement and voice, and this influence will waft in and out on impulse. Allow the Laban vocabulary to be a leaping-off point—a stimulant, not an end in itself.

- In silence, use your imagination to motivate moving on CPT Pathways. What are the qualitative differences among them? Do you feel the relationship between CPT Pathways and the Modes of Shape Change? When in locomotion, do you recognize the Floor Patterns?
- Stand in active stillness and motivate describing your kinesphere through CPT Pathways using just your voice with both unstructured and structured sounds.
- Continue to explore CPT Pathways with your voice and body. Allow your body to respond by mirroring the Pathways your voice is revealing. The physical responses may be revealed in your whole body or through individual body parts. Keep in mind that in this exercise, *the voice is leading the body*.
- Now *let the body lead the voice*. Explore CPT Pathways with your body and let your voice mirror the Pathways chosen by your body.

What is the difference between the body leading the voice and the voice leading the body? Remember, there are no "right" or "wrong" answers. There is only your experience and, consequently, your response to the question may vary over time as you continue to explore. The following exercises feel like patting your head and rubbing your tummy simultaneously, but they are well worth the effort to discover the complex relationships possible.

- Working alone, explore one Pathway with movement and simultaneously a different one with sound. For instance, move your body on a Central Pathway while your voice reflects a Transverse Pathway.
- Here is a real challenge: Can you move your arm on a Central Pathway and reflect the Carving Mode in your sound?
- Repeat the previous exercises, changing up the combinations.

- With a partner, improvise with CPT Pathways and the Modes of Shape Change. The choices your body and voice make are predicated on how you are affected by your scene partner and vice versa; however, the limitation of the exercise is that all impulses are directed through CPT and the Modes of Shape Change. Your voice may respond with both structured and unstructured sounds on impulse.
- After you intuit the end of the improvisation, recuperate.
- Share your experiences.

When you share your experiences, focus on your connectedness to yourself and your ability to affect and be affected by your partner. Share any imaginary circumstances or characters that were sparked by the exploration. Compare how your articulators responded to the exercise. What was the balance of structured to unstructured sounds? Did you and your partner create some new structured sounds with your articulators?

Vowels and diphthongs pertain to **Shape**, while consonants tend to pertain to **Space**. Remember, **Shape** reveals our emotional state, while **Space** answers the question, "Where am I going?" In relation to speech, the concept **Space** functions metaphorically and answers the questions: "Where is this thought leading me? Am I changing the direction of my thinking? Are my thoughts moving toward a conclusion?" Vowels express the emotion of the speaker and the consonants put boundaries on the emotional flow by creating limitations on the vowel sounds. Without the constraints imposed by consonants, we would have a very difficult time understanding anything beyond the emotional content of the speaker. The consonants reveal the facts; they tell us *where* this story is going. Take a moment to sing a song and notice that it is the vowels that are manipulated through pitch and duration to express the feeling of the song. With this perspective, it is easy to understand that unstructured sounds, sound-shapes, and the structured mouth-shapes of the vowels and diphthongs have much in common. Perhaps during some of your explorations there was a melding of the sound-shapes with recognizable vowels/diphthongs blurring the distinction between the two? If that happened, that is good!

CHAPTER NINE
Consonants: Articulation and Rhythmic Explorations
Time Frame: Fifteen one-hour sessions

A consonant sound is produced when the articulators interrupt or impede the flow of the breath on the exhalation. There are twenty-six consonant sounds; therefore, it may be helpful to examine the consonants in the framework of a large extended family. Like most families, the traits you choose to examine determine to which family unit or category an individual consonant belongs. For instance, you can categorize a consonant based on which articulators are employed, how the breath is used, or what kind of sound is made.

As described in chapter 6, the English language is full of inconsistencies, and spelling is often not an indication of pronunciation. Relative to consonant sounds, sometimes "*TH*" represents the sound in "*TH*in," and other times it represents the sound in "*TH*en." Another example is the letter "*S*." Sometimes it represents the sound of "*S*" as in "pre*SS*," and sometimes it represents the sound of "*Z*," as in "clue*S.*" Consequently, as suggested in chapter 6, it is recommended that you invest in a book of lexical sets. Let's begin with the broadest designation for the consonant sounds: *voiced* and *unvoiced*.

Put your fingers lightly on your Adam's apple and speak the consonant sounds:*
*M, N, L, Z, B, D, G, V, W (W*ell), *NG* (ri*NG*), *ZH* (vi*S*ion), *TH* (*TH*en), *DZH* (*JuDG*e), *R* (*R*eap), *Y* (*Y*ou), *H* (be*H*ind). Can you feel the vibration in your Adam's apple? This is the sensation of a *voiced consonant*. Now speak the consonant sounds: *P, K, T, F, S, CH* (*CH*oke), *TH* (*TH*in), *SH* (*SH*eet), *WH* (*WH*ite), *H* (*H*e). Can you feel the absence of vibration in your Adam's apple? These are *unvoiced consonants*.

To be more specific, we can divide the consonants into smaller family units using the following six surnames: fricatives, stop-plosives, nasal consonants, affricates, glide consonants, and a single lateral consonant.

The **fricatives** form the largest family: *F, V, S, Z, R, TH* (*TH*in), *TH* (*TH*en), *H* (*H*e), *H* (be*H*ind), *SH* (*SH*eet), and *ZH* (vi*S*ion). These are called fricatives because the articulators impede but do not stop the breath flow, thus creating audible friction on the outgoing breath. Put your fingers close to your lips and speak the fricatives. Can you feel a bit of air touching your fingers as you phonate?

The next largest consonant family is comprised of the **stop-plosives**: *P, B, T, D, K,* and *G*. To produce the stop-plosives, the articulators stop the outgoing breath stream and then suddenly release

---

*Speak the sounds, not the consonants' names. For instance, "M" is "mmmmmm," not "em."

it, causing an explosion of air. Again, put your fingertips close to your lips and phonate the stop-plosives. Can you feel the explosion of air on your fingertips?

The **nasal consonants** are a family unit of three: *M*, *N*, and *NG* (ri*NG*). With your fingers lightly touching either side of your cheeks close to your nose, speak each nasal consonant. Can you feel the vibration in your face? Now plug your nose and try to say them. No cheating, really plug your nose! You hear no sound but probably feel pressure in your sinuses that may even cause your ears to pop. The nasal consonants are dependent on the vibrations in the nasal cavities to be heard and felt; therefore, the soft palate is relaxed downward. For most spoken English phonemes, the effort is to keep the soft palate gently raised to avoid excessive nasality. Obviously, the nasal consonants are the exception.

The **glide consonants** also have three family members: *WH* (*WH*ite), *W* (*W*ell), and *Y* (*Y*ou). The sounds of these consonants are "vowel-like" in that there is little or no friction involved. To form a glide consonant, the articulators begin in a specific shape for a vowel and then quickly glide into another vowel or diphthong shape during the phonation of the consonant. For instance, when you speak the word "woe," your lips begin in the "OO" shape and glide into the "OH" shape. When you speak "yodel," the back of your tongue assumes the shape for "EE" and glides downward during the phonation as your lips move into the "OH" shape. It is interesting to note that the glide consonants are always followed by vowels or diphthongs and never appear at the end of a word.

With only two members, **affricates** are the next consonant family. The only two affricates in spoken English are *DZH* (*JuDGe*) and *TSH* (*CH*eap). The blending of one stop-plosive and one fricative forms each affricate. The affricate sound *DZH* is formed from the voiced stop-plosive "*D*" and the voiced fricative *ZH* (vi*S*ion). The "*CH*" sound is formed from the unvoiced stop-plosive "*T*" and the unvoiced fricative *SH* (*SH*eet). When put together, they form the phonological symbol "*TSH.*"

Lastly, living by itself is the **lateral consonant** "*L.*" This consonant sound is made with the tip of the tongue touching the alveolar ridge and the blades of the tongue relaxed downward. In this posture, the breath stream passes over the sides of the tongue to produce the "*L*" sound. Although "*L*" lives alone as a lateral consonant, it does have cousins, *N*, *D*, and *T* which are also formed by touching the tongue tip to the alveolar ridge. It is the pressure of the tongue tip against the gum ridge that will determine which *alveolar consonant* is produced. *L*, *N*, *D*, and *T* are the principal *alveolar consonants*. In addition to the *alveolar consonants*, there are designations called *bilabial*, *labio-dental*, *palatal*, *velar*, *glottal*, and *dental*.

- Additional *alveolar consonants*: Speak: *S*, *Z*, *SH* (*SH*eet), *ZH* (vi*S*ion), and *R*. Can you feel the tip of your tongue pointing toward but not touching your gum ridge? Because the tip of the tongue rises toward the ridge but does not touch it, these consonants fall into a secondary *alveolar* category. The exception could possibly be "*S*" and "*Z.*" For instance, if you form your "*S*" with the tongue tip remaining behind your lower front teeth and you have a clear "*S*" sound, then it is not necessary to conform to the prescribed alveolar placement. Additionally, the affricates "*DZH*" (*JuDGe*) and

"*TSH*" (*CH*eap) are considered alveolar because they blend two *alveolar consonants* (one is a stop-plosive and the other a fricative) to form one sound.

- *Bilabial:* Speak: *P, B, M, WH,* and *W.* Notice that they are articulated by using both lips.
- *Labio-dental:* Speak *F* and *V.* Both of these fricatives use the lower lip and the upper teeth.
- *Palatal:* Intend to say "you" but stop on the very first sound, which is "*Y*," and feel the placement of the tongue. The placement for this sound is *palatal* because it requires arching the front of the tongue in relationship to the hard palate.
- *Velar:* Speak: *K, G,* and *NG* (ri*NG*). These are considered *velar consonants* because a relationship is formed between the back of the tongue and the soft palate.
- *Glottal:* Speak the words "*H*e" and "be*H*ind." These words represent the two sounds for "*H*." They are considered *glottal consonants* because they are both articulated in the throat. The sound "*H*," as in "*H*e," is formed with the back of the tongue arching toward the hard palate. The other is formed with the tongue relaxed down, as in "be*H*ind." The difference between the two is almost indistinguishable on an auditory level. Nonetheless, the fact that the voiced version will only appear between two vowel sounds gives us some guidance. Luckily, the occasions where the distinction between the two is important are minimal and mostly will arise during dialect acquisition. Consult a book with lexical sets for more examples of this subtle distinction.
- *Dental:* Sound the voiced and unvoiced "*TH*" (*TH*ough and *TH*ud) one after the other several times. These are *dental consonants* because they both are produced with the tip of the tongue in contact with the upper teeth.

Your personal speech patterns may vary from these descriptions. As you work through the muscular activity for the consonants, observe which ones you produce as described and which ones vary. What does it feel like to interrupt your habitual placement and attempt a new one? This is not to imply that your habits are unacceptable or substandard in any way, but rather to help you develop alternatives. Even if you opt to retain your habitual consonant placements in everyday life, remember that your goal is to gain an "extra-daily technique" for your work as an actor. Therefore, you want to challenge your articulators to move in less familiar ways.

Just as dancers have specific warm-ups at the barre, actors also need specific functional practices that condition the articulators to be able to acquire the unique speech patterns required of a character. Therefore, do not think of the consonant explorations as "getting it right" but as an opportunity to expand your choices. Additionally, just as the whole body can employ efficient and less efficient ways of moving, so can the articulators. The described placements tend to make the most efficient use of the muscles that control the articulators and thus support simple, clearly spoken English that can be easily understood by a diverse population of English speakers.

Consonant Chart

Consonants	Voiced	Unvoiced	Fricative	Stop-plosive	Nasal	Glide	Affricate	Glottal	Lateral	Alveolar	Bilabial	Labio-dental	Palatal	Velar	Dental
B	X			X							X				
D	X			X						X					
F		X	X									X			
G	X			X										X	
H (*He*)		X	X					X							
H (be*h*ind)	X		X					X							
K		X		X										X	
L	X								X	X					
M	X				X						X				
N	X				X					X					
NG (ri*NG*)	X				X									X	
P		X		X							X				
R*	X		X							X					
S*		X	X							X					
T		X		X						X					
V	X		X									X			
W (*W*ell)	X					X					X				
W (*WH*ite)		X				X					X				
Z*	X		X							X					
ZH* (vi*S*ion)	X		X							X					
SH* (*SH*eet)		X	X							X					
TH (*TH*in)		X	X												X
TH (*TH*en)	X		X												X
TSH** (*CH*eap)		X					X			X					
DZH** (Ju*DG*e)	X						X			X					
Y (*Y*ou)	X					X							X		

* Secondary Alveolar Consonants. The tongue tip reaches for the gum ridge but does not touch it. However, many individuals form S and Z with the tongue tip resting behind the lower front teeth.

** The affricates are a combination of primary and secondary alveolar placement.

More Muscular Activity for the Articulators

We will start with the "barre" practice for the *alveolar consonants*: L, N, D, and T. We are beginning with the principal *alveolar consonants* because they are probably the most challenging. When you have mastered them, the rest of the consonant explorations will fall into place easily. The purpose of the following exercises is to develop the appropriate strength and accuracy in the tip of the tongue to articulate the *alveolar consonants*.

Before you begin, review the articulators in the Anatomy Illustrations and warm up your tongue and lips with the Modes of Shape Change as described in chapter 7. During each of the following exercises, use a mirror to observe the action of your articulators. Until instructed otherwise, stand in active stillness in neutral dynamic alignment.

Between each series of exercises, recuperate by doing the following:
- Shake out the Jaw: Drop your jaw, clasp your hands together, and vigorously shake them back and forth, a motion to which your jaw will respond by also shaking back and forth.
- Massage the Masseter Muscles: Drop your jaw, and massage your masseter muscles with the heel of your palm and/or slide the heel of your palm down the length of this muscle.
- Tongue Waggle: Bend over and place your hands on your thighs for support. Look at the floor and let your tongue hang out of your mouth. Shake your head back and forth, letting the tongue waggle with the motion.
- Buzz out your lips on an exhalation. You will sound a bit like a horse.

Exercises for the Principal Alveolar Consonants
Mime-Through: This first exercise is a preparation for articulating L, N, D, and T.

- Drop your jaw from your temporomandibular joint with the feeling of a yawn and rest the tip of your tongue behind your lower front teeth. The distance between your front teeth will approximate the width of the tips of your index and third fingers. Allow the body of the tongue to relax so that you can see your uvula.
- Curl the tongue tip up to touch your alveolar ridge and then drop it down again behind your lower front teeth.
- Repeat ten times.
- Recuperate.

On the following exercises, control the exhalation with the abdominal muscles while keeping the rib cage expanded until the end of the whole sequence. The symbol "^" indicates where the abdomen relaxes, thereby allowing the new breath to drop into the lungs. Although you are capable of longer phrases, the exercise is designed to teach you how to phrase. A phrase is a series of words or movements that form a distinct unit within a longer passage. The organization of the breath is essential to effective phrasing because it arranges the units or phrases sequentially in time. Think of the following exercises as long passages with the symbol "^" dividing the passages into distinct units. In addition to phrasing, the purpose of the exercises is to find the appropriate pressures in the tip of the tongue to produce the *alveolar consonant* sounds.

Breathe-Through:
- Breathe in on six counts (three to the ribs and three to the abdominals). Drop your jaw the width of the tips of your index and third fingers.

- *Breathe-Through:*

LAH-LAH-LAH ^ LAH-LAH-LAH ^ LAH-LAH-LAH ^
LAH-LAH-LAH-LAH ^ LAH-LAH-LAH-LAH ^ LAH-LAH-LAH-LAH ^
LAH-LAH ^ LAH-LAH ^ LAH-LAH ^

(At the end of the whole sequence, relax your intercostal muscles.)

- Repeat the exercise on *N*, *D*, and *T*.
- Recuperate.

Intone:
- Breathe in on six counts (three to the ribs and three to the abdominals). Drop your jaw the width of the tips of your index and third fingers.
- *Intone* on your center pitch:

LAH-LAH-LAH ^ LAH-LAH-LAH ^ LAH-LAH-LAH ^
LAH-LAH-LAH-LAH ^ LAH-LAH-LAH-LAH ^ LAH-LAH-LAH-LAH ^
LAH-LAH ^ LAH-LAH ^ LAH-LAH ^

(At the end of the whole sequence, relax your intercostal muscles.)

- Repeat the exercise on *N*, *D*, and *T*.
- Recuperate.
- Repeat the exercise again, this time raising or lowering the pitch on each new phrase. To ensure that you don't gravitate to the same two or three pitches over and over, use your pitch pipe.
- Recuperate.

Can you feel the abdominal muscles moving in during each phrase? Can you feel the abdomen relax outward as the air drops in? Can your ribs remain floating until the end of the entire sequence? If it is too taxing to keep your ribs buoyant through the whole sequence, then relax the ribs after each line. Is your jaw remaining relaxed or is it tightening, thereby reducing the space between the teeth? Your jaw is most likely to tighten on "*D*" and "*T*" because they are the most challenging. If your jaw is tightening, then shake out the jaw and massage the masseter muscles after each line.

Be aware that the more difficult the feat is for the tip of the tongue, the more likely you are to resort to tensing the jaw and abdomen to produce the sound. Your goals are to let the jaw hang freely with a two-finger drop between the teeth and for the breath to be easy while the tongue does its gymnastics. The burden, therefore, remains with the tongue to gain the appropriate strength to produce the consonant sounds with ease and precision.

If you are a beginner, the jaw will probably not remain at a two-finger drop, especially for "*D*" and "*T*." The remedy for *some* actors is to place the index and third fingers between the teeth for part of the sequence or to place a cork the size of two fingers between the teeth. There are also aids manufactured for this purpose called "bone props," which actually hook onto the teeth to keep the space. These three choices—fingers, a cork, or a bone prop—are known collectively as "speech props."

The purpose of a speech prop is to help build independence of the jaw from the lips and tongue, thus allowing the articulators to function with precision very quickly. A speech prop is useful for creating maximum space in the back of the mouth because it encourages the soft palate to lift and the back of the tongue to relax downward. However, some individuals have a short lingual frenulum, which is responsible for loosely attaching the tongue to the bottom of the mouth. The short lingual frenulum causes a shorter tongue reach. If you have a "short tongue" that will not reach the gum ridge with a speech prop between your teeth, you can adapt the prop to fit the length of your tongue. When the prop is removed, the exercise should be repeated immediately without the device to observe the benefit. Thereafter, recuperate by shaking out your jaw, lips, and tongue, and massaging your masseter muscle.

Caution: As effective as the speech props are, they must be used with caution and are not recommended for everyone. If you suffer from temporomandibular joint dysfunction, hear clicking as you open and close your jaw, grind your teeth at night, or have any pain in your jaw hinge during your daily activities (speaking, singing, yawning), then the speech props are contraindicated. In this situation, if there is pain, there will be no gain. When using a speech prop, it is crucial that you do not bite it to keep it in place and that you never leave the prop between your teeth longer than one sequence of an exercise.

The next element we need to include with our speech gymnastics is rhythm. Plato was perhaps the first to write about the importance of rhythm to aesthetic activities. Through the ages, many esteemed individuals in the arts have repeated the theory that rhythm is the most important element to all artistic endeavors. Without rhythm, art lacks *form*, and without *form* there can be no communication. Consequently, comprehension largely hinges on the rhythms with which we speak. Say a sentence with an even meter. This means giving every word you speak equal "time" and "weight." You probably sound robotic at best. Now speak the same sentence with an objective and feel how some words naturally are given more "weight" than others. Also, notice how some words take longer to say, while your mouth skips quickly over others. Change your intention and see which words now become prominent.

Rhythmic Explorations for Consonants Married to Vowels/Diphthongs

The purpose of the following exercises is to sensitize you to the rhythmic possibilities of spoken English. To practice the specific rhythms, you need to recognize the symbol "∪," which indicates that the sound is *unstressed*, and the symbol "/," which indicates that the sound is *stressed*. How the symbols are combined determines the rhythm. We will explore four basic rhythms: iambic (∪/), trochaic (/∪), anapestic (∪∪/), and dactylic (/∪∪). Be careful not to confuse rhythm with pitch and volume changes. It will be tempting to raise the pitch or speak louder on the stressed sounds. This is certainly an option when telling a story or making a point, but for now, resist these inclinations and see what happens if you work purely from the rhythm. Notice that the first rhythm (iambic) mimics the beat of your heart.

- *Rhythm*: Speak the exercises with the following rhythms on your center pitch and observe the markings for the breath organization represented by "∧."

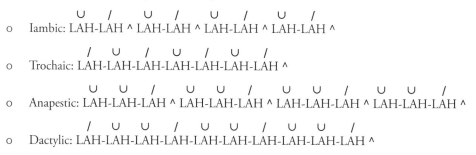

  - Iambic: LAH-LAH ∧ LAH-LAH ∧ LAH-LAH ∧ LAH-LAH ∧
  - Trochaic: LAH-LAH-LAH-LAH-LAH-LAH-LAH ∧
  - Anapestic: LAH-LAH-LAH ∧ LAH-LAH-LAH ∧ LAH-LAH-LAH ∧ LAH-LAH-LAH ∧
  - Dactylic: LAH-LAH-LAH-LAH-LAH-LAH-LAH-LAH-LAH-LAH ∧

- Recuperate.
- Repeat the exercise on the consonants *N*, *D*, and *T*. If you are using a speech prop, do the sequence twice for each consonant—once with and once without the prop. At each "∧", can you feel the breath dropping into your abdomen while you maintain a buoyant rib cage?
- Recuperate.
- Repeat the sequences, but this time raise or lower the pitch with each change of rhythm.
- Recuperate.
- In silence, "dance" the rhythms with your whole body.
- Add the articulation sequence into your "dance." You can relate your movement and sound to the space, to objects in your environment and, if present, to other people.
- Improvise with a partner, marrying the rhythmic articulation sequences with movement. As the improvisation develops, do not hold fast to the breath organization or the precise rhythms. Instead, let the breath, pitches, and rhythms evolve as your communication and intentions shift.
- Return to active stillness and repeat the sequences *as written* on voice.
- Recuperate.

You have been exploring dynamic alignment, breath control, center pitch, vocal range, resonance, articulation, phrasing, rhythms, and communication through the concepts of **Space** and **Shape**. Additionally, you have created relationships with the objects and persons in your environment. Congratulations!

Now let's marry the mouth-shapes for the sounds "OO" and "OH" with *L, N, D,* and *T* consonant actions. During the next set of exercises, use a mirror to observe your mouth and stand in active stillness in neutral dynamic alignment until instructed to move.

- *Mime-Through*: LAH-LOO ^ LAH-LOH ^ LOO-LOH ^ LOH-LAH.
- Repeat, substituting the consonants *N, D,* and *T* for *L*.
- *Breathe-Through:* Breathe in on six counts, three to the ribs and three to the abdomen. Keep the rib cage expanded as you breathe-through the previous exercise, replenishing your breath at the symbol "^." Do you feel your abdominal muscles moving toward the spine on the phonations and relaxing outward on the inhalations?
- At the end of the sequence, relax your intercostal muscles and recuperate.
- Repeat on *N, D,* and *T*.
- *Intone*: Repeat the exercise, intoning on your center pitch.
- At the end of the sequence, relax your intercostal muscles and recuperate.
- Repeat intoning the exercise and raise or lower the pitch by half steps at each consonant change.
- *Spoken with Iambic Meter*. Using the model below: On your center pitch, *speak* the exercise (rather than intone) with the iambic meter. Observe the new breath organization. Allow your abdominal muscles to relax at each "^," thus allowing the new breath to drop in.

  o LAH-LOO-LAH-LOH-LOO-LOH-LOH-LAH ^

  o NAH-NOO-NAH-NOH-NOO-NOH-NOH-NAH ^

  o DAH-DOO-DAH-DOH-DOO-DOH-DOH-DAH ^

  o TAH-TOO-TAH-TOH-TOO-TOH-TOH-TAH ^

- *Vocal Range*: Repeat the previous sequence with the rhythm and either raise or lower the pitch with each consonant change. Use your pitch pipe to guide you.
- **Shape, Space,** and **Relationship**: Repeat the articulation sequences and let your body explore the Modes of Shape Change and CPT on impulse. Relate your improvisations to the objects in your environment and/or improvise with a partner. Allow the pitch, tempo, rhythm changes, and breath organization to evolve as your intentions change. As always, the shifts happen as a result of your communication, which in turn affects the intention motivating your movement and speech.

- With a partner, stand in active stillness and, as if the exercises are the dialogue of a scene, repeat the articulation and rhythm sequences *as written*. Speak the sequences to each other, not as speech exercises but as *communication*. Even though your speech at present is organized senselessness, it can still be filled with intention.

The next speech hurdle raises the bar significantly for the muscular activity of your articulators. The following sequence includes all of the vowels and diphthongs that you know so far, married to *beginning* and *ending* consonant sounds. When a consonant appears at the beginning of a word, it is called a *beginning consonant* (<u>B</u>ow). When it appears at the end of a word (ea<u>T</u>), it is called an *end consonant*. And, for future reference, when the consonant sound appears in the middle of a word (beau<u>T</u>iful), it is called a *medial consonant*.

An additional challenge is to avoid a glottal attack on the vowel sounds that initiate words, such as in "<u>EA</u>sy" or "<u>OO</u>ze." A glottal attack is a sudden violent interruption of the breath flow through the throat. Generally, glottal attacks are undesirable in spoken English because they can prevent the listener from understanding the words and, if used frequently, can cause damage to the speaker's vocal folds. The symbol "↳" between the consonant sound and the following vowel or diphthong sound indicates that you are linking the consonant to the very next sound to avoid a glottal attack.

- *Mime-Through*:

  LOO-LOH-LAW-LAH-LER-LAY-LEE ^ EEL-AYL-ERL-AHL-AWL-OHL-OOL
                                  ↳   ↳   ↳   ↳   ↳   ↳

Substitute *N*, *D*, and *T* for *L*.
- Recuperate.
- Repeat the sequence on a breathe-through.
- Recuperate.
- Intone the previous exercise first on your center pitch and then on a new pitch each time you change the consonant sound.
- Recuperate.
- Repeat the sequence, speaking rather than intoning. Be careful not to glottal-attack the vowel sounds that come before the consonant.
- Recuperate.

Notice that the "ER" vowel sound is not in the following sequence. The purpose of dropping it out is to accommodate the rhythm. You can drop any of the units to make a sequence of twelve rather than fourteen.

- *Speak* with the dactylic meter (/∪∪) on your center pitch:

    /   ∪   ∪   /   ∪   ∪   /   ∪   ∪   /   ∪   ∪
  LOO-LOH-LAW-LAH-LAY-LEE ^ EEL-AYL-AHL-AWL-OHL-OOL
                              ↳   ↳   ↳   ↳   ↳

Substitute *N*, *D*, and *T* for *L*.

- Repeat the exercise, raising or lowering the pitch with each consonant change.
- Recuperate.
- Iambic and dactylic meters: Mime-through, breathe-through, and speak on your center pitch:

$$\cup \quad / \quad \cup \quad / \quad \cup \quad / \quad \cup \quad /$$
LAH-LOO-LAH-LOH-LOO-LOH-LOH-LAH ^

$$/ \quad \cup \quad \cup \quad / \quad \cup \quad \cup \quad / \quad \cup \quad \cup \quad / \quad \cup \quad \cup$$
LOO-LOH-LAW-LAH-LAY-LEE-EEL-AYL-AHL-AWL-OHL-OOL

Substitute: *N*, *D*, and *T* for *L*.

- Recuperate.
- Speak the exercise and raise or lower the pitch on each consonant change.
- Recuperate.
- **Shape**, **Space**, and **Relationship**: Repeat the articulation sequences and let your body explore the Modes of Shape Change and CPT on impulse. Relate your improvisations to the objects in your environment and/or improvise with a partner. Allow the breath organization, pitch, tempo, and rhythm to evolve as your intentions change.
- Return to active stillness. With a partner, repeat the sequences *as written*. Treat the sequences as if they are the dialogue of a scene and, therefore, can be filled with intention.
- Recuperate.

Be patient, persistent, and consistent with your practice. You may need to practice four times a week for several weeks in order to train your articulators to be precise. The good news is that the muscles of the mouth train very quickly, *if* you do the practice. Of course, attention to detail is necessary in order to develop the desired strength and flexibility in the articulators.

Due to the distance between the teeth and the position of the tip of the tongue, the consonants *L*, *N*, *D*, and *T* are very challenging. Mastering them will support an easy transition into exploring the balance of the consonants. To test this theory, repeat this chapter, substituting other consonants for the principal *alveolar consonants*. In this way, you will begin to fine-tune the functional and expressive relationships among the vowels, diphthongs, and consonants that occur with each new combination.

CHAPTER TEN
Effort Life of Voice and Movement
Time Frame: Ten ninety-minute sessions

There is probably no better vocabulary for inspiring and defining expressiveness than the descriptive words housed under the heading **Effort**. This is because **Effort** addresses the "feeling" qualities of movement and speech. **Effort** embodies our attitudes toward the Effort Factors: Time, Weight, Space, and Flow. Each Effort Factor operates on a continuum "bookended" by two *effort elements*.

Continuum of the Effort Factors
- Time = *sustained* ↔ *quick*
- Space = *direct* ↔ *indirect*
- Weight = *strong* ↔ *light*
- Flow = *bound* ↔ *free*

Effort fills the containers we call **Body**, **Shape**, and **Space** with specific emotional content that enriches the story. **Body** addresses the mechanics of movement and speech. **Shape** is the outward reflection of our inner state of being. **Space** locates "where" it all takes place and, as will be explained later, is separate and distinct from the Effort Factor, Space. **Effort** is the "filling" for those containers. Here is an example of what is meant by the word "filling." Perhaps you move your whole body along a Central Pathway and gesture with your right arm in a Carving Mode of Shape-Change. You can "fill" the choreography with *quick* or *sustained time*, *strong* or *light weight*, *direct* or *indirect space*, *bound* or *free flow*. You can emphasize one *element*, or, if you draw from separate Factors, two or three *elements* can be emphasized simultaneously. By clarifying and complicating your **Effort** life, the "pure movement" of the choreography becomes a story that includes specific emotional content. That is not to ignore the fact that there is interdependence between function and expression that affects the outcome of **Effort**. The purpose of the following exercises is to play with whatever the vocabulary for **Effort** means to you at this point. Do not concern yourself with "right" or "wrong." Play.

Experiments with Effort
Write the eight *effort elements* on separate pieces of paper. Divide them into four bags according to the Factors. Each Factor Bag will contain the two *elements* belonging to the same Factor. For instance, the Weight Factor Bag will contain *strong* and *light*. In the exercises that follow, I have suggested a simple "choreography," but feel free to invent your own. The important thing is that the choreography is short

and repeatable. However, keep in mind that you are not moving for moving's sake; the movement must have the potential for purpose and intent. I say "potential" because, as you experiment, the intention of the movement will not remain fixed, but will change with the **Effort** life. To experience the changes in intention, keep the same choreography for each experiment.

- Pull an *element* out of one of the Factor Bags. Emphasize this quality—whatever it means to you organically—as you move your whole body on a Central Pathway while gesturing with your right arm in a Carving Mode of Shape-Change, or substitute your own choreography.
- Repeat the exercise until you have, in turn, pulled an *element* from each Factor Bag.
- Pull *one element* each out of *two* different Factor Bags. Repeat the exact choreography, emphasizing *both effort elements* simultaneously.
- Repeat the experiment, pulling from different Factor Bags.
- Pull *one element* each from *three* different Factor Bags. Now you will emphasize those *elements* (as simultaneously as possible) with the same choreography.

Does the story change depending on your attitude toward Time, Weight, Space, and Flow? Do you tell a different story if you emphasize *one element*, *two elements*, or *three elements*? In this experiment, the constants are **Body**, **Shape**, and **Space**. **Effort** is the variable and it fills the choreography with new meaning and emotional specificity with each repetition. **Effort** offers a kaleidoscope of possibilities because many simultaneous combinations of *effort elements* are possible, as long as each *element* is drawn from a separate Effort Factor.

Beginning with chapter 1, you have been addressing **Effort** (albeit with your own vocabulary) every time you answered the question, "How does this make me feel?" But describing feelings can be a psychologically slippery slope for some individuals. **Effort**, on the other hand, offers a vocabulary that is not typically threatening. The language of **Effort** allows you to dig deep and, hopefully, challenges you toward heretofore unexplored expressiveness in psychological safety. Having said that, please note that words are powerful symbols, and even the simplicity of the descriptive words for the *effort elements* may evoke judgments that are not useful. For instance, you may unconsciously assume that *free flow* is better than *bound flow*. That statement is as erroneous as the declaration "*Quick time* is better than *sustained time*," or "*Strong weight* is better than *light weight*."

Through Laban's lens, there are no pejorative implications attached to the descriptive words. Balanced human beings shift easily along the continuum of each Effort Factor in order to accomplish everyday life efficiently. Yet it is also true that most of us tend to have inclinations toward one end or the other of the Factor's spectrum. Therefore, one of the goals of this chapter is to identify your personal affinities or inclinations and how they impact your work as an actor. Additionally, you will identify and strengthen your "disaffinities" for the purpose of broadening and deepening your expressive choices. The term "disaffinity" was coined by the Laban community to describe qualities that are not logical or natural to a particular activity. It also describes qualities that seem foreign or unlike a given individual's inclination. For instance, the *up* direction in **Space** is affined with *lightness* and disaffined with *strength.* Likewise, an individual may have a natural propensity toward accomplishing tasks with an attitude of *quickness.* A person so inclined may find *sustainment* (prolonged movement, no urgency) unnatural or inorganic, making this quality a personal disaffinity. The following are descriptions of the qualities that each Effort Factor governs.

Flow

The Flow Factor provides the underpinnings for the other Factors. We are never without a relationship to Flow in either a constrained manner (*bound*) or a released manner (*free*). Flow describes *continuity* and it answers the question, "How?" Your attitude toward Flow is *free* if you engage in the activity with such abandon that it is difficult to stop or interrupt it. For instance, think of a child running down a hill with no restraint. He is unable to stop and finally falls. Or, think of a person whose emotions pour out in an unconstrained manner. Someone who inclines toward *free flow* may be an individual for whom ideas come with such abandon that her problem-solving capabilities are amazing or her creative output seems endless.

Your attitude is *bound* when you are performing a task that needs restraint, such as assembling a model airplane or handling fine china. You can also bind the flow of your emotions by withholding your emotional response to a situation. Or, you may bind the flow of your words in order to carefully phrase your point. In other words, *bound flow* is present when you wish to gain or remain in control and lies along the *condensing/fighting* end of the Flow continuum. *Free flow* is present when you wish to indulge or give over to the circumstances, and therefore lies along the *indulging/expanding* side of the Flow continuum (see **Effort** graph on page 121).

Weight

The Weight Factor addresses the force with which we accomplish a task or carry ourselves. The Weight Factor describes *intention* and answers the question, "What?" It does not relate to how big or small an individual is relative to pounds carried on the skeletal frame. Although physique might influence how we perceive an individual's relationship to weight, we cannot let it blind us to the person's intention relative to the activity.

Whether engaging in *light* or *strong weight,* you have an intention, which causes you to use your weight effectively to achieve your objective. If your intention is to move a boulder from the roadway, no one will argue that this action will require your *strong weight* against the boulder. If you wish for your argument to win the day, you may fill your voice with *strong weight* to have an impact on the listeners. Or, perhaps your intention is to bully (physically or metaphorically), which will result in "pushing your weight around."

While *strong weight* is condensed and tends toward the *fighting/condensing* side of the continuum, *light weight* lives along the *indulging/expanding* end. When engaging *light weight,* your attitude may be one of tenderness, such as touching an infant's fingers one by one. Depending on the listener, one may also win an argument by stating one's points moderately. Similarly to *strong weight,* your intention in *light weight* is to overcome the obstacles, not give in to them. *Light weight* can be seen and felt with the same clarity as *strong weight.*

There are a few pitfalls relative to the observation and exploration of the Weight Factor. When exploring *strong weight*, do not confuse it with "straining" against an object, opponent, or idea. When you are straining, your use of Weight is inefficient; therefore, the possibility of overcoming the obstacle diminishes. Straining is often considered a precursor or pre-effort to *strong weight*. Another pitfall is identifying "passive weight" as *strong* or *light*. When you give in to an obstacle, rather than actively attempt to overcome it, you are engaged in a passive relationship to Weight. To an observer, an individual engaged in passive weight may appear to be weak, overcome by gravity, or displaying a hopeless attitude. The descriptions of "straining" and "passive weight" are not meant to be judgmental, but only to say that they are neither *strong* nor *light weight*. In fact, expressively they could be useful to an actor in specific situations.

Time

The Time Factor relates to your *decision-making* efforts. Time answers the question, "When?" We are all familiar with ten minutes feeling like an eternity in one instance and feeling too quick in another. You may indulge in combing your hair for a full ten minutes, giving the activity an air of leisure (*sustained*). But that same ten minutes could feel urgent (*quick*) if that is all the time you have to get your child ready for school. Try as we might, it is difficult not to relate this Factor to the duration and tempo of an activity. Yet fundamentally, the Time Factor does not describe either duration or tempo, but rather *your attitude* toward a given amount of time. However, the fact remains that when your attitude toward Time (whether *sustained* or *quick*) is revealed in your body and voice, the result often includes an adjustment of the tempo and possibly an increase or decrease in the duration.

That said, there are times when you do not adjust the tempo or duration of the activity, regardless of your attitude toward Time. For instance, imagine that you are a scientist with two minutes to save the world by filling a vial with a liquid substance without spilling a drop. Your attitude toward those two minutes will no doubt be urgent, but to increase the tempo (causing a spill) or duration (missing the deadline) will result in disaster. What you will feel and what the viewer will observe is your attitude toward those two minutes, but the tempo and duration of the activity will not change. In fact, this is a ploy used by many a TV cliffhanger which depicts an urgent situation that defies an increase in tempo or change in duration. *Quick* lives along the *condensing/fighting* side of the continuum and *sustained* lives along the *indulging/expanding* side.

Space

The Space Factor addresses *attention* to space. Relative to **Effort**, the Space Factor does not necessarily answer the question, "Where?" in the sense of location. Rather, it clarifies one's attitude toward this location in space. The Space Factor is related to "thinking" and how one attends to the "Where?" You can attend to a location along the continuum of *direct ↔ indirect*. *Direct* lives along the *condensing/ fighting* side of the continuum, while *indirect* lives along the *indulging/expanding* side.

For example, imagine that you have walked into a fabulous penthouse apartment for the first time. Deeply impressed, you scan the environment, which means you are attending to the space *indirectly*. Then, after a bit, you start to focus on specifics of the architecture and decorative features one by one. Now your attention to the space is *direct*, because you are pinpointing your attention on one specific item at a time.

With regard to personality, you may be a person who can juggle multiple ideas and/or activities (*indirect*), or one who likes to focus and concentrate on a single idea or activity at a time (*direct*). Relative to communication, a person may speak about an issue in a roundabout manner (*indirect*), or be to the point (*direct*). Our individual proclivity toward being *direct* or *indirect* in conversation is often the culprit that causes misunderstandings. To a person who values *indirectness*, a *direct* person may seem rude and blunt. To an individual who values *directness*, an *indirect* person may appear wily or devious. This is a simplification, of course, but it is food for thought for both our lives and our art.

EXERCISES FOR EXPLORING THE *EFFORT ELEMENTS*

As previously stated, unbeknownst to you, you have been exploring **Effort** in almost all of the previous exercises. You were only lacking the LMA vocabulary to describe all the ways in which your body and sound were responding. This chapter began by speaking of **Body**, **Shape**, and **Space** as containers for **Effort**. Now, we are going to explore how Effort influences and changes your relationship to **Body**, **Shape**, and **Space**.

- Start with the Flow Factor. Physically and vocally manifest *bound flow* in the extremis.
- Once you have established the extreme end of *bound flow*, begin to move and sound along the continuum from extreme *bound flow* toward extreme *free flow*.
- Repeat the experiment, substituting the *elements* of the other Effort Factors: Time, Weight, and Space.
- *Stand in active stillness* and explore each continuum with unstructured sound.

The first time you attempt move and sound along a continuum, you will probably leap from one end of the spectrum to the other without much variance in between. It is simply easier to identify the extremes than the subtle gradations. With practice, you will begin to feel the entire spectrum between the two extremes. When you have a "taste" for each continuum in your body and voice, continue with the next exercises.

- Take a notebook and go out into the world. Find an example in real life of each *effort element* and write down what you see and hear. You will have eight separate examples. These observations are necessarily *very short* because you are looking for the few moments when a particular *element* seems to be most salient.
- Return to the studio and reproduce each of the observations in *your* body. This includes your specific observations relative to **Body**, **Shape**, and **Space**. If your subject made any sound, incorporate those as well. Be very specific in your recreations. Do not generalize. Your movement may last under a minute, but it will be rich in the details.

Partner Work:

As you experiment with the following exercises, keep in mind that while it is possible to emphasize a particular *element* or combinations of *elements*, it is not possible to move exclusively from those elements for any length of time. What you are attempting to do is make the chosen *elements* the *most salient* in your phrase of movement and/or sound. Consequently, your improvisations either alone or with a partner will be short snippets. If the exploration goes on too long, then *effort elements* other than those you intended will emerge and blur what you wanted the observers to see. You achieve this by directing your impulses to move and sound through your chosen *elements*. While this can be frustrating, even in small doses, it is often the limitations imposed that provoke the richest imaginative journeys.

- Work with a partner. Each of you, independently, decides on an Effort Factor to explore. Do not tell each other your decision. Improvise with body and voice, emphasizing the *effort elements* of *your* Factor moment to moment in response to each other. Remember, you are improvising only a snippet of interaction.
- When you and your partner intuit the end of the improvisation, share your experience. What questions can you answer with only a minute or two of exploration? Who were you? Who did your scene partner become to you? What circumstances were you in? Where were you? What was the conflict? Remember, your partner was probably moving and sounding from a completely different set of impulses filtered through his/her chosen *elements*.
- Repeat the previous exercise, but this time improvise *only* with your *voice*. The body remains in active stillness. Respond vocally to each other moment to moment, directing all your impulses through the *effort elements* of your Effort Factor.
- When you and your partner intuit the end of the vocal improvisation, recuperate.
- Share your experiences.

The following exercise needs several minutes to develop. The purpose is to discover how your voice, which will be exploring the *effort elements* on impulse, can influence the movement of the group. The limitation of the exercise is that *you will remain in active stillness.*

- Work with a group. If this is not possible, you may remain with a single partner. Have a group of actors stand in front of you with their backs to you. You will remain in active stillness. The group members will respond to the sound of your voice with movement, but they do not make sound. Move your voice with the intention to move the group and the *elements* will appear. Although silence and stillness may occur organically, your sound will mostly pour forth and their bodies will be in motion fairly continuously. You should not think about or plan the movement of your voice. The group members will respond physically to what they hear.

- When you intuit the end of the experience, take the time for feedback. The group members will discuss how their imaginations were affected by your voice and you will share how it felt to move their bodies with your voice.

Listen carefully to the feedback; it is important that you begin to discover your personal affinities by recognizing how frequently or infrequently you may expose a particular *element* or combination of *elements* in your voice and body. For instance, you may discover that you are very at home (affined) with *light weight* and *indirect space* and do not often gravitate toward *directness* or *strong weight* (disaffined). Keep a diary noting your affinities and disaffinities. Recognizing your personal inclinations is essential self-knowledge that will help you grow as a human being and artist.

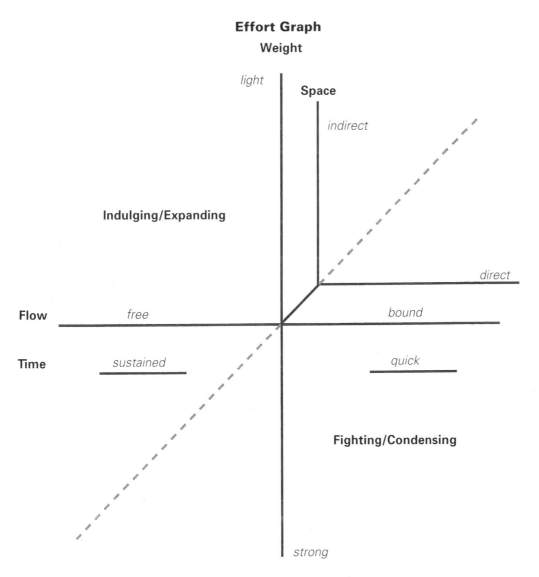

Effort Graph

CHAPTER ELEVEN

Effort Life and Precise Articulation
Time Frame: Twenty ninety-minute sessions

In this chapter, you are going to discover how **Effort** can manifest itself through the muscular activity of the individual consonant and vowel sounds. For instance, the stop-plosive "*T*" tends to lend itself more to *quick*, *bound*, *light*, and *direct*. If you try to produce the "*T*" with its disaffinities, it will no longer be a "*T*," but some other sound. On the other hand, the continuant "*M*" tends to lend itself toward being *sustained*. However, relative to the other *effort elements*, "*M*" has the capability of moving easily along the remaining continua without marring its clarity.

CONSONANTS AND EFFORT LIFE

- Warm up your articulators with the muscular activity exercises described in the chapters 6, 7, and 9.
- Speak the consonants and let the action of the articulators for each consonant provoke your body to move.
- Play with the *effort elements* and discover which *elements* best allow the inherent properties of each individual consonant to "shine." You are investigating each consonant to discover its affinities.
- For fun, play with the consonant actions and their disaffinities. For instance, try to produce the stop-plosive "*D*" with a *sustained* relationship to Time and an *indirect* relationship to Space. Perhaps you will invent a new language.

Group Exploration:
- With as many partners as are available, imagine that you all live in a land where the only means for vocal communication are the consonants. Create your world of movement and sound around this limitation.
- When the group has intuited the end of the improvisation, recuperate.
- Share your experiences.

An improvisation of this nature can take twenty minutes or more to develop. It is helpful to begin with movement and let the consonant articulations be the result of the *need* to speak. Discovering the impulse that leads to speech is crucial for the actor and it will serve you well when working on text. Ideally, we don't speak just because the next line in the play is ours. We speak because the needs of the character bring us to *those* words at *that* moment. The words of the play must ultimately be *inevitable*.

VOWELS/DIPHTHONGS AND EFFORT LIFE

It is particularly rewarding to explore the vowel sounds with **Effort**. Principally, this is true because there is no obstruction of the breath; therefore, the vowels and diphthongs can move easily along the continua of the *effort elements*.

- As you did in the previous chapter, randomly pull out *effort elements* from your Factor Bags (never two from the same Bag).
- Stand in active stillness. Fill the vowel/diphthong mouth-shapes that you know so far with the *effort elements* that you pulled. You may choose to work with one, two, or three *elements* at a time. For instance, perhaps for the vowel "OO" you pulled *light* from the Weight Factor Bag and *direct* from the Space Factor Bag. Produce the vowel with these *elements* either consecutively or simultaneously, according to your impulse.
- As your experiment continues, gradually shift along the continua. For instance, if you are sounding "OO" with *light weight* and *direct space*, then gradually move along the continua until the sound is filled with *strong weight* and *indirect space*.
- Add movement.
- Return to active stillness and explore the *elements* again through the vowels and diphthongs.

At present, your vocabulary of vowels/diphthongs is somewhat limited. Therefore, to take full advantage of **Effort**, it is time to include more pure vowel sounds, diphthongs, as well as triphthongs!

Short Vowels

First, let's look at "short vowels." Short vowels are pure vowels that are short in length, such as the "a" sound in "b*a*t." For our purposes, we will examine eight short vowels. They are: "oo" (b*oo*k), "o" (b*o*x), "uh" (l*u*ck), "a" (b*a*t), "e" (b*e*d), "i" (s*i*t), and *schwa*. A *schwa* is a sound of indeterminate quality. It is also unstressed and always weak. Some call it the "tofu" of English because it takes on the flavor of whatever is around it. Examples of the *schwa* sound are: fath*er*, dram*a*, *u*pon, *a*mid, J*a*pan, and poss*i*ble. These are just a few possibilities. Rest assured that you use *schwa* all day long to deemphasize the insignificant part of the word or to produce a weak form of a word within a phrase—typically an article, auxiliary verb, personal pronoun, preposition, or conjunction. Therefore, though possessing no definitive stand-alone sound, the *schwa* does have rhythmic value and, consequently, helps create sense.

If you have mastered the mouth-shapes for the long vowels and diphthongs (OO, OH, AW, AH, ER, AY, EE), then the muscular activity for the short vowels will be easy. As you experiment with the following descriptions, don't forget to keep the tongue tip resting behind the lower front teeth. The short vowel "oo" (b*oo*k) is a back vowel, and its lip position rests between "OO" and "OH." The "o" (b*o*x) sound is also a back vowel with a slightly forward lip position, and lives between "AW" and "AH." The "uh" (l*u*ck) sound is a mid-vowel that is produced with relaxed lips while the middle of the tongue arches toward the place where the hard and soft palates meet. The arch of the tongue lies between "AH" and "ER." *Schwa* is also considered a mid-vowel. In this instance, the tongue arches to a position that lies between "uh" and "ER." The short front vowels begin with "a" (b*a*t). The body of the tongue arches toward the hard palate, finding a placement that is a bit higher and more forward than "ER." The short vowel "e" (p*e*t) follows "a" and is articulated with another slight rise in the arch of the tongue toward the hard palate. With another lift in the arch of the tongue toward the hard palate, you will articulate the final short front vowel sound, "i" (b*i*t), which lives between "AY" and "EE." I recommend that the lips remain neutral during the front vowels. However, in some training programs the lips are encouraged to slightly spread on these sounds. The slight "smile" will increase face resonance. If you tend to lack sufficient nasal resonance, then you may want to experiment with a slight smile, or a lift of the cheek muscles as you phonate the front vowels. Likewise, you can mitigate an overabundance of nasal resonance, or "thin" voice, by phonating the front vowels with relaxed lips.

Collectively we will call the five long vowels (OO, AW, AH ER, and EE), six short vowels (oo, o, uh, a, e, and i) and two diphthongs (OH and AY) *The Sound-Sequence*. The illustration titled *The Sound-Sequence* depicts the gradation of lip openings and tongue raisings to achieve the progression, which moves from the smallest lip rounding (OO) to the highest arch-of-the-tongue position (EE). As stated in chapter 6, the trickiest aspect of recognizing sounds in words is not to be fooled by the spelling. For instance, the letter "a" appears in the word "bake" and in the word "sand," but as you know, one is a diphthong and the other is a short vowel. Switch the vowel sound in the words "bake" and "sand." There you go again, creating your own language! Now let's do some practice.

The Sound-Sequence

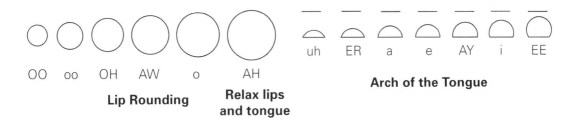

- Stand in front of a mirror in active stillness. Open and close your lips just like a fish eating food from the top of the water's surface as you say:

WOO→WOO→WOO→WOO→WOH→WOH→WOH→WOH→
WAW→WAW→WAW→WAW→WOW→WOW→WOW→WOW!

- Repeat the sequence several times.
- Recuperate by shaking out your jaw in this manner: Clasp your hands together and shake them back and forth with a relaxed jaw.
- Stand in front of a mirror in active stillness. Rest your tongue tip behind your lower front teeth, drop your jaw from the temporomandibular joint, and gradually arch the body of your tongue from the bottom of your mouth toward the hard palate and back again, producing:

$$AH \rightarrow AY \rightarrow EE \rightarrow AY \rightarrow AH$$

- Repeat several times and recuperate.
- Stand in front of a mirror in active stillness. Mime-through, breathe-through, and speak *The Sound-Sequence*. Observe the "catch breath" on each "^" symbol.

OO ^ oo ^ OH ^ AW ^ o ^ AH ^ uh ^ ER ^ a ^ e ^ AY ^ i ^ EE

- Repeat several times and recuperate.

Practice this sequence until you are secure with the breath organization, order, and precise mouth-shapes required. As you practice, check to make sure your ribs are expanded and the breath is dropping toward your abdomen. The action of the "catch breath" on each "^" is similar to panting. This means that as you phonate, the abdomen swiftly moves in toward the spine, and as the new breath drops in, the abdomen moves forward. Most importantly, make sure that you do *not* glottal attack the vowel/diphthong initiations. It will help to put a slight "h" just before the vowel. Although there are a fair number of nonsense "words," treat every combination as if it were a real word. When recognizable words do appear, enjoy the recognition.

- Add beginning and end consonants to *The Sound-Sequence*:

LOO ^ Loo ^ LOH ^ LAW ^ Lo ^ LAH ^ Luh ^ LER ^ La ^ Le ^ LAY ^ Li ^ LEE
OOL ^ ooL ^ OHL ^ AWL ^ oL ^ AHL ^ uhL ^ ERL ^ aL ^ eL ^ AYL ^ iL ^ EEL

   Substitute N, D, and T for L.
- Speak the previous exercise with other consonant substitutions.

Did you notice that you said seven "real" words? They were: "low," "law," "lay," "Lee," "eel," "ale,"and "Earl." You also spoke seven real words when "L" followed the vowel/ diphthong sound, and when you used an "h" sound to avoid glottal attacks on the vowel initiations. They were: "whole," "haul," "Hal," "hell," "hail," "hill,"and "heel." What recognizable words showed up when you substituted other consonants for "L"? Now that you know *The Sound-Sequence*, let's celebrate with a dance incorporating **Effort!**

THE SOUND-SEQUENCE DANCE

OO: Draw a winding pathway on the floor with your toe: *sustained/light/indirect.*

oo: Shake something off your toe toward someone/thing in the room: *quick/light/direct.*

OH: Circle your knees: *sustained/strong/indirect.*

AW: Press your palms to the back as your hips press forward: *sustained/strong/direct.*

o: Turn palms forward: *quick/ light/indirect.*

AH: Swing your arms around your body at waist level: *sustained/light/indirect.*

uh: Slap your belly with your open palms: *quick/strong/direct.*

ER: Press your palms into your sternum and drop your head back: *sustained/strong/direct.*

a: Tap your sinus cavities with your fingertips: *quick/light/direct.*

e: Flick your palms to face forward: *quick/light/ indirect.*

AY: Bend over and massage the sinus cavities: *quick/strong/indirect.*

i: Flick your fingers up from the top of your ears: *quick/light/indirect.*

EE: Press your hands up toward the ceiling: *sustained/strong/direct.*

Make up your own *Sound-Sequence Dance* and choose the *effort elements* that express what you want to say.

More Diphthongs

In the following exercises, you are being challenged to add beginning and ending consonants to new diphthong articulations and to add **Effort**. Before diving into **Effort**, take your time and use a mirror to observe the precise mouth-shapes necessary for clarity. Be particularly aware of the strength and organization needed to produce a clear consonant ending. Resist pulling the tongue tip away from the lower front teeth on the diphthong sound. Keep the tongue tip forward until the consonant action lifts the tongue tip up to the "shelf" between the back of the teeth and the alveolar ridge. Also, be careful not to glottal attack the initiating diphthong sounds. You will find that these exercises produce a fair amount of gibberish, but they also produce many "real" words. See if you can find them as you speak the exercise. In all of the following exercises, the symbol "^" represents a catch breath.

OW ("AHoo" = <u>loud</u> c<u>ow</u>) is composed of two back vowels. The first sound is the long vowel "AH" (f<u>a</u>ther) and the second sound is the short vowel "oo" (b<u>oo</u>k). The stress is on the first sound and the second is treated as a grace note: *quick* and *light.*

- Drop your jaw from the hinge. Approximate a two-finger drop between the teeth, which is the width of the tips of your index and third fingers together. The tip of your tongue remains behind the lower front teeth for the duration of the diphthong.
- Sound an "AH."
- Move your lips forward with *quickness* and *lightness* from "AH" into an "oo" (b<u>oo</u>k) position.
- Mime-through, breathe-through, and speak:

AH ^ oo ^ AH ^ oo ^

AHoo ^ AHoo ^ AHoo^

Add consonants:

LAHoo ^ NAHoo ^ DAHoo ^ TAHoo ^

AHooL ^ AHooN ^ AHooD ^ AHooT ^

Did you notice the "real" words: "now, "Dow," "howl," and "out"?

- Explore *effort elements* through this diphthong. First include movement, then repeat in active stillness.

OI ("AWi" = <u>oi</u>led b<u>oy</u>) is composed of the back vowel "AW" (w<u>a</u>ll) and the short front vowel "i" (b<u>i</u>t). The stress is on the "AW" while "i" is *quick* and *light.*

- Drop your jaw from the hinge. Approximate a space between the teeth that is slightly smaller than a two-finger drop. The tip of your tongue remains behind your lower front teeth for the duration of the diphthong.
- Turn your lips out for the "AW" mouth-shape and give it sound.
- Quickly relax the lips to neutral as the body of the tongue arches with *quickness* and *lightness* toward the hard palate, producing "i" (b<u>i</u>t).
- Mime-through, breathe-through, and speak:

AW ^ i ^ AW ^ i ^

AWi ^ AWi ^AWi ^

Add consonants:

LAWi ^ NAWi ^ DAWi ^ TAWi ^

AWiL ^ AWiN ^ AWiD ^ AWiT ^

Did you find the words: "toy" and "oil"?

- Explore *effort elements* through the diphthong. First include movement, then repeat in active stillness.

I ("@i" = br<u>igh</u>t s<u>ide</u>) is composed of the two short front vowels. In order not to confuse the initiating sound of the diphthong with any other sound previously described, I am representing this sound with the symbol "@". The "@" sound is actually the first of the short front vowels. The arch of the tongue lies between "AH" and "a" (b<u>a</u>t), and words that contain the option for this sound are part of a designated group called the "Ask" List. The "@" has not been included in our round of short vowels until now because in contemporary Neutral American speech, it is not used except as part of the aforementioned diphthong. It can be heard, however, in specific American regional dialects such as Boston (P*ar*k the c*ar* in H*ar*vard y*ar*d), parts of Long Island, and the South. The British, however, make more use of this sound, often substituting the "@" for "AH" in words such as "adv*a*nce" or, in honor of the list's name, "*a*sk." This adjustment may be a sign of the evolution of the British dialect toward a more American sound on words that were traditionally pronounced with the long "AH," such as "p*a*st." In some American training programs, the "@" remains a mainstay of the Mid-Atlantic dialect (also called Standard Stage Speech), while other programs no longer emphasize "@" except as part of the diphthong "@i" (br*i*ght). Consult a book with extensive lexical sets to discover the words for which this short vowel may be used. As with most diphthongs, the stress is on the first phoneme and the second sound is treated as *quick* and *light*.

- Drop your jaw from the hinge. Approximate a two-finger drop between the teeth, which is the width of the tips of your index and third fingers together. The tip of your tongue remains behind your lower front teeth for the duration of the diphthong.
- *Slightly* arch the body of the tongue as you articulate the "@" sound.
- Raise the body of the tongue higher with *quickness* and *lightness* to produce the "i" (b*i*t) sound.
- Mime-through, breathe-through, and speak:

@ ^ i ^ @ ^ i ^

@i ^ @i ^ @i ^

Add consonants:

L@i ^ N@i ^ D@i ^ T@i ^

@iL ^ @iN ^ @iD ^ @iT ^

Did you find the words: "lie," "nigh," "die," "tie," "hide," and "height"?
- Explore the *effort elements* through the diphthong. First include movement and then repeat in active stillness.

EW ("yOO" = c*ue*, ref*u*se, n*ew*, b*eau*tiful, *you*) is also called the liquid "u" because it is composed of the vowel-like consonant glide "y" and the long vowel "OO" (gl*oo*m). In this case, the first phoneme is *quick* and *light* and the second sound carries the stress. In other speech systems, the first sound is characterized as an "i" as in "b*i*t." You will get a better result on this exercise if you substitute an "i" sound for "y."

- Drop your jaw from the hinge. Approximate a two-finger drop between the teeth, which is the width of the tips of your index and third fingers together. The tip of your tongue remains behind your lower front teeth for the duration of the diphthong.

- Arch the body of your tongue toward your hard palate and articulate the sound of "i" as in "b*i*t."
- With *quickness* glide the tongue downward while the lips simultaneously move forward into the "OO" mouth-shape.
- Mime-through, breath-through, and speak:

i ^ OO ^ i ^ OO ^

iOO ^ iOO ^ iOO ^

Add consonants:

LiOO ^ NiOO ^ DiOO ^ TiOO ^

iOOL ^ iOON ^ iOOD ^ iOOT ^

Did you find the words: "new," "dew," and "hewn"?

- Explore the *effort elements* through the diphthong. First include movement, then repeat in active stillness.

The Diphthongs of "r"

We name the diphthongs of "r" such because the second sound for each one has only a small "hint" or "coloring" of an "r" sound. The sound is similar to how the British diminish the presence of the "r." This reduction in the "r" sound applies when "r" *does not* initiate a word or appear between two vowel sounds. The "r" coloring is actually a version of the *schwa* sound because, although it leans toward the vowel sound "ER," it is actually in a very weak and unstressed position. For our purposes, the "r" coloring will be represented by "er."

During the following exercises, use a mirror to observe the precise movements of the articulators. Make sure you are not bringing any excessive tensions to the activity. It is crucial that the tip of your tongue remain relaxed behind your lower front teeth throughout the diphthong. Therefore, keep an eye on your tongue tip, as there may be a strong inclination to retract it back toward the throat, which can cause constriction in the action of the vocal folds. As you have previously discovered, diphthongs are very rhythmic. For each of the diphthongs of "r," the stress is on the first sound and the second sound is treated as a "grace note," *light* and *quick*. Keep adding the slight "h" sound to avoid glottal attacks on the vowel initiations.

EAR ("**ier**" = b**eer**, h**ear**)

- Drop your jaw from the hinge. Approximate a two-finger drop between the teeth, which is the width of the tips of your index and third fingers together. The tip of your tongue remains behind your lower front teeth for the duration of the diphthong.

- Arch the body of your tongue toward the hard palate, producing an "i" (b*i*t) sound.
- Release the body of the tongue to a lower arch to produce the *schwa*.
- Mime-through, breathe-through, and speak:

i ^ er ^ i ^ er

ier ^ ier ^ ier ^

Add consonants:

Lier ^ Nier ^ Dier ^ Tier ^

ierL ^ ierN ^ ierD ^ ierT ^

Did you find the words: "Lear" (leer), "near," "dear" (deer), and "tear (tier)"?

- Explore the *effort elements* through the diphthong. First include movement, then repeat in active stillness.

AIR ("**Eer**" = c**are**, b**ear**, f**air**)

- Drop your jaw from the hinge. Approximate a two-finger drop between the teeth, which is the width of the tips of your index and third fingers together. The tip of your tongue remains behind your lower front teeth for the duration of the diphthong.
- Arch the body of the tongue toward the hard palate to produce the short front vowel "e" as in "p*e*n."
- Release the body of the tongue downward *slightly* to produce the *schwa* (er).
- To avoid confusion, we will use "E" as the symbol for the "e" sound in this exercise. Mime-through, breathe-through, and speak:

E ^ er ^ E ^ er ^

Eer ^ Eer ^ Eer ^

Add consonants:

LEer ^ NEer ^ DEer ^ TEer ^

EerL ^ EerN ^ EerD ^ EerT ^

Did you find the words: "lair," "Nair," "dare," and "tear"?

- Explore the *effort elements* through the diphthong. First include movement, then repeat in active stillness.

OR ("**AWer**" = d**oor**, f**our**, c**ore**)

- Drop your jaw from the hinge. Approximate a space between the teeth that is slightly smaller than a two-finger drop. The tip of your tongue remains behind your lower front teeth for the duration of the diphthong.
- Turn your lips out to the mouth-shape for "AW" and give it sound.
- With *quickness*, relax your lips as the body of your tongue *slightly* arches toward the place where the hard and soft palates meet to produce the *schwa*.
- Mime-through, breathe-through, and speak:

AW ^ er ^ AW ^ er ^
AWer ^ AWer ^ AWer ^

Add consonants:

LAWer ^ NAWer ^ DAWer ^ TAWer ^
AWerL ^ AWerN ^ AWerD ^ AWerT

Did you find the words: "lore," "nor," "door," "tore," and "hoard"?

- Explore the *effort elements* through the diphthong. First include movement, then repeat in active stillness.

OOR ("ooer" = p<u>oor</u>, t<u>our</u>)

This is a challenging diphthong because most speakers tend to substitute "AWer" (roar, door) in "ooer" words. To discover other words that can be pronounced with this diphthong, consult a book with lexical sets.

- Assume the mouth-shape for the short vowel "oo" and give it sound.
- With *quickness*, release your lips to neutral as the body of the tongue arches slightly toward the place where the hard and soft palates meet to produce the *schwa*.
- Mime-through, breathe-through, and speak:

oo ^ er ^ oo ^ er ^
ooer ^ ooer ^ ooer ^

Add consonants:

Looer ^ Nooer ^ Dooer ^ Tooer ^
ooerL ^ ooerN ^ ooerD ^ ooerT ^

Did you find the words: "lure," "dour," and "tour"?

- Explore the *effort elements* through the diphthong. First include movement, then repeat in active stillness.

AR ("AHer" = c<u>ar</u>, l<u>ar</u>d, h<u>ear</u>th)

- Drop your jaw from the hinge. Approximate a two-finger drop between the teeth, which is the width of the tips of your index and third fingers together. The tip of your tongue remains behind your lower front teeth for the duration of the diphthong.
- Produce the vowel sound "AH" (f<u>a</u>ther).
- With *quickness*, slightly arch the body of the tongue toward the place where the hard and soft palate meet to produce the *schwa*.
- Mime-trough, breathe-through, and speak:

AH ^ er ^ AH ^ er ^

AHer ^ AHer ^ AHer ^

Add consonants:

LAHer ^ NAHer ^ DAHer ^ TAHer ^

AHerL ^ AHerN ^ AHerD ^ AHerT ^

Did you find the words: "tar," "hard," and "heart"?

- Explore the *effort elements* through the diphthong. First include movement and then repeat in active stillness.

Triphthongs

There are two triphthongs in spoken English. They are named such for the obvious reason that they are made up of a diphthong and a pure vowel sound so closely blended together that they may be perceived as one sound. Again, the tip of the tongue must remain behind the lower front teeth during the triphthong. The stress is on the first phoneme; the second two are treated as "grace notes," *light* and *quick*.

OWER ("AHooer" = fl<u>ower</u>, fl<u>our</u>) This triphthong is a combination of the diphthong AHoo (s<u>ou</u>nd) and the *schwa* "er."

- Mime-through, breathe-through, and speak:

AH ^ oo ^ er ^ AH ^ oo ^ er ^

AHoo ^ er ^ AHoo ^ er ^

AHooer ^ AHooer ^ AHooer ^

Add consonants:

LAHooer ^ NAHooer ^ DAHooer ^ TAHooer ^
AHooerL ^ AHooerN ^ AHooerD ^ AHooert ^

Did you find the words TAHooer = tower and AHooerD = Howard?

- Explore the *effort elements* through the triphthong, first with movement, then in active stillness.

IRE ("@i er" = f<u>ire</u>, ch<u>oir</u>, p<u>yre</u>, l<u>iar</u>) This triphthong is comprised of the diphthong "@i" (s<u>i</u>de) and the *schwa* "er."

- Mime-through, breathe-through, and speak:

@ ^ i ^ er ^ @ ^ i ^ er ^
@i ^ er ^ @i ^ er ^
@ier ^ @ier ^ @ier ^
Add consonants:

L@ier ^ N@ier ^ D@ier ^ T@ier ^
@ierL ^ @ierN ^ @ierD ^ @iert ^

Did you find the words: "liar," "dire," "tire," and "hired"?

- Explore the *effort elements* through the triphthong. First include movement, then repeat in active stillness.

Our family of sounds is growing!

The Family Tree (Long and Short Vowels, Diphthongs, and Triphthongs)

Sound-Sequence (with "@"):	OO	oo	OH	AW	o	AH	uh	ER	@	a	e	AY	i	EE
Diphthongs:	iOO			AWi		AHoo			@i					
Diphthongs of "r":		ooer		AWer		AHer					Eer		ier	
Triphthongs:						AHooer			@ier					

Create Your Own Culture of Sound

The sounds of spoken English need to be produced with clarity and ease to ensure that your message will reach the largest number of listeners possible. Just like with the gross body, if you are hampered by extraneous tensions or are static, communication may be marred. Practicing the mouth-shapes is the "workout" through which the muscles of the articulators gain flexibility and strength. Though effective and practical, the mouth-shapes described in this chapter and previous ones are by no means the only ways the articulators can move. The following exercises are an opportunity to remove the onus from "correctness" by creating a heretofore unheard-of family of diphthongs. This family of new diphthongs will be the language of your "new" culture. The exercises require a partner or, even better, a group.

- Put pieces of paper with each of the pure vowel sounds (no diphthongs or triphthongs) into a bag and pull them out two or three at a time. Create your own diphthongs and triphthongs from this sound bank.
- Teach your diphthongs/triphthongs to your partner or group and vice versa.
- With a single partner or a group, improvise with the new sounds. Let your body move on impulse, filled with **Effort** life and influenced by the new muscular actions of the articulators and the sounds that are produced.
- In active stillness, improvise with the sounds of your new culture. Again, let your **Effort** life impulsively fill the sound improvisation.
- Return to the precise mouth-shapes for recognizable sounds of spoken English and repeat the last two exercises.

Did the distinction between your made-up language and English blur? If so, this is good. Expressively, all sounds are created equal regardless of whether or not they have all been given a specific recognition in spoken English. However, while it is true that emotional expressiveness is not diminished, intellectual sense for the listener will no doubt be elusive.

The next two experiments take time to develop. You should have a minimum of twenty minutes for each experiment and you need a group of actors.

- The group divides itself in half. Half will be the consonant group and half the vowel/diphthong/triphthong group. The entire group "goes to sleep," and when they "wake up," half the group will have only vowels/diphthong/triphthongs with which to communicate, and the other half only consonants. The groups will intermingle and improvise with body and voice using only their designated sound bank.
- When the group has intuited the end of the improvisation, recuperate.
- Share your experiences.

- This exercise requires a "leader." The group is told that they will go to sleep and wake up in a culture where they can speak *only* with the consonants. Vowels do not exist. The group begins to improvise with body and voice. When the improvisation begins to "cook," the leader whispers to one individual that he/she now has access only to the vowel/diphthong/triphthong sounds. The leader observes and the participants experience what happens when one member speaks differently.

- As the improvisation progresses, the leader whispers to more and more actors that they, too, now possess only vowel/diphthong/triphthong sounds, until a sole member is left who has only consonants as a means of vocal expression.
- When the group intuits the end of the improvisation, recuperate.
- Share your experiences.

These last two experiments address the impulse to speak and the desire to be understood, as well as the social implications of "sounding different." The exercises also highlight how the body is affected by open, unobstructed sounds (vowels/diphthongs/triphthongs) and sounds that are formed by impeding or stopping the breath stream with the articulators (consonants). Conversely, the movement of the body certainly may influence the articulators toward certain kinds of sounds. The "culture of consonants" no doubt provoked different manifestations of **Body**, **Effort**, **Shape**, and **Space** than the "culture of vowels/diphthongs/triphthongs."

Back to the Beginning

To reach this point of clarity and expressiveness in body, voice, and speech is quite an achievement. Yet it is always good to go back to the beginning and incorporate the new skills with previous exercises. So here we go, back to the beginning.

- Return to the Bartenieff Fundamentals described in chapter 2. Practice each Fundamental and randomly incorporate the vowel/diphthong/triphthong sounds. What does it feel like to sound an "OH" (b*oa*t) as you do a Thigh Rotation, or the short vowel "a" (b*a*t) with a Thigh Lift? What is it like to explore the triphthong "@ier" (*fire*) with Body Half Rolls?
- Incorporate into the Fundamentals the muscular activity exercises for the articulators introduced in this chapter and in previous chapters. The descriptions of the potential breath organizations described with the Fundamentals will be very helpful as you explore articulation.
- As you continue to practice the Fundamentals with the precise articulation sequences for speech, heighten your awareness of how you use your body and the inherent presence of **Shape**, **Space**, and **Effort**. For instance, how is a Forward Pelvic Shift affected if your attitude toward Time is one of indulgence rather than urgency?
- Re-explore the exercises that emphasize **Shape** from floor to standing and apply muscular-activity exercises for articulation and **Effort**. Such an exercise is "Shaping Your Body Through Levels from One to Ten described in chapter 4.
- Review CPT and Modes of Shape Change, adding **Effort** choices and articulation exercises.
- Travel, exploring the Floor Patterns with the articulation exercises and **Effort** life. Keep in

mind that traveling can manifest itself in many forms, such as crawling, running, leaping, skipping, etc.

At the beginning of this chapter, you divided the *effort elements* into Effort Factor Bags. You were instructed to pull one, two, or three *elements*, each from a different Factor Bag. When you simultaneously moved with two *elements* in equal proportions, you were moving in a State. When you moved emphasizing three *elements* in equal proportions simultaneously, you were moving in a Drive. When you practiced *The Sound-Sequence Dance*, you were attempting to emphasize three *elements* simultaneously and were therefore in a Drive.

As you have no doubt discovered, it is very difficult to move while emphasizing only one *element* for very long. Naturally, the body needs recuperation, so other *elements* begin to appear consecutively or simultaneously. This is a testament to our complexity as human beings. We are never just one thing. The *elements* emerge and disappear, folding into one another, traveling side by side at times and, at other times, consecutively. One or two *elements* become predominant; then something happens and a third joins the party, only to have the whole bunch evaporate as two or three different *elements* emerge and take their place. The intricate behavioral and psychological patterns that emerge from the *effort elements* can be likened to the patterns made by the varied shapes of the colored glass tumbling within the kinesphere of a kaleidoscope. In the next two chapters, which begin the advanced section of this book, we will name the specific States and Drives and, of course, explore them physically and vocally. The final chapter is an introduction to Space Harmony, married with all that you have explored in Levels One and Two.

Level Three

"The word is born—Air and earth are mated—"

–Rudolf Laban

CHAPTER TWELVE

Revealing Your State of Mind
Time Frame: Ten one-hour sessions

Before we continue, let's look at your accomplishments so far. You have practiced muscular activities for articulation; therefore, your articulators are gaining accuracy and ease. In addition, you have married articulation to breath, tone, and range of voice. By applying Bartenieff's Nine Principles to the Fundamentals and the subsequent **Shape**, **Space**, and **Effort** explorations, your body has become a barometer for how much physical release, coupled with virtuoso expressiveness, you can bring to your creative activity. At this juncture, you understand that excessive tension anywhere in your instrument will mar both your functional and expressive capabilities.

One of the rewards for your dedicated practice is the opportunity to speak text. Your text need not be long. A juicy ten lines will suffice. The exercises in this chapter are expansive, and texts that can hold up to the pressure will be the most rewarding. Ten lines from a Greek play can be very useful for our purpose. If that doesn't appeal to you, there are also contemporary texts that meet the criteria. Plays by Tennessee Williams, August Wilson, Charles Mee, Tony Kushner, David Hare, David Rabe, Tom Stoppard, Caryl Churchill, Edward Albee, and Samuel Beckett (to name just a few), as well as the modern European classics by Chekhov, Strindberg, Ionesco, Anouilh, and Ibsen, all fit the bill nicely. Of course, Shakespeare is the king of the mountain, and all the exercises you have and will explore can help unlock the verse. The point is, never cheat yourself. Choose superb writing by genius playwrights from the past and of the present. Regardless of the text you use, it is important that you let go of any preconceived notions of how to speak the words and let the explorations provide you with a smorgasbord of possible choices with which to craft the text.

In the previous chapter, you experimented with the *effort elements* singly and in random combinations. In order to make the language of **Effort** convenient for inspiring and describing expressive aspects of voice, speech, and movement, it is important to give specific names to the States (two *elements*) and Drives (three *elements*), as well as examine each for its qualitative properties.

States

There are six States: Awake, Dream, Remote, Near/Rhythm, Stable, and Mobile. Laban also called these "incomplete efforts" because they utilize two *effort elements* as opposed to "complete efforts," which employ three *elements* and are called Drives. States form a link or pathway from one Drive to the next. While Drives express the heightened moments in life, the States are the moment-to-moment stepping-stones between the Drives.

Awake   Space & Time *indirect/sustained, direct/sustained,*
                              indirect/quick, direct/quick

The Awake State describes awareness, whether certain or uncertain, quick or gradual. It can be all encompassing or very focused. You may awaken to a new idea, to your surroundings, or to your given circumstances. In an Awake State, you possess an inner attitude of alertness. Alertness may happen quickly or gradually, directly or indirectly: "She came to realize that she wasn't getting the promotion." "She heard her name and immediately bounced up out of her seat, realizing she had won the prize."

Dream   Weight & Flow *light/free, strong/free,*
                              light/bound, strong/bound

The Dream State is the dynamic opposite of the Awake State, and therefore describes sensing and unawareness. You may exhibit unawareness of others, the environment, or even ideas: "He is a dreamer—his ideas cannot come to fruition in reality." "Thank goodness for the dreamers of the world; they push the envelope of what is possible." "It was so unreal, it was like a dream." The disconnection from Space makes this State less connected to reality and more connected to sense of self.

Remote   Space & Flow *indirect/free, direct/free,*
                              indirect/bound, direct/bound

Remote States can describe detachment or a level of concentration that may be filled with carefulness or abandon. In a Remote State, the focus may be concentrated on oneself or a single activity. An individual in a Remote State may be focused on the total environment as well as multiple activities, as long as he is directed toward a single end: "He was so focused on getting the dance right that I could not get his attention." "The actor's concentration was so deep that nothing could make him forget his lines." "She was so focused on her book that she didn't notice the child crying." People walking down the street chatting on their cell phones are often in a Remote State. They are directed toward the person they are speaking to on the phone, often to the exclusion of all else; hence the danger of driving while speaking on the phone.

Near/Rhythm   Time & Weight *sustained/light, sustained/strong,*
                                   quick/light, quick/strong

Near/Rhythm State describes the dynamic opposite of Remote. Rather than detachment, Near/Rhythm describes attachment. It also includes presence and impact that may be physical or emotional, superficial or deep. On a physical level, playing the drums, tap dancing, clicking your tongue, snapping your fingers to the music, or conducting an orchestra are examples of the Near/Rhythm State. On an emotional level, a child who cannot bear to let go of mother's hand or an individual who draws a friend near in time of crisis or joy are also examples of this State. A person may be in a Near/Rhythm State when he says, "It is an honor to shake your hand!" "Near" was the name Laban originally ascribed to this State, and it makes logical sense in relation to literally drawing near to an object, person, or idea. In recent years, it has also been called Rhythm State, due to its close relationship to rhythmic activities.

Stable   Weight & Space *strong/direct, strong/indirect,*
light/direct, light/indirect

Stable State describes resoluteness that may be the result of stubbornness or sensitivity. It can also depict all-encompassing powerfulness or a delicate pinpointing of issues. A person in a Stable State is not likely to waver, give in, or crumple under pressure. Some examples are: "We hired her because she is a very stable individual. She is flexible but strong in her opinions. She is not likely to be bullied and is willing to listen to and apply advice as long as it helps her achieve her stated goal." "We did not hire him because he was absolute in his stance. Nothing could budge him." The Stable State is present in both of these individuals.

Mobile   Time & Flow *quick/free, quick/bound,*
sustained/free, sustained/bound

The dynamic opposite of Stable is Mobile, which describes adaptability that may be easy or difficult. It may gradually manifest itself over time, or suddenly, with urgency. An individual who is in a Mobile State can be described as changeable. For instance: "We need new hires who are not fixed in their ideas, but rather are willing to adapt and change their minds if necessary." "Her ideas are so changeable that it is in difficult to pin her down." Birds flying on the wind are constantly adapting their flight both quickly and gradually by binding and releasing their flow as the wind shifts.

Exercises for Exploring the States

Before adding text, it will be helpful to explore the States in your body with sound-shapes. Keep in mind that the goal of your experiments is not to prove mastery of a particular State by sustaining it twenty minutes or more, but rather to enter the State and go on whatever journey it initiates. Entering a State is a beginning point, not the end product. This is true whether you are emphasizing a single *element*, a State, or eventually a Drive. They all serve as buoys in the ocean of your imagination, so to speak. The following exercises are places of departure for your imagination. Have fun.

- Write the States (Awake, Dream, etc.) on separate pieces of paper and put them in a bag. Pull one out. Move your whole body and make sound-shapes on impulse filtered through that State. Your movement can be very abstract. Remember, being a complex creature, you cannot move for long in only that State, but the State you chose will be dominant throughout your exploration.
- Repeat the previous exercise until you have explored each State.
- Write your own description of what each State represents to you. The descriptions of the States in this book are only guidelines to get you started. Your descriptions will be far more valuable and meaningful to you.

- Make observations in the real world. Keep a notebook handy and jot down examples of the States as you recognize them. Be very specific and keep the examples short—a moment in time, not a whole scene. Find at least one example of each State. At this juncture, the importance of real-world observations for the development of the actor cannot be overstated. Our affinities and disaffinites are often revealed through what we are able to see or not see.
- Return to the studio and recreate your observations in your body and voice. Does each State *feel* like what it looked/sounded like?

During the following exercises, you will incorporate text. For the exercises to have benefit, it is crucial that you know your text extremely well. "Teach the words to your lips, so that you can forget them with your brain," was the advice of Laurence Olivier. To that end, you will first employ a series of exercises designed to assist in teaching the text to your lips. Take the time to work out any difficult hurdles for the articulators.

- Mime-through each thought with your articulators. Feel the muscular activity of each word.
- Speak the passage.
- Repeat the previous two steps five times.
- Recuperate.

- Mime-through only the operative words (words that are most important to the sense).
- Speak the text with all the words restored.
- Repeat the previous two steps five times. (You may vary which words you deem to be operative.)
- Recuperate.

- Breathe-through each line for consonant energy.
- Speak the passage.
- Breathe-through only the operative words.
- Speak the text with all the words restored.
- Repeat the previous four steps five times. (You may vary which words are operative.)
- Recuperate.

- Intone the passage on your center pitch.
- Intone again, but change the pitch to above or below your center pitch on each thought change.
- Speak the passage.
- Intone only the operative words.
- Speak the text with all the words restored.

- Repeat the previous five steps five times. (You may vary which words are operative.)
- Recuperate.

- Explore orchestrating where you will breathe for the purpose of delineating the thoughts. (Observing the punctuation will be very helpful as a starting place.)
- Change the breath organization and discover how the change may impact the sense of the passage.
- Recuperate.

- Explore the exercises for **Shape** (Modes of Shape Change), **Space** (CPT), and Floor Patterns described in chapters 7 and 8 with your text.
- Explore single *effort elements* through body and text.
- Stand in active stillness and speak the text.
- Recuperate.

By now, you have learned your text accurately, which means DLP (Dead Letter Perfect)! Additionally, speaking the text should reflect a flexible, fluid, and unfixed approach to interpretation. If that is the case, you are ready to move on to the exercises for States. You will not be concerned with the playwright's intention. Instead, you will be bending the text in new, possibly extreme, and certainly illogical ways, but you may also "trip" into some real possibilities should you ever perform this text.

Each State has *four* possible combinations of *effort elements*. In other words, don't get stuck in the assumption that Stable State is always *strong/direct*. It can also emerge as *light/direct*, *strong/indirect*, and *indirect/light*. Refer to the Effort Table on page 147 as a reference for the combinations of *elements* that comprise a State. As you experiment, don't try to be perfect or exacting and thus overwhelm yourself with the details of the language of **Effort**. Instead, use the terminology as a stimulus for your sound and movement. The operative words are *experiment* and *play*.

- Explore each State with body and text. Sometimes a character will emerge, sometimes a given circumstance, or both. Keep notes on your impressions of each State.
- Execute everyday activities imbued with the States. For instance, peel an orange in a Remote State, then in a Near/Rhythm State. Repeat the activity, adding your text.
- Develop scenarios that involve an evolution from one State to another. For example, perhaps in your "scene" you are walking down the street in a Dream State when you remember you forgot something at home (Awake State), so you turn around and in a Mobile State begin your trek home. If you have an impulse to speak, add text, but feel no obligation to speak all of it.
- Experiment with the States by filtering them through the text while you remain in active stillness. Can just your voice and speech reflect the State(s)? Can you find an internal justification for speaking the text: Dream→Awake→Mobile?

- Choose a new combination of States and repeat the previous two exercises.

The following exercises, which emphasize character development and communication, require a partner. It is of no importance that your texts may be from different sources. You will treat your words as if they were meant to be a response to your partner's words. You have to be "Awake" to the impulse to speak, and listen to your scene partner with your whole body to know when to respond with your words. Your improvisations do not have to be lengthy. Short is good.

- You will each decide on a State that your character will value above all the other States. Do not tell each other your decision. Improvise with body and text influenced by your State. Keep in mind that you are not trying to guess your scene partner's State. You are responding to each other moment to moment through the lens of your State.
- When you intuit the end of the improvisation, share your experience.
- Stand with your partner in active stillness and repeat the last exercise with just your text.
- When you intuit the end of the exercise, share your experience.
- Keep a journal on the States to which you have easy access and those that are more difficult for you. Take note of the specific *effort elements* that your affined and disaffined States contain.

It is not always the most interesting choice for the body and voice to be in the same State simultaneously. Remember the kaleidoscope. The **Effort** qualities are wafting in, out, and around, up and down, moving toward and away from each other, revealing the complexity of human behavior. **Effort** is a fluid system, not a fixed one. And, as an artist, you are not at its mercy; you are in the driver's seat. Therefore, as an experiment, try the following:

- Pick a simple activity like peeling an orange, and do it in a Dream State while speaking your text in a Stable State.
- Switch. Peel the orange in a Stable State and speak in a Dream State.

Your success at inhabiting one State in your body while speaking in another is not as important as the *attempt*. An honest attempt can be enough to produce complex, expressive possibilities.

Effort Table

Effort Factors:	Time	Weight	Space	Flow
Elements:	*(quick ↔ sustained)*	*(strong ↔ light)*	*(direct ↔ indirect)*	*(bound ↔ free)*

- *Quick*: Fighting/condensing decision in time. Spark-like, excited, rushed.
- *Sustained*: Indulgent/expansive decision in time. Leisurely, prolonged, endless.
- *Strong*: Fighting/condensing intention in weight. Having an impact.
- *Light*: Indulgent/expansive intention in weight. Delicate or fine touch.
- *Direct*: Fighting/condensing intention in space. To the point, aimed, blunt.
- *Indirect*: Indulgent/expansive attention in space. Flexible, multi-overlapping foci.
- *Bound*: Fighting/condensing emotions or continuity. Careful, restrained, controlled.
- *Free*: Indulgent/expansive emotions or continuity. Abandoned, uncontrolled, unlimited.

States: A combination of equal parts of two *effort elements*.
- Dream State = Weight + Flow (*light/free, strong/free, light/bound, strong/bound*)
- Awake State = Space + Time (*indirect/sustained, direct/sustained, indirect/quick, direct/quick*)
- Near/Rhythm State = Time + Weight (*sustained/light, sustained/strong, quick/light, quick/strong*)
- Remote State = Space + Flow (*indirect/free, indirect/bound, direct/free, direct/bound*)
- Mobile State = Time + Flow (*quick/free, quick/bound, sustained/free, sustained/bound*)
- Stable State = Weight + Space (*strong/direct, strong/indirect, light/direct, light/indirect*)

Drives: Combinations of equal parts of three *effort elements*.
    Action Drives: Time, Weight, Space
- Punch Action Drive = *quick + strong + direct*
- Dab Action Drive = *quick + light + direct*
- Slash Action Drive = *quick + strong + indirect*
- Flick Action Drive = *quick + light +indirect*
- Press Action Drive = *sustained + strong + direct*
- Glide Action Drive = *sustained + light + direct*
- Wring Action Drive = *sustained + strong + indirect*
- Float Action Drive = *sustained + light + indirect*

Transformation Drives:
- Passion Drive = Time + Weight + Flow
- Vision Drive = Time + Space + Flow
- Spell Drive = Weight + Space + Flow

CHAPTER THIRTEEN

Drives: Expressing Heightened Moments
Time Frame: Twenty two-hour sessions

The term Drive is culled from the German word *Antrieb*, which literally means "on drive." In LMA, a Drive is the simultaneous manifestation of three *effort elements* in equal proportions. An individual moves and sounds in a Drive during the heightened moments of daily living. For instance, you are longing for an ice cream cone on a very hot day. When you take that first lick and feel like you have gone to heaven, you are in a Drive. Or you see someone breaking into your car and you rush forward and hit the individual with your backpack as you yell, "Police!" You are in a Drive. When you walk into a fabulous rose garden and feel your heart lighten as you slowly take it all in with a gasp and a sigh, you are in a Drive. Drives are enormously energetic and difficult to sustain for very long. So each of these examples is a moment in time that passes quickly into a State.

You already began to work with Drives in chapter 10 when you were instructed to move and sound with three *effort elements* in equal proportions simultaneously. You also explored Drives during *The Sound-Sequence Dance* in chapter 11. Each movement and sound had three *elements* attached to it. When you made up your own dance, you assigned three *elements* to each of your moves and allowed your sound to follow suit. Before embarking on the new experiments in this chapter, take the time to revisit the **Effort** exercises in chapters 10, 11, and 12.

There are two categories of Drives: Action Drives and Transformation Drives. Transformation Drives include Passion, Vision, and Spell Drives. Each Drive, whether an Action Drive or one of the Transformation Drives, emphasizes *effort elements* from three of the four Effort Factors. The three *effort elements* that comprise a Drive are considered *primary*. The fourth Factor, sometimes referred to as the "missing" Factor, is either devalued or missing altogether.

Action Drives

An Action Drive is a combination of *elements* culled from the Effort Factors: Time, Space, and Weight. Flow is of diminished importance. There are eight Action Drives: Float, Punch, Glide, Slash, Dab, Wring, Flick, and Press. For actors, the Action Drives are of particular value. The word "action" pretty much sums it up. How often have you heard that the vital components of acting are "action" and "reaction"? Action Drives are particularly beneficial because they emphasize *intention* (Weight), *decision* (Time), and *attention* (Space), and de-emphasize *emotion* (Flow). All of which underscore

Stanislavski's revelation that emotion is a byproduct of action, and only action creates truthful physical behaviors. In this instance, Flow can be likened to the shifting sand under the waves of Space, Time, and Weight. Flow is always present, but it is just not running the show. For the actor, the Action Drives address and clarify the basic tenets in the craft of acting: a) identifying the "wants" and "needs" of the character, b) living truthfully in the given circumstances, and c) choosing a course of action with which to overcome the obstacles. As previously stated, the States serve as the links between the Drives. The States that lead to Action Drives are Awake, Near/Rhythm, and Stable.

Passion Drives

As with the Action Drives, each of the Transformation Drives also has eight possible combinations of *effort elements*. The Passion Drives are a combination of *effort elements* culled from the Time, Weight, and Flow Factors. During a Passion Drive, the individual is self-involved because the Flow is now prominent, along with Time and Weight. During a Passion Drive, Space is not present. Here are some examples: Someone who attacks another person in a fury, stabbing wildly without focus in a hit-or-miss fashion is committing a "crime of passion." In the throes of sex, the teenagers fail to notice parents entering the room. When a child throws a tantrum, it is all about him to the exclusion of all else. The description earlier of the first lick of ice cream on a hot day is also an example of a Passion Drive, albeit one that lasts only a few seconds.

Besides relating to given circumstances, Passion Drives can also support character development. For instance, someone who is always governed by her emotions may be unreasonable in the eyes of others. An individual who is passionate about a particular topic can take others to task, challenging the opinions of others to the exclusion of listening to opposing views. Passionate individuals also give us great art, books, and science. A Passion Drive may be born out of Rhythm/Near, Dream, and Mobile States.

Vision Drives

The Vision Drives combine *elements* from the Space, Time, and Flow Factors. The importance of the Weight Factor is diminished. Consequently, one of the hallmarks of a Vision Drive is that it *lacks clear intention*. On stage, without intention there is no acting. However, as with the Passion Drives, Vision Drives can be useful to the actor in particular circumstances, such as when a character is envisioning possibilities. The "visions" can reveal themselves instantly or over time, directly or indirectly. Relative to character, philosophers and creative thinkers of all sorts have visionary aspects to their personalities. One who "sees" the future, the past, or abstract concepts with *quickness* or *sustainment*, but has *no clear purpose*, is living in a Vision Drive. Visionaries tend not to live in the here and now, but are "lost in the stars"—weightless. Such a character would be interesting to watch (and portray), provided the play is balanced with other characters who are full of action. The Vision Drives grow out of Remote, Mobile, and Awake States.

Spell Drives

The Spell Drives combine *elements* from the Space, Weight, and Flow Factors. The Time Factor is diminished. Because the Time Factor is connected to decision-making and rhythm (two vital elements for acting), the uses of Spell Drives may be highly selective for the actor. The diminished importance of Time renders the individual "actionless" because there is no discernable impending need for action. However, this Drive still has value for the actor expressively. For instance, someone who appears transfixed or trancelike after a car accident is in a Spell Drive. Or, difficulty processing good or bad news may cause an individual's internal rhythm to become fixed or "timeless." The Spell Drives are born from Remote, Dream, and Stable States.

The Drives can be helpful to craft a performance from beginning to end, relative to mapping out the character's affinities and disaffinities, as well your character's reactions to the given circumstances and subsequent events of the play. Important questions to this task are: "How does your character attempt to overcome the obstacles in the play?" "To what degree does your character move away from her affinities toward her disaffinites?" For instance, you may play a character that comfortably inhabits a Vision Drive, but the events of the play force the character to evolve toward an Action Drive. It is the evolution that captivates the audience. It is important to question whether your character is transformed forever or if the transformation is momentary. In the alternative, perhaps you are playing a character that is metaphorically "immovable." All such questions and explorations are grist for the mill, and the answers are made known to the audience through your body, your voice, and how you articulate the words.

Although each of the Drives has eight possible combinations of *effort elements*, it is interesting to note that Laban only gave formal names to the eight Action Drives. Obviously, Passion, Vision, and Spell Drives also have as many permutations, and why Laban didn't formally name them is unknown. One theory is that while working for the British government on time and motion studies, he found the Action Drives were the most applicable to the tasks he was observing.

For fun, and to level the playing field, as you explore Spell, Vision, and Passion Drives, invent your own descriptive vocabulary for the individual Transformation Drives within each category. Move and make unstructured sound that reflects each Drive.

Exercises for Exploring the Drives in Body and Voice

Action Drives (Flowless)

- Float: *indirect, sustained, light*
- Punch: *direct, quick, strong*
- Glide: *direct, sustained, light*
- Slash: *indirect, quick, strong*
- Dab: *direct, quick, light*
- Wring: *indirect, sustained, strong*
- Flick: *indirect, quick, light*
- Press: *direct, sustained, strong*

- Return to *The Sound-Sequence Dance* in chapter 11 and name the Action Drives. (Some are named for you.)

Passion Drives (Spaceless)

- Invent names for each combination:

  - *Free, sustained, light*
  - *Bound, quick, strong*
  - *Bound, sustained, light*
  - *Free, quick, strong*
  - *Bound, quick, light*
  - *Free, sustained, strong*
  - *Free, quick, light*
  - *Bound, sustained, strong*

Vision Drives (Weightless)

- Invent names for each combination:

  - *Indirect, sustained, free*
  - *Direct, quick, bound*
  - *Direct, sustained, free*
  - *Indirect, quick, free*
  - *Direct, quick, free*
  - *Indirect, sustained, bound*
  - *Indirect, quick, bound*
  - *Direct, sustained, bound*

Spell Drives (Timeless)

- Invent names for each combination:

  - *Indirect, free, light*
  - *Direct, bound, strong*
  - *Direct, bound, light*
  - *Indirect, free, strong*
  - *Direct, free, strong*
  - *Indirect, bound, strong*
  - *Indirect, bound, light*
  - *Direct, free, light*

At first, it may be difficult for you not to gravitate toward Weight and Time, respectively, during the Vision and Spell Drives. That is because *bound flow* is often confused with *strong weight* and/or *sustained time*. Similarly, *free flow* is often confused with *light weight* and/or *quick time*. No worries. The more you improvise with the *elements*, the clearer they will become in your body and voice. You may find that you are only able to nail each Drive for a second or two. The rest of the time you are moving and sounding with the related States on your way toward or away from a Drive. That is absolutely fine. That is how real life works and, likewise, how you will orchestrate your performance. Enjoy the imaginative journeys that the States and Drives can inspire.

The following exercises return to the task of observing real life. Some actors may find that Vision and Spell Drives are a challenge to notice, as well as to experience. This may be due to the fact that actors are dedicated to "action." If this is true for you, don't get discouraged. Part of the exercise is to learn to "see," and that takes time. You will sometimes notice the Drives when you are relaxed and not consciously looking for them. Keep that notebook handy and record your observations in as much detail as possible.

- Gather examples from real life of *each* Action Drive. As a result, you will have eight *short* examples. Also, catalogue examples of Passion, Vision, and Spell Drives.
- At home, take each of the observations into your own body and voice (if there was sound). Be very specific. Recreate as much detail as possible—no approximations or generalizations.
- Record in your journal the Drives that were easiest and hardest to "see."
- Write about your experience of embodying each Drive. Which felt the most available to you? Which the least? Make particular note of the *effort elements* that your affined and disaffined Drives contain.
- Compare today's experience with past notes on your personal affinities/disaffinities relative to *elements* and States.

The importance of knowing yourself and the impact that self-knowledge can have on your acting cannot be overstated. How can we walk truthfully in someone else's shoes if we don't know first who we are? How can we expand our expressiveness if we don't know our personal baseline from which we wish to expand?

The following exercises are experiments in how many different stories you can tell if you choose a different **Effort** life each time you repeat the exact same movements and the exact same words. Keep in mind that while these experiments are not very long, they are very *precise*. Using a lot of your text or a long movement phrase is not the point. Evolution and change are. Remember to keep the activity simple, and don't be concerned about speaking your whole text from start to finish.

- Stand in active stillness. Speak a few lines of your text several times, emphasizing a different Drive each time. Make notes after each experiment about what it felt like you were "doing." For instance, if you spoke the text in the Punch Drive, you may have felt that you were punishing the listener. Of course, the actual words will influence how the Drive manifests in relation to action. For instance, if "I'm sorry" is your line and you say it in a Punch Drive, you may feel like you are defending yourself or perhaps attacking the other person.

- Choose three Drives. As you speak the text, each of the three Drives must show up at some point. You can, if you wish, orchestrate exactly when each Drive will manifest itself, or you can explore more randomly. But each time you repeat the text, make sure you are changing the order of the Drives. How does switching up the order of the Drives change the intention of the words?

- Choose simple everyday activities (combing your hair, brushing your teeth, setting the table, folding the laundry, etc.) and explore each one in a Drive. Remember, the actual moments that you are in the Drive will most likely be brief. The corresponding States lead you to and from the Drive.

- With a simple everyday activity, build a movement phrase that includes your text. Begin with an emphasis on one *effort element*, then evolve to a State, and finish in a Drive. Then repeat the movement phrase and change up the **Effort** life. For example, you may be holding a bowl and mixing imaginary cake batter with a *sustained* relationship to Time. As you mix, you slowly become Awake to a bubble in the batter. You then become very *direct* with your spatula as you try to get rid of the bubble while maintaining a *sustained* attitude toward Time. Unable to burst the bubble, you add more and more weight to the spatula until you are using *strong weight* in equal proportions to Time (*sustained*) and Space (*direct*). You are now in a Press Action Drive. In your attempt to Press the bubble out of the batter, you dislodge the bowl from your arm, and it crashes to the floor, splattering your imaginary batter everywhere.

- Continue to experiment with everyday activities and change up the specific *elements*, States, and Drives to discover how the story changes.

- Speak your text in one Drive while you do an activity in another! Anytime you mix it up with body and sound, the challenge increases, along with the complexity of what you produce. Let's face it: body and voice are not always in perfect accord with one another. The actor needs to be adept at revealing discord as well.

Diction with Drives

As you have discovered from your practice of the muscular activity exercises for articulation, the vowels and consonants have distinct personalities, both individually and as groups of phonemes. **Effort** exploration will help you further distinguish these personalities.

- To warm up your articulators, review the vowel, diphthong, triphthong, and consonant sounds for their precise mouth-shapes. Review the muscular activity exercises for articulation in chapters 9 and 11.

- Explore *each* vowel, diphthong, triphthong, and consonant sound with *each* Action Drive. Let your body follow the voice.

- Repeat the previous exercises, experimenting with Passion, Spell, and Vision Drives. What are the qualitative differences?

Don't try to do all the possible permutations in one session. Enjoy yourself. Take your time and indulge in the exercise over several days. There is much to discover and, besides, the practice is effective for training your articulators to become both precise and flexible.

What is so important about exploring each sound with all the Drives? The process will expand your expressive choices by conditioning the muscles of your mouth and body to respond to any impulse that arises. The practice will also stimulate your imagination in new ways. As you turn the kaleidoscope, revel in each new pattern that is revealed. With practice, you will sensitize yourself to the value of recognizing (functionally and expressively) what the repetition of sounds coupled with precise articulation can teach you about acting the text. For instance, when a text has an abundance of diphthongs in close proximity, they will, if articulated precisely, affect your instrument very differently than if the short vowels are numerous and in close proximity. Here is an example from Shakespeare's *Richard III*. The following is the first fifteen lines of Queen Anne's speech in Act I, scene iii:

> Set down, set down your honorable load,
> If honor may be shrouded in a hearse,
> Whilst I awhile obsequiously lament
> The untimely fall of virtuous Lancaster.
> Poor key-cold figure of a holy king!
> Pale ashes of the house of Lancaster!
> Thou bloodless remnant of that royal blood!
> Be it lawful that I invocate thy ghost
> To hear the lamentations of poor Anne,
> Wife to thy Edward, to thy slaughter'd son
> Stabb'd by the selfsame hands that made these
>   wounds!
> Lo, in these windows that let forth thy life,
> I pour the helpless balm of my poor eyes.

How will you speak this text? The given circumstance is a funeral procession and Lady Anne is mourning her father-in-law, King Henry VI, who was killed by Richard, Duke of York, as was her husband. Notice that, of the ninety-nine words, almost a third of them contain diphthongs. This is a striking number, and it is not an accident: It is by design. Lady Anne "wrings" and "presses" through the diphthongs, igniting in herself the qualities of grief and manipulation. Queen Anne cries for her father-in-law and wishes to manipulate the public against Richard through her display of mourning. Therefore, the Wring and Press Action Drives are both a cry to the ghost of Henry and a manipulation of whoever may be watching and listening. The nature of the diphthongs makes them well affined with Wring and Press, and the repetition heightens and reinforces the feelings. You may ask: Why can't the actor just play "grief stricken" and "revengeful"? The simple answer is that "grief stricken" and "revengeful" are not actions; they are *feelings*. Anne's feelings of grief and revengefulness are a byproduct of her "wringing" and "pressing" through the repetitions of the diphthongs for the purpose of making others witness and feel her grief. Perhaps you amend your question to be, Why can't the actor play "to grieve" or "to seek revenge"? She could. These are actions, but they still do not clarify the specific quality of the grieving or revenge because one can filter either action through any number of Drives, which would alter the quality of the actions. Consequently, the actions "to grieve" or "to seek revenge" could still put the actor in danger of playing generalizations. **Effort** life provides specificity. Let's see how her speech continues. There is only a catch breath between the last line and the next portion of the speech. Without warning, the diction changes drastically.

> Cursed be the hands that made these fatal holes!
> Cursed be the heart that had the heart to do it!
> Cursed the blood that let this blood from hence!
> More direful hap betide that hated wretch
> That makes us wretched by the death of thee,
> Than I can wish to adders, spiders, toads,
> Or any creeping venom'd thing that lives!
> If ever he has child, abortive be it,
> Prodigious, and untimely brought to light,
> Whose ugly and unnatural aspect
> May fright the hopeful mother at the view;
> And that be heir to his unhappiness!
> If ever he have wife, let her be made
> As miserable by the death of him
> As I am made by my young lord and thee!

The actor is dealing with fifteen lines again, but this time there are one hundred and twenty words, among which only twenty-two contain diphthong sounds. Additionally, the listener has the impression that the tempo has picked up due to the inclusion of more words, though not that many more syllables, in the same amount of lines. But most importantly, the predominance of stop-plosives and short vowels is suggestive of Drives such as Punch and Slash. With these Action Drives, Anne is literally "driving" home her point. Does this analysis mean that you couldn't make other choices? No, it doesn't. You could decide that Anne is in a Vision Drive. The content of the lines tell us that Anne is envisioning her revenge. The elements of the Vision Drive in this instance are *quick time*, *direct space*, and *bound flow*. The challenge would be to diminish the Weight Factor. The passage is so rhythmic that to lessen the importance of Weight would be very difficult, but not impossible. Try it. The point is, a good actor can bend the text to her will. "Flexing the script" is an essential part of an actor's development of a role. It is also a skill that is essential in this age of performing deconstructions of important texts. However, the ability to sense the playwright's intention is crucial to making coherent choices that possess the satisfying quality of *surprising inevitability*. If you choose to do otherwise, *know* that you are doing it.

It is almost cheating to use Shakespeare as an example because his writing is so attuned to the relationship between the muscular articulation of the words and action. He didn't write about revenge. His words become revenge itself: revenge made actual in sound. Any very good writer possesses this craft and talent. You need to become "Awake" to these possibilities as you study your script.

Scene Work

The next sets of exercises explore the application of **Effort** to scene work. You may use an open scene, converge your monologues as if they were meant to be a scene, or use a scene from a play. It is important that you have the scene or monologue memorized because if you are fighting for words, you will have a tough time letting go. Likewise, if you hold your script, it will be difficult to move on impulse in all the ways you may be inspired to respond. The exception to this is converging your monologues into a scene. As long as both partners know their individual monologues well, the convergence will happen moment to moment during the course of the experiment.

- Put all the Action Drives in one bag. Pull a Drive from the bag and do not share it with your partner. Your partner will do the same. At some point during the scene, the Drive must manifest at least once. You must justify this Drive through your own internal logic and your moment-to-moment responses to your scene partner.
- Repeat the experiment, pulling new Drives each time, until all the Drives have been explored.
- Share your experiences with each other.

If you are using a scene from a play, no doubt some of what you explored is totally unsuitable for the play. (Though, hopefully, it was fun.) However, some of the explorations may have surprised you with their viability. How did the meaning of the story change as you altered the **Effort** life despite using the same words? Clearly, once you are engaged in scene work, the challenge becomes even more interesting. Were you able to stay true to your **Effort** actions and still remain flexible and adaptable to your scene partner? The following experiments include the Transformation Drives.

- Put your scene aside for now and work alone. Put the words Action, Spell, Vision, and Passion in a bag. Pull two Drives from the bag. Decide what combinations of *effort elements* you will emphasize to fulfill the Drives. (Use the Effort Table in chapter 12 as a reference.) Improvise with those Drives. You can be as abstract physically and vocally as you like. Keep in mind: abstract does not imply imprecise.
- Return to your scene partner, who also has been working with two Drives. Do not reveal which Drives you are using, and improvise with your scene partner. You are not using the scene at this point, so be as abstract as you wish with body and voice.
- When you intuit the end of the improvisation, give each other feedback but do not reveal your Drives.
- Return to the actual scene and do a dumb show (silent show) of the scene with the same Drives. Where the Drives manifest themselves in the scene may vary from your last experiment.

- Repeat the scene with the text. Again, where the Drives manifest themselves may vary from your last experiment.
- Share your experiences.

The question often arises: "How does the actor go from big abstract movements and sounds to realistic/naturalistic behavior?" The substitute for size is *precision*. To that end, try the following experiments:

- Working on your own, pull a Drive (Action, Vision, Spell, Passion) from the bag. Decide which combinations of *effort elements* will be used to reveal the Drive. Pick one simple everyday activity such as folding the laundry, sweeping the floor, stirring a pot, etc. Improvise with this activity, knowing that the Drive must manifest itself at some point.
- Add text.
- Return to your partner and the text of your scene. You are each building toward your Drive step by step until it manifests and then diminishes. One of you may be in a State while the other is in a Drive. Or, you may both explode into your Drive simultaneously.
- Do the scene again, mostly in active stillness. Impulses to move will be redirected through text. You may use gestures, but they must be very economical. Your voice and speech carry most of the responsibility for expressing the Drive.
- Recuperate and share your experiences.

We have been using **Effort** in concrete ways to achieve an objective. But, as described earlier in this chapter, it is also important to explore **Effort** as a leaping-off point for creating character. What kind of personality lives principally in Punch Action Drive? What do you know about someone who tends to Dab his words? You can recreate all the exercises you just did with your scene partner, but this time explore **Effort** as an entry into character.

One of the most fulfilling ways to experiment with character is to create a character who values one Drive, but due to an event in the play, ends up valuing another. For instance, perhaps your character is a high-powered Wall Street investor who values all aspects of the Press Action Drive in order to make his fortune. He has a near-death experience that stops him literally and figuratively in his tracks, and he "*sees* the error of his ways." As he returns to health, he learns meditation and becomes very quiet, no longer anxious to do, do, do. Content to sit and ponder, he becomes more dedicated to a Vision Drive than the Press Action Drive. This is not to suggest that Action and Vision are all that reveal themselves over the course of the play; they simply "bookend" the arc of his character development. Can you examine your own life for times when your values or goals changed, thus altering how you moved through the world?

The following is a "freestyle" **Effort** exploration. The idea of using a grid was borrowed from *Rasaboxes*, a practice based on the Sanskrit words to describe emotion, and adapted for actors by Richard Schechner. In this version, we are substituting the **Effort** vocabulary for the Sanskrit words. You need a large space and several participants. With spiking tape, mark a huge grid on the floor that looks like the following diagram:

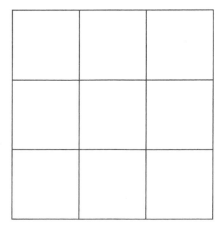

The Setup: There are nine squares, each approximately 2-½ square feet in size. Label the eight squares around the perimeter with either the **Effort** *elements* or the Action Drives. The middle square remains unlabeled and is completely open to the actors' impulses—a wild card, so to speak.

The Agreements: The group can agree to work with or without sound or text. Likewise, the group can also agree to try a round with *just* sound and text; therefore, large body movements would manifest themselves only when traveling from one square to another. Let the games begin!

- The group surrounds the perimeter of the grid.
- You may come and go from the playing area on impulse.
- When you enter a square, you explore that particular *element* or Drive for as long as you remain in the square. Be alive to whether you are inclined to emphasize character or to play imaginary given circumstances inspired by the **Effort** life.
- You may move from square to square on impulse. The transformation from square to square happens instantaneously. No time for thinking.
- You may communicate with the actors in other squares or even join another actor in one square.

Here is another possibility for this game:

- Assign a group leader. Two claps of the leader's hands signals that you may enter or leave the grid.
- If you are on the grid, a single clap signals that you must enter a new square.

Obviously, you can change out the Action Drives for the Passion, Vision, and Spell Drives, or mix them up. To avoid confusion, the group needs to agree on the names for each Transformation Drive. Think of the grid as a sandbox full of toys—you want to eventually play with them all! Be greedy!

The opportunities to explore with **Effort** seem endless. You can make up exercises until the cows come home and seemingly never run out of possibilities. In fact, the experiments that are born out of your curiosity and interest will be even more meaningful to you. There is nothing sacrosanct about the exercises written here. They are examples of how you can play with the material. The hope is that you will be inspired to create your own explorations. Rest assured, there cannot be any "bad" or "incorrect" experiments. Go to town! Keep in mind, however, that you will not effectively apply **Effort** to your craft without the support of **Body**, **Shape**, and **Space**. Unless your body and voice are well tuned to these other spheres, your **Effort** life may remain a thought, a word, an idea, or a concept, but not become actualized in your body and voice. Most actors at some point have heard the comment from a coach or director, "Play the action 'to seduce.'" And you, with frustration, thought, "I *am* playing 'to seduce'!" Ah, but you weren't. It was all in your head. The explorations described here will ensure that your choices will radiate into the environment with clarity of purpose for all to witness and hear.

In the beginning of chapter 10, **Body**, **Shape**, and **Space** were referred to as containers for your **Effort** life. But **Effort** is also a container for **Body**, **Shape**, and **Space**. This was proven when you moved with the *effort elements* and noticed how they affected your **Body**, **Shape**, and relationship to **Space**.

CHAPTER FOURTEEN
Space Harmony for Voice, Speech, and Movement
Time Frame: Twenty two-hour sessions

Laban's theory of Space Harmony was introduced at the end of chapter 5 and was further developed in chapter 8. In this, the final chapter, we will look at Space Harmony from the practical point of view of how it serves the actor. **Space** is what allows us to radiate into the environs the dynamic union of **Body**, **Effort**, and **Shape**, thus making our creative endeavors seen, heard, and felt. Additionally, we will explore **BESS-R**, which is the **Relationship** among **Body**, **Effort**, **Shape**, and **Space**, as it applies to LMA concepts and their component parts described throughout this book. First, let's look at foundational information, followed by elemental practices.

Laban's theory of Space Harmony is predicated on his belief that just as there are harmonies in music, there are also harmonies produced by the body as it responds to the *spatial pulls* inherent in nature. According to his theory, each point in **Space** has a corresponding affinity to **Body**, **Effort**, and **Shape**. As you connect the points through movement, you create a dynamic relationship among the components simultaneously, much like striking a chord on the piano. These relationships resonate into the environs, confirming that there is no such thing as "empty space." Furthermore, Laban did not believe that movement ended at the furthest extension of the body's limbs. Instead, he proposed that movement produces "trace lines" that continue to travel beyond the corporeal self, a phenomenon that we will call "body resonance." This possibility can be likened to an echo or perhaps the tone that lingers when a musician has stopped singing or playing an instrument, or maybe the bright lines that trail after a Fourth of July sparkler waving in the night. Laban developed specific movement sequences called Scales as a means to "connect the dots" in space, which in turn allow the body to capitalize on the possibility of harmonizing internally and externally with the universe at large. More specifically, Laban theorized that harmony between **Space** and **Body** could be achieved if one moved sequentially through the points of the platonic solids, or the "crystalline forms" (as Laban preferred to call them). The movement sequence that creates a Laban Scale is based on the most efficient and expressive pathway between each point. For our purposes, we will be considering the tetrahedron, octahedron, cube, and icosahedron (see illustration page 162).

On a purely practical level, moving through Laban's Scales can be likened to a musician practicing musical scales. The purpose of the practice is to ready the artist for his specific expressive activities. For the musician, the task is to play an instrument or sing a composition. For the actors, the task is

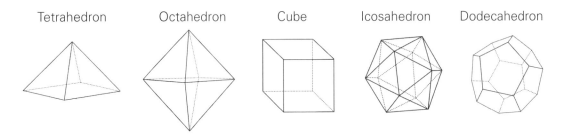

Tetrahedron   Octahedron   Cube   Icosahedron   Dodecahedron

to "play" the play. Actors have many possible practices, but few that simultaneously address the whole "instrument" (body, voice, and articulators) on both functional and expressive levels. The Scales help decompartmentalize the actor's training and provide "wholeness." Laban believed that "wholeness" was possible because practicing the Scales is an activity of the spirit as well as the flesh. Inspired by the musical scales, martial arts, and crystalline forms, the Scales are among Laban's most profound and elegant contributions to movement. Though not developed exclusively for actors, they serve actors' needs effectively.

The integration of Laban's Scales with voice and speech creates a complex and dynamic "chord" composed of movement, voice, and speech "notes." And, contained within each note of this chord are more "harmonies," which are produced by the predominant **Body**, **Effort**, **Shape**, and **Space** (BESS) qualities in **Relationship** to one another at any given moment. One can think of the manifestation of Space Harmony as chords within chords or layers of harmonies.

To penetrate the environs with these harmonies means that the actor is able to fill the environment with his presence. Much is made of the need for the actor to develop presence. What is "presence"? Simply put, an actor's presence is felt when the totality of his body, voice, and speech ignites the atmosphere, compelling an audience to watch and listen. Practical exercises based on the theory of Space Harmony assist the actor to achieve the goal of heightened physical and vocal presence.

Of all the ideas we have explored, **Space** is perhaps the most elusive concept for the actor to absorb. Conversely, **Space** and its relationship to **Body** is what dancers, gymnasts, and, frankly, gifted athletes of all types understand, capitalize on intuitively, and develop further with each practice. Actors, however, can be prone to remain focused internally or only on their scene partner, forgetting that, in the theatre, there is a larger environment to be filled with dynamic energy. Film and television acting has done much to remove the actor from a kinship with **Space**. Consequently, the exercises included here are an attempt to reunite the actor with **Space**. A performer's inclination toward acting in film or on the stage may be linked to the actor's connection to **Space** or the lack thereof. With practice, you, the actor, will be able to adjust this relationship according to the medium in which you are working.

To further understand the value of **Space** explorations to the actor, we must also consider Laban's assertion that **Space** has psychological impact on the mover. Your inclinations relative to **Space** reveal subtle aspects of your personality, your relationships to others, and the given circumstances of the moment. As with **Effort** and **Shape**, once you gain self-knowledge in regard to **Space**, it is a short distance to apply your understandings to character development and craft a performance.

Dimensions and Planes

The Vertical, Horizontal, and Sagittal Dimensions and Planes represent the components of **Space**. Refer to the illustrations titled "Dimensions and Planes," and note that a Dimension is composed of two opposing *spatial pulls*, while the Plane can be described as two *spatial pulls* acting on the body simultaneously. When two *spatial pulls* on opposite poles act on the body simultaneously, the *diameter of a plane* becomes apparent.

Dimensions and Planes

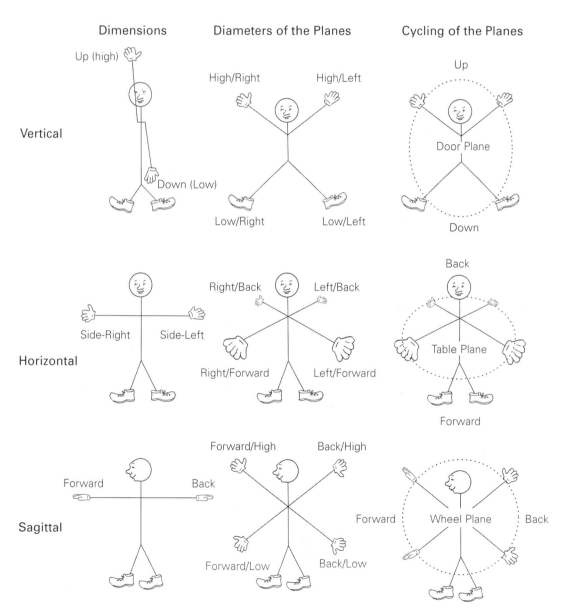

On an imagistic level, the Vertical Dimension relates to issues of self-esteem and the Vertical Plane encompasses "becoming someone" (*ascending*) or "losing yourself" (*descending*). The Horizontal Dimension encompasses the feeling, needing, giving aspects of your personality and desires. While acting in the Horizontal Dimension, you are engaged in how you feel and satisfying your emotional needs. The Horizontal Plane is the spatial equivalent of embracing (*enclosing*) or longing (*spreading*). The Sagittal Dimension emphasizes relationships to *others*. Operating in the Sagittal Dimension may manifest itself as imposing your will, instructing, guiding, rejecting proposals, or making counteroffers. When the Sagittal Plane is dominant, you are engaged in taking action (*advancing*) or rejecting action (*retreating*). You may have noticed that the descriptions for moving in **Space** are supported by the terms that describe the Modes of Shape Change (chapter 7). The terms for Shape Change help describe and reveal the "feeling" aspects of moving toward or away from specific destinations, and give you a peek at the symbiotic relationships among **BESS**.

Because we are complex beings, we are rarely relegated to one Dimension for very long. We are much more complicated than that. Consequently, we often engage the *diameters of the planes* and sometimes even three directions in space simultaneously. When we employ *planar* movement, as opposed to purely *dimensional* movement, the world in which we engage exponentially expands to include deeper feelings of connectedness with the environs. We interact as part of a whole rather than as a single entity. Perhaps embedded in *planar* movement is equality of status, resulting in cooperative behavior born of togetherness.

The following explorations give you the opportunity to "play" in the Vertical, Horizontal, and Sagittal Dimensions and Planes for the purpose of discovering, "Who am I in relation to **Space**?" As always, it is important to observe yourself and others in real life. What are your personal affinities and disaffinites relative to **Space**? How do others use **Space**? How do these observations affect your perception of personality and needs, or influence the tactics chosen to accomplish an objective? It is fun to create characters that value the Vertical, Sagittal, or Horizontal Dimension or Plane above all else. What kinds of people would these be? What do they want? How do they satisfy their needs? How do they speak?

To explore the potential of Space Harmony and marry it with voice and speech, you need to be well versed in the affinities among the components within **BESS**. To accomplish this, we begin our exploration by exploring the *dimensions of the planes*, the *diameters of the planes*, and the *planes*. Before continuing, it will be helpful to review the Modes of Shape Change and CPT Pathways described in chapters 7 and 8 because they describe "feelings" or "attitudes" embedded in the directions in **Space**. Once you have done your review, explore moving guided by the illustrations titled "Dimensions and Planes," and see what you can teach yourself about Planes.

Perhaps you have already noticed that when moving on the *dimensional axes* or the *diameters of the planes*, you employ Central Pathways, and when *cycling the planes*, you engage in Peripheral Pathways. Additionally, take note that each Dimension is affined with *one* **Shape** quality and *one* direction in **Space** as well as *one effort element*, at each end of the spectra, whereas the *diameters of the planes* are affined with *two effort elements* at each end of the spectrum as well as *two* directions in **Space** and *two* qualities of **Shape** and are, consequently, *two-dimensional*. When you *cycle the planes*, you connect the dots between the *dimensions* and the *diameters of the planes. Cycling the planes* is considered to be primarily *two-dimensional* even though there are brief moments of one-dimensionality during the cycles.

Body and Voice Meet Space

If you haven't done so in a while, review the areas of vocal resonance described in chapter 5. The exercises in this chapter build on those initial explorations of resonance. Now turn your attention inward and begin with the Shape Flow of the breath. Imagine that the *dimensions of the planes*, *diameters of the planes*, and the *cycles of the planes* are living in the center of your torso. The following exercises explore "inner space." These explorations will be very subtle but rich.

- Sit on the floor with your eyes closed and envision the inside of your torso. Breathe, feeling the breath *lengthen* and *shorten* the spine on the Vertical Dimension.
- Allow the exhalations to evolve from a breathe-through to a fully resonant sound.
- As your torso moves with the breath and the vocal resonance develops, explore the specific areas of resonance, i.e., head, face, mouth, and chest. Do not hold your breath at any point, but do feel the pause or suspension of the breath as your body awaits the next impulse to breathe in. As you produce sound, imagine the resonances are traveling up and down your spine.
- Repeat on the Horizontal Dimension and feel the torso *widen* and *narrow* with breath and resonance.
- Repeat on the Sagittal Dimension and feel the torso *hollowing* and *bulging* with breath and resonance.
- Repeat the above exercises along the *diameters of the planes* and then *cycle the planes*. Feel the deep engagement of the trunk as you focus on the inner architecture of your torso and the Shape Flow of the breath.

During the following exercises, as your body follows your voice into the environs, you may find yourself lying on your right or left side in the Horizontal Dimension, or lying flat out on your back or front in the Sagittal. Don't go beyond the point that the impulse of the breath and sound propel your body. If the impulse is sufficiently energetic, your body will be at full extension along the floor while the voice continues its journey beyond your corporeal reach. Although Dimensions are affined with the Spoke-like Directional Mode and Central Pathways, we are expanding the possibility that one can move and *sound* on a Central Pathway with the qualities of the Carving Mode as well. From this point forward, we will designate that moving on the *dimensions of the planes*, *diameters of the planes*, and the *cycles of the planes* as simply "exploring the Dimensions and Planes." You will alternate between working alone and with a partner.

- Work alone. Remain seated but open your eyes. Repeat the previous exercises, and allow the limbs to follow the voice, reflecting either the qualities of the Spoke-like Mode, Arc-like Mode, or Carving Mode. For instance, move your arms Spoke-like one at a time on the Vertical Dimension. Then repeat the movement, filling it with *ascending/descending* (Carving Mode). Though the direction in **Space** remains the same (up/down), is there a qualitative difference between filling the direction with Spoke-like or Carving Modes?

• Add sound. Feel the vocal resonance describe the Vertical Plane and be propelled beyond your body. Again, be careful not to hold your breath at any point, force the inhalation, or squeeze out the sound at the end of the breath.

• Repeat, substituting the Horizontal Plane (Spoke-like or Arc-like: *side-across/side-open*, or Carving: *enclosing/spreading*).

• Repeat, substituting the Sagittal Plane (Spoke-like or Arc-like: *backward/forward*, or Carving: *retreating/advancing*).

• Instead of using your arms, *move any other body part* along with your vocal resonances to explore the Planes.

• In active stillness, repeat the exercises *with just your voice*. Can your voice describe the Dimensions and the Planes? You may use unstructured sound, muscular activity exercises for articulation, or text for this purpose.

• Recuperate.

• Make notes on how each Dimension and Plane affected you physically and vocally. Did you feel more at home in one over the others?

• Sit opposite a partner and repeat the exercises. You and your partner may stay with core connections or reach with any body part from a seated position. The progression of this exercise is dependent upon the relationship between you and your partner, as well as the imagery that is affecting you.

• When you have intuited the end of the improvisation, share your experiences.

• Without a partner, come to standing and explore with sound and movement the Dimensions and Planes. You may find yourself in locomotion. For instance, *cycling* the Horizontal Plane can manifest itself as a small circle made by your arms (as if dusting a tabletop), or your whole body may cycle the perimeter of the studio. It is important that the breath and voice support the movement and vice versa.

• Recuperate.

• With a partner, improvise, describing the Dimensions and Planes with sound and movement. Again, let the relationship dictate how your improvisation unfolds. For instance, you may be *cycling a plane* with your whole body and your partner may respond by moving along the *diameters of a plane* only within the torso. The bottom line is that you must let your partner affect you and you must be aware of how you are affecting your partner. This communication will influence how the movement and sound develop between you. Relative to sound, you may use unstructured sound, muscular activity exercises, or text.

- You do not need to move and sound all the time. Explore the interplay between movement and stillness, silence and sound.
- When you have intuited the end of the improvisation, share your experiences. Did each Plane have a unique effect on your communication?

- Stand in active stillness with a partner. Improvise, describing the Planes with unstructured sound, muscular activity exercises for the articulators, or text.
- When you have intuited the end of the improvisation, share your experiences.

Exploring the Platonic Solids

Tetrahedron

Although Laban did not build a Scale precisely for the tetrahedron, it is the most stable form in nature and the crystal upon which all other crystalline forms (platonic solids) are built, and therefore deserves a bit of attention. It is interesting to note that almost all positions the body can assume are related to the tetrahedron.

- Look at the illustration of the tetrahedron on page 162. Imagine you are stepping into the center of the form. This form is now your whole world. Treat the tetrahedron as if you landed there by accident and it is entirely new and unfamiliar territory. Notice where the "corners" are located. Outline the tetrahedron with various body parts and let your voice be led by your body. Investigate it thoroughly, exploring the flat surfaces as well. In other words, you are not just looking. You are "touching" the structure with your body and voice. What does it smell like? Taste like? Does it have a resonance of its own? If you jump, does it shake? Is there a way out? Can you come and go as you please? Does it have a rhythm?
- Explore taking on the shape of the tetrahedron. For instance, your right toe strives toward the highest point of the form, your head reaches toward a forward point on the floor and your hands to the other two points. Your whole body is now a tetrahedron of sorts. Find out how many different arrangements of your body you can make to reflect this form, which may be stretched and rotated in any direction. How is your voice affected as it moves with your body into each new permutation of the tetrahedron?
- With a partner, repeat the last two exercises by placing yourselves inside the octahedron. Negotiate exploring the space together. Can the two of you replicate this form with your bodies?
- With three partners, repeat the previous exercise by placing yourselves inside the cube.

- Explore alone. Now that you know the tetrahedron, octahedron, and cube inside-out (so to speak), devise an order for connecting the corners of each form. You may use a limb or your whole body to "draw" your journey. If you are using a body part (leg, arm, elbow, foot, knee, etc.), you must decide to lead with either the right or the left side and not change sides until you return to your starting point. You are drawing a map of the form and thus are devising your own Scale.

- Memorize your personal Scale for each of the forms. In other words, you want to be able to repeat them.
- Explore how the voice can travel through your Scales using unstructured sound, muscular activity exercises for articulation, or text for this purpose.

- Teach at least one of your Scales to a partner. Learn at least one of your partner's Scales.
- With your partner, improvise with sound and movement, using your Scales as the script. The movements may be very abstract and the sound unstructured.
- When you have intuited the end of the improvisation, share your experiences.

Laban's Scales

Now that you have explored the crystalline forms and devised your personal Scale for each form, you are poised to investigate a few of Laban's Scales. For our purposes, we will investigate Laban's Dimensional Scale, Defense Scale, Diagonal Scale, and A-Scale. You will also examine a devised Peripheral Scale.

The Dimensional Scale (Illustration page 169)

The Dimensional Scale is literally one-dimensional, and the mover passes through center along each Dimension. Imagine that you are standing in active stillness in the center of the illustration for the Dimensional Scale with your back to the viewer. The *cross of axes* are passing through your center.

- Using the illustration as your map, experiment with moving through the Dimensional Scale, first initiating with the right arm and then the left. (Step 3 on the illustration becomes 4 and step 4 becomes 3.)
- Embody the **Space**, **Shape**, and **Effort** affinities. Make sure each move is initiated from the breath and remember that you are forming a bridge between yourself and something in the environment. You must motivate each gesture.
- Complete the following statements as you move:
    o On impulse, the right arm moves up with the feeling of *ascending* with *lightness* to reach for . . .
    o On impulse, the right arm moves down with the feeling of *descending* with *strength* to reach for . . .
    o On impulse, the right arm moves across the chest toward the left side of the body with the feeling of *enclosing* with *directness* to take or give away . . .
    o On impulse, the right arm opens to the right side with the feeling of *spreading* with *indirectness* to receive or give away . . .

Dimensional Scale

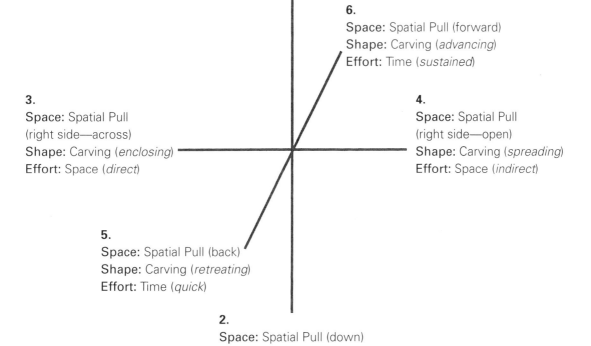

Right Side Leading

1.
Space: Spatial Pull (up)
Shape: Carving (*ascending*)
Effort: Weight (*light*)

6.
Space: Spatial Pull (forward)
Shape: Carving (*advancing*)
Effort: Time (*sustained*)

3.
Space: Spatial Pull
(right side—across)
Shape: Carving (*enclosing*)
Effort: Space (*direct*)

4.
Space: Spatial Pull
(right side—open)
Shape: Carving (*spreading*)
Effort: Space (*indirect*)

5.
Space: Spatial Pull (back)
Shape: Carving (*retreating*)
Effort: Time (*quick*)

2.
Space: Spatial Pull (down)
Shape: Carving (*descending*)
Effort: Weight (*strong*)

- o On impulse, the right arm reaches back with the feeling of *retreating* with *quickness* away from . . .
- o On impulse, the right arm moves forward with the feeling of *advancing* with *sustainment* toward . . .
- o Use other body parts as initiators and *always have an objective.*
- Add unstructured sound.
- Try to repeat the Scale with just your sound.
- Repeat the Scale with movement and add muscular activity exercises for the articulators and/or text. Relative to muscular activity for the articulators, experiment with sounding through OO, OH, AW, AH, AY, EE, EE, AY, AH, AW, OH, OO as you pass through the six points of the scale, once on the right and then immediately on the left. Add

beginning and ending consonants as you did in chapter 9 and keep changing up the body parts that are describing the Scale.

- Initiate the Scale with your whole body. This can include jumping, falling, and some manner of traveling (crawling, hopping, running etc.). For instance, the whole body *advances* with *sustainment* toward . . .
- Repeat the exercises with a partner. You and your partner will move through the Scale simultaneously.
- Recuperate and discuss the quality of the communication and the "actions" you played.

Remember, this is a *journey*. The endpoints exist only because the paper illustration is finite; your imagination and "body resonances" are not. Additionally, it is crucial that you move with *intention*. Without an objective, the move is senseless and will have nothing to do with "Where?" which is the domain of **Space**.

The Defense Scale

The Defense Scale takes place within the octahedron, and like the Dimensional Scale, it is built on the *dimensional cross of axes*, but unlike the Dimensional Scale, it alternates between Central and Peripheral Pathways. As its name suggests, the Defense Scale reflects an "attack and defend" mode and will tend to appear when two people have disparate points of view. Because the Defense Scale travels on Central and Peripheral Pathways, it is affined with Spoke-like or Arc-like Modes. However, as established previously, it is possible to travel on Central and Peripheral Pathways with the qualities of the Carving Mode. This "complication" becomes increasingly more tantalizing because of the inclusion of voice and speech. Refer again to the illustration of the Dimensional Scale. The order of the moves for the Defense Scale duplicates the Dimensional Scale, but the intention of the movements during the Defense Scale is "to defend." Therefore, the motivation for moving is as follows, with the right arm leading:

- Up—to defend the head (Central)
- Down—to defend the right flank between the hip and ribs (Peripheral)
- Side-across—to protect the left jugular (Central)
- Side-open—to protect the right jugular (Peripheral)
- Back—to protect the left flank (Central: the right arm moves across the body to left/back)
- Forward—to protect the abdomen (Peripheral)

Creating a Peripheral Scale for the Octahedron (Illustration on page 172)

This version of a Peripheral Scale moves only on the periphery of the octahedron. While this Scale is not technically a typical Peripheral Scale, it has been devised to give you an opportunity to discover the effect on the body and voice to remain on the periphery of an issue, an event, or even life itself. When one is dedicated to Peripheral movement, the individual displays more objectivity and less passion than would arise from an attacking or defended stance. Perhaps the person who values a

Peripheral relationship to **Space** would make a good mediator or counselor, i.e., someone with an objective point of view. Or, it is also possible that she may suffer from separateness that comes from a lack of involvement. When you are moving on the periphery of the form, there is less stability than there was in the Defense Scale, which allowed you to return to center. Take note of the qualitative differences between Central and Peripheral Pathways to *you*. The illustration on page 172 is numbered for the right side leading.

- Imagine that you are standing in active stillness in the center of the illustration for the octahedron with your back to the viewer. In the order of the numbers on the illustration, motivate your right arm to lead the body along the edge of the form. Allow the **BESS-R** qualities specified on the illustration to manifest themselves, and don't forget to support all the movement from your core support and personal imagery.
- Switch to your left arm and repeat the sequence. (Step 3 on the illustration becomes 4 and step 4 becomes 3.)
- Repeat the Peripheral Scale and add unstructured sound, muscular activity exercises for the articulators, and/or text with the movement. Relative to muscular activity for the articulators, experiment with sounding through OO, OH, AW, AH, AY, EE, EE, AY, AH, AW, OH, OO as you pass through the six points of the Scale, once on the right and then immediately on the left. Add beginning and ending consonants and keep changing up the body parts that are describing the Scale. It is very important that you are truly moving and sounding from your core, supported by the Shape Flow of your breath and motivated by something in the environment or by something inside yourself toward the environment.

Of course, as an actor, you don't always want everything you do to be so "harmonious." You will be playing all sorts of complex characters in extraordinary circumstances, and *ascending* may not always be *light*. Once you know the Scales for their affinities, move through the Scales investigating the disaffinites for each journey. Incorporating "minor chords" into the Scales poses some very sophisticated possibilities, such as moving up with the feeling of *descending*, or forward with the feeling of *retreating*. And what about the sound? Is it always in lock step with the movement? Here is another fun challenge that is crucial to increasing your expressiveness. Can you physically *advance* with *sustainment* while your text is filled with *quickness*? Can you *descend* with *strength* as you fill your text with *ascending* and *lightness*? As you turn the LMA kaleidoscope, new patterns emerge.

Take your time with these experiments. As always, it is important that you allow your imagination to be engaged. Some actors will stimulate their imagination by experimenting with movement and voice to "see what happens." Those actors are working from the outside→in. Others actors first will perceive an image or stimulate an emotion to which they allow the body and voice to respond. They are working from the inside→out. Both are valid approaches to this creative activity, and it is useful for you to know to which strategy you tend to gravitate. If you are in the latter group, then the vocal and physical impulses that arise from the image must still be directed through the Scale.

Creating a Peripheral Scale for the Octahedron

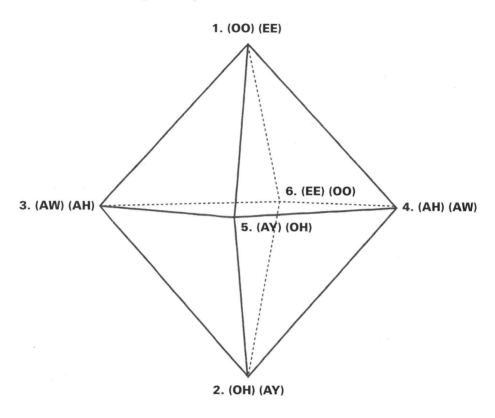

1. (OO) (EE)

6. (EE) (OO)

3. (AW) (AH)

4. (AH) (AW)

5. (AY) (OH)

2. (OH) (AY)

1. OO
Space: Spatial Pull (up)
Shape: Carving (*ascending*)
Effort: Weight (*light*)

2. OH
Space: Spatial Pull (down)
Shape: Carving (*descending*)
Effort: Weight (*strong*)

3. AW
Space: Spatial Pull (right side—across)
Shape: Carving (*enclosing*)
Effort: Space (*direct*)

4. AH
Space: Spatial Pull (right side—open)
Shape: Carving (*spreading*)
Effort: Space (*indirect*)

5. AY
Space: Spatial Pull (back)
Shape: Carving (*retreating*)
Effort: Time (*quick*)

6. EE
Space: Spatial Pull (forward)
Shape: Carving (*advancing*)
Effort: Time (*sustained*)

Repeat with your left side leading.

The following exercises require a partner. Once you are working with a partner, some of the challenges of answering the question, "Where?" are solved. But consider that not every movement is directed toward and away from your partner. You both may be affected by imaginary circumstances that cause you to focus on the environs and *not* each other, although the communication between you remains palpable. The first exercise has an abstract result, but the remaining exercises guide you toward more naturalistic behaviors. It is important to honor the feelings the Scales provoke in you and to reflect the qualitative differences between the Scales and their potential for altering tactics in communication.

- Start by facing your partner. You do not have to remain facing each other, but you do need to be in good communication throughout.
- Repeat the Scales with the affinities for each point in **Space**. Treat the Scales as if they are the physical "script" for an abstract "scene."
- The Scales are short; therefore, keep looping the Scales and alternate leading with the right and left sides of the body until you and your partner intuit the end of the exercise.
- Repeat, adding unstructured sound, muscular activity exercises for the articulators, or text.
- When you intuit the end of the improvisations, recuperate.
- Share your experiences.

- With your partner, sit in chairs opposite each other. Have a "conversation" through the Scales with *just your torsos*—first in silence and then with unstructured sound or text.
- Repeat the previous exercise, but this time *do not be concerned with the order of the moves dictated by the Scales or their affinities*. Instead, you and your partner will respond to each other on impulse moment to moment. For instance, if you witness your scene partner's torso *ascending* with *lightness*, you may be compelled to respond by *retreating* with *sustainment*, which is disaffined. All impulses to gesture should be redirected through your torso. That is not to imply that the arms and hands are dead or totally passive. Most actors tend to overuse their arms and hands in unsupported, meaningless gestures. This is an opportunity to radiate your expressiveness from your core.
- Repeat the previous exercise, and this time add gestures as the impulses arise. Your gestures may manifest in *near*, *intermediate*, or *far reaches* (chapter 8). Don't forget that gestures can manifest not just in the hands, but also in a foot, whole leg, elbow, fingers, knee, head—in other words, virtually any body part.
- When you intuit the end of your improvisation, recuperate.
- Share your experiences.

- Come to standing and continue to improvise with your scene partner, using the Scales as the basis. Your impulses to gesture or move your whole body must be directed through the basic moves of the Scales, but the prescribed order of the moves is now unimportant. Depending on how you apply **BESS-R**, your behavior may be abstract, realistic, or even a melding of the two.

- When you intuit the end of the improvisation, recuperate.
- Share your experiences.

- In *active stillness*, improvise with your partner using unstructured sound, muscular activity exercises for the articulators, or text. All of your impulses to move must be redirected through your voice and speech.
- When you intuit the end of the "scene," recuperate.
- Share your experiences.

Cube: Diagonal Scale (Illustration page 175)

The Diagonal Scale takes place in the cube and is a representation of three-dimensionality. It is developed around the *diagonal cross of axes* as opposed to the *dimensional cross of axes*. Three-dimensionality becomes apparent when "diagonality" is present. The Diagonal Scale also represents emotional extremes. Refer to the **Effort** affinities on the illustration. Talk about going from zero to sixty! You are traveling from one emotional extreme to another with *every journey* from corner to corner. Whew!

- Stand in the center of your imaginary cube. Start with your right arm and gesture toward all eight corners of the cube in any order you like, once again devising your own Scale. No matter what point or corner of the cube you are inclined toward, keep your hips facing forward. In other words, *do not turn your hips toward the corner to which you are inclined.*
- As you move from point to point, feel your body's evolution through the Still Shape Forms.
- Repeat, leading with your left arm.

The corners of the cube represent a "major chord" struck by **BESS-R**. Relative to **Effort**, each corner represents an Action Drive. This means that *three* Factors (Time, Weight, and Space [*direct/indirect*]) are represented in equal proportions. Flow is present but secondary. There are eight corners in a cube and eight Action Drives. In addition to a chord of Effort Factors, **Space** is also acting on the body with three equal *spatial pulls*. Likewise, there are three equal qualities of **Shape** represented through the body. This is all happening simultaneously during the moments that you are fully inclined toward a particular corner in the cube. For instance, stand in the cube and incline your body, led by your right arm, toward the high-right-forward corner. When you reach the apex, your body is moving high, right, and forward *simultaneously*. This pulls the body off-center into a diagonal. (Keep hips forward. Do not turn toward the corner.) Relative to **Shape** and **Effort**, you *simultaneously ascend* with *lightness*, *spread* with *indirectness*, and *advance* with *sustainment*. As you recall, equal parts of *lightness*, *indirectness*, and *sustainment* comprise the Float Action Drive.

The most important aspect of moving through the Diagonal Scale is that you are increasing your awareness of your continually adaptive journey toward each corner in the cube. The *journey* is what is interesting and attention grabbing, not the *destination*. As you progress from corner to corner, you are moving along the continua of **BESS-R** until there is a moment of harmony at each corner, which produces a "major chord" in **Space**.

Cube: Diagonal Scale

Right Side Leading

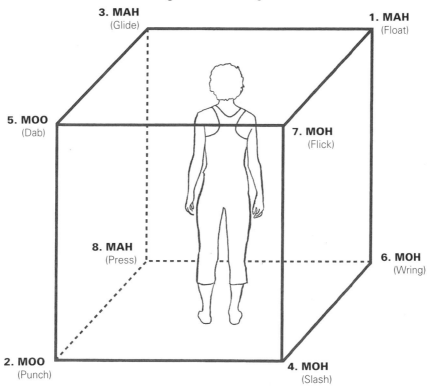

3. MAH (Glide)

1. MAH (Float)

5. MOO (Dab)

7. MOH (Flick)

8. MAH (Press)

6. MOH (Wring)

2. MOO (Punch)

4. MOH (Slash)

1. MAH
Space: Spatial Pull (high, right, forward)
Shape: Carving *(ascending, spreading, advancing)*
Effort: Float Action Drive

2. MOO
Space: Spatial Pull (low, left, back)
Shape: Carving *(descending, enclosing, retreating)*
Effort: Punch Action Drive

3. MAH
Space: Spatial Pull (high, left, forward)
Shape: Carving *(ascending, enclosing, advancing)*
Effort: Glide Action Drive

4. MOH
Space: Spatial Pull (low, right, back)
Shape: Carving *(descending, spreading, retreating)*
Effort: Slash Action Drive

5. MOO
Space: Spatial Pull (high, left, back)
Shape: Carving *(ascending, enclosing, retreating)*
Effort: Dab Action Drive

6. MOH
Space: Spatial Pull (low, right, forward)
Shape: Carving *(descending, spreading, advancing)*
Effort: Wring Action Drive

7. MOH
Space: Spatial Pull (high, right, back)
Shape: Carving *(ascending, spreading, retreating)*
Effort: Flick Action Drive

8. MAH
Space: Spatial Pull (low, left, forward)
Shape: *Carving (descending, enclosing, advancing)*
Effort: Press Action Drive

Repeat, leading with any body part on the left side.

To make another example, let's begin where we left off with inclining toward the Float corner of the cube. At the Float corner, something happens that drives your right arm across your body, toward the low-left-back corner: *descending* with *strength*, *enclosing* with *directness*, and *retreating* with *quickness*. By the time you arrive at the low-left-back corner you are manifesting a Punch Action Drive. But a lot has happened between Float and Punch. It is important to be aware of the evolution of the continuum you are riding on as you progress from Float to Punch. You want to sensitize yourself to the whole journey not just the "corner"—which is artificial at best, since **Space** extends beyond our immediate environs. Therefore, we ultimately don't know exactly where each corner is. We do know the directions in which they lie and can incline our bodies toward these directions.

All the exercises that you explored on the previous Scales are excellent for experimenting with the Diagonal Scale as well. It is very important that each move toward or away from a corner is motivated through intention. You want to be aware of the dynamic journey between the corners, not just the Action Drives affined with the corners. Refer to the illustration for the Diagonal Scale and use it as a map for moving through the Scale, following the numbers and incorporating **BESS-R**.

- Move through the Scale, leading first with your right arm and then the left.
- Vary which body parts are initiating the Scale. For instance, can you explore the sequence with your right hip or left toe?
- Repeat the sequence with *just voice* while your body remains in active stillness. Moving the voice along the diagonals with intention will develop your vocal variety, which includes range, volume, rate, and resonance. Experiment with unstructured sound, the muscular activity exercises for articulation, and text. Relative to muscular activity for the articulators, experiment with the exercise MAH-MOO, MAH-MOH, MOO-MOH, MOH-MAH. Change up the consonant with each repetition.
- Explore the Scale with movement *and* sound.
- Recuperate.

- Move through the Scale, exploring the disaffined Effort for each corner in the Cube. For instance, Punch is disaffined with the Float corner.
- Move on the diagonal toward a corner, honoring its affinities in your movement, but produce sound or speak with the disaffinities and vice versa.
- Recuperate.

- Repeat the exercises with a partner. When including a partner, your communication with each other must be palpable. You are not moving through the cube by rote; you are reflecting the communication between the two of you. You can experiment with abandoning the strict order and let the journeys toward the corners come up in any order, guided by your imagery, impulses, and the communication between you and your partner.
- Recuperate and share your experiences.

Icosahedron: The A-Scale (Illustration page 178)

To challenge you further, you are going to investigate Laban's A-Scale joined with *The Sound-Sequence*. The A-Scale travels on Transverse Pathways (review CPT in chapter 8) within the icosahedron, touching the twelve corners of the three planes. The order of the planes is Vertical→Sagittal→Horizontal, repeated three times until all twelve points of the form have been passed through.

The A-Scale is often traditionally described as the "female" Scale. But there is irony in this assertion because qualitatively, the Scale begins rather reserved and evolves to assertive in the second half. There is another Scale called the B-Scale that is designated as the "male" Scale; it also transverses the icosahedron. Here is some more irony: The B-Scale begins aggressively and is quite reserved by the end. The challenge of either Scale is to keep up with the constantly changing diagonals as you transverse the inner space of the form toward each point. In life, if someone is affined with the A-Scale, she may be an individual who is in constant flux, embarking on numerous adventures, never in one place for very long. She might be an individual who has a "slow burn," but once she takes off or takes a stand, there is no stopping her. The Transverse Pathways within the Scale speak to someone who likes to be involved, in the middle of things, who enjoys change, and who is not afraid of being off balance or caught off guard. In relationship to others, she may be very difficult to pin down or keep up with. Just try to get her attention for any length of time!

The A-Scale and *The Sound-Sequence* are perfect accompaniments for each other. Numerically they are symbiotic because on the last sound of the *Sequence*, you have arrived back at the first corner in the icosahedron. Speaking *The Sound-Sequence* is enhanced by the journey through the A-Scale because the Scale enlivens your voice with the ever-changing dynamics of **BESS**, particularly since the torso must be pliable to accomplish the Scale. Otherwise, *The Sound-Sequence* is in danger of becoming stuck in the Sagittal Dimension, which could make it sound very pedantic, attacking, or lacking in nuance. Therefore, moving through the A-Scale with text is beneficial for challenging yourself toward even greater expressive flexibility with spoken thought. Additionally, *The Sound-Sequence* enhances the A-Scale by encouraging you to be very clear about your trajectory within the form, as you evolve from diagonal to diagonal, adjusting your relationship to **Effort**, **Shape**, and **Space** over and over. For those of you who are already well versed in Laban's Scales, I am emphasizing the imagery of the three associated diagonals to the A-Scale, hence labeling the progression with the Action Drives. Attempt to investigate the A-Scale using the illustration "Icosahedron and *The Sound-Sequence*" as your map. *When you stand in the center of the form, your back is to the reader and you are facing the solid lines and the dotted lines are to your back.*

Presented in this book are just a few of Laban's Scales. For more information about the Scales, I recommend Laban's book *The Language of Movement: A Guidebook to Choreutics* and *The Geometry of Movement: A Study in the Structure of Communication: Parts 1 and 2* by Ellen Goldman. Both are listed in the bibliography.

Icosahedron and *The Sound-Sequence*

Right Side Leading

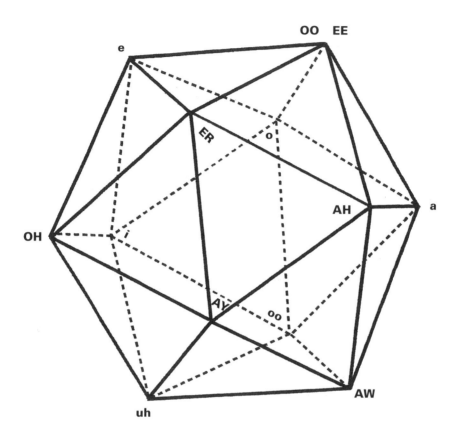

Float/Punch
1. OO (gl<u>oo</u>m), right/high, *spreading/ascending*
2. oo (c<u>oo</u>k), back/low, *retreating/descending*

Glide/Slash
3. OH (s<u>ou</u>l), left/forward, *enclosing/advancing*
4. AW (b<u>aw</u>l), low/right, *descending/spreading*

Dab/Wring
5. o (h<u>o</u>t), back/high, *retreating/ascending*
6. AH (f<u>a</u>ther), right/forward, *spreading/advancing*

Punch/Float
7. uh (l<u>u</u>ck), low/left, *descending/enclosing*
8. ER (b<u>ir</u>d), forward/high, *advancing/ascending*

Slash/Glide
9. a (s<u>a</u>t), right/back *spreading/retreating*
10. e (p<u>e</u>n), high/left, *ascending/enclosing*

Wring/Dab
11. AY (b<u>a</u>ke), forward/low, *advancing/descending*
12. i (s<u>i</u>t), left/back, *enclosing/retreating*

Return to Float
13. EE (s<u>ea</u>t), high/right, *ascending/spreading*

Group Exploration with an Emphasis on Space

Move to music! To continue to play with *dimensional axes*, *diameters of the planes*, and *cycles of the planes*, and to further explore the Scales—both your invented Scales and Laban's—move to music that has strong **Space** qualities. (Recommendations are Carl Orf's *Carmina Burana* or the soundtracks of *Star Wars* and *Lord of the Rings*, all available on CD.)

The following exercise is best explored with a group of at least eight actors. How the actors enter and exit the playing area is as important as their time in the playing area. An actor enters and exits on impulse. With a group of eight or more, the exercise typically needs about twenty to thirty minutes to give everyone an opportunity to participate.

- In a large studio, the group sits around the perimeters of the space, forming a circle. All movement takes place within this circle.
- Play the music. On impulse, an individual enters the playing area and begins to explore **Space** (*dimensions of the planes*, *diameters of the planes*, *cycling the planes*, or the prescribed and/or personal Scales) motivated by the music. The individual may create relationships with the group along the perimeter and/or the imaginary environment created by the music and movement. The actors are not required to be true to the strict sequences of the Scales or to stay with one aspect of **Space**. The aspect of **Space** that is evident is governed by the actors' moment-to-moment impulses.
- On impulse, another individual enters the playing area and, through an emphasis on **Space**, forms relationships with the first player, the witnesses along the perimeter, and/or the imaginary environment created by the music and the movement.
- As many as three players are permitted into the playing area at one time. When a fourth individual enters, someone has to make an exit and return to the perimeter of the playing area. Individuals may enter and exit as often as they are motivated to do so.
- During the course of the experiment, the participants in the playing area do not have to move all the time. The impulse for active stillness is honored.
- When everyone has participated at least once in the playing area, then the last players will intuit the end of the experiment and come to active stillness. They will pause long enough to signal "the end."
- The group recuperates together and shares their experiences.
- Repeat the entire experiment, but without the music. On impulse, the participants will add unstructured sound, muscular activity exercises for the articulators, and/or text.

Experimentations in Transformation

Let us turn our attention to creating characters. You have explored the transformative possibilities of **Body**, **Effort**, and **Shape** in previous chapters. Now it is time to incorporate **Space** as inspiration for character and allow all of **BESS-R** to inform your body and voice. This chapter began with a discussion of the emotional/psychological impact of the Planes on personality; now let's make applications. The statement, "The questions are more important than the answers," is absolutely correct. And, in that spirit, I offer you the following questions based on **BESS-R** that can inspire character development.

- How is your imagination affected if you create a being who is dedicated to Verticality and who *ascends* with the disaffinity *strong weight*?
- Or, how is your imagination affected if you create someone dedicated to the Horizontal and *spreads* with the disaffinity *directness*?
- Or, perhaps you are building a character who is action oriented (*advancing*) and therefore values the Sagittal Plane. But perhaps he also tends to be *indirect* and *sustained* as well. Is it possible to be *indirect* and still forward-action oriented? It is possible that only his use of speech is *indirect*.
- Discover someone who dedicates herself to the down direction of the Vertical Dimension but whose essence lives in the Float Action Drive. Is this possible? Maybe her voice lives in a Float Action Drive but her body *descends* toward a Ball Shape with *strong weight*.

The words and images are *starting points* to entice your body and voice into places you might not discover otherwise, and will assist in avoiding generalizations and clichés. The attempt to discover these potential characters will take you on a creative road to somewhere new and surprising. That is the joy of it! Use LMA as a backdrop for your experiments born out of your curiosity, and, of course, *ask questions* and see what emerges. Additionally, the value of self-knowledge to the acting process cannot be overstated. If you know *who you are* and *how you are perceived by others* in regard to your personal **BESS** affinities, then it is easy to diminish those aspects of yourself that vary from the character, and heighten the ones that you share. Each character you explore will be born out of you and yet not *you*. Armed with self-knowledge and craft, you now possess transformative powers.

The devised explorations based on Space Harmony are many, and the ones recorded here are only suggestions. The experiments that *you* create from this material will be just as valid and useful. Your goal is to be functionally proficient and expressively inexhaustible. Do not wait to be cast to engage in developing your craft. That is like starting your training for a twenty-six-mile marathon the day before the race. Instead, create your "gymnasium" for acting and "work out" regularly. Your reward will be the development of your voice, speech, and movement beyond the level of simple, isolated skills, and they will assume their rightful places as the cornerstones of your craft.

FINAL THOUGHTS

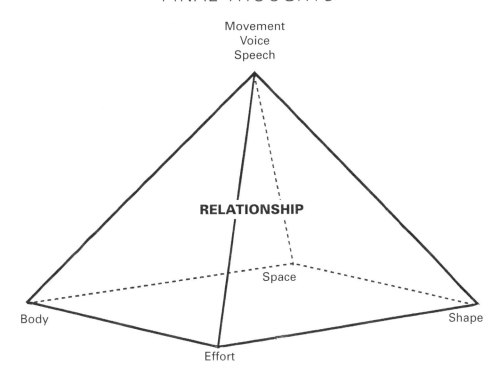

During the experiments in this book, you have integrated **BESS** and formed **Relationships** (BESS-R) with other actors and the environs dictated by your moment-to-moment impulses. Your ability to direct these impulses into the specifics of **BESS-R** speaks to your skill in crafting a performance that is dynamic and unpredictable, yet inevitable—because your progression has both an internal and an external logic that the audience can see, hear, and feel.

You have now completed one lap around the LMA material formulated for actor training. One lap does not a winner make! Now it is time to advance to the beginning of the book. I say "advance to the beginning" because the beginning exercises will now be advanced. It will be impossible for you to ignore the collective impact that your newly acquired, well-earned understanding of **BESS-R** has on your voice, speech, and movement. Whether inventing a simple hand gesture or a complex organization for the whole body, sounding with the primeval basics of unstructured sound, or delivering intricate text, your instrument is now functionally and expressively responsive to inner and outer stimuli moment to moment, and you have dramatically increased your range of dynamic creative choices. Each pass you make through this book will inspire new questions and ignite original explorations, thus expanding your artistry as an actor.

BIBLIOGRAPHY

Aikin, W. A., MD. *The Voice*: *An Introduction to Practical Phonology*. London: Longmans, Green and
   Co., 1951.

Alexander, F. M. *The Use of Self*. London: Orion Books Ltd., 2001.

Barba, Eugenio. *The Paper Canoe*: *A Guide to Theatre Anthropology*. New York: Routledge, 1995.

Barker, Sarah. *The Revolutionary Way to Use Your Body for Total Body Energy*. New York: Bantam
   Books, 1978.

Bartenieff, Irmgard. *Body Movement*: *Coping with the Environment*. New York: Gordon and Breach
   Science Publishers, 1980.

Berry, Cicely. *The Actor and His Text*. New York: Charles Scribner's Sons, 1988.

Bertram, Joseph. *Acting Shakespeare*. New York: Theatre Arts Books, 1969.

Brodnitz, Freidrich. *Keep Your Voice Healthy*. Boston: College Hill Publications,
   1988.

Calais-Germain, Blandine. *Anatomy of Breathing*. Seattle: Eastland Press, Inc., 2006.

_____. *Anatomy of Movement*. Seattle: Eastland Press, 1993.

Dell, Cecily. *A Primer for Movement Description*: *Using Effort-Shape and Supplementary Concepts*.
   New York: Dance Notation Bureau Press, 1993.

Feldenkrais, Moshe. *Awareness Through Movement*. San Francisco: Harper Collins Publishers, 1977.

Fletcher, Patricia. *Classically Speaking*: *Dialects for Actors*. Victoria, BC : Trafford Publishing, 2007.

Forgerty, Elsie. *Speech Craft*. New York: E.P. Dutton and Co., 1931.

Goldman, Ellen. *The Geometry of Movement*: *A Study in the Structure of Communication*. *Part 1*: *The
   Defense Scale*. New York: Self-published. 1999.

_____. *The Geometry of Movement*: *A Study in the Structure of Communication*. *Part 2*: *The
   Axis Scales*. New York: Self-published. 2005.

Hackney, P. *Making Connections: Total Body Integration through Bartenieff Fundamentals*.
   Amsterdam: Gordon Breach Publishers, 1998.

Haelser, Sebastian. "Programmed for Speech." *Scientific American Mind* (June/July 2007): 67-71.

Hartley, Linda. *Wisdom of the Body Moving: An Introduction to Body-Mind Centering*. Berkley: North
   Atlantic Books, 1995.

Hodge, Alison, ed. *Twentieth Century Actor Training*. New York: Routledge, 2000.

Kapit, W. and L. M. Elson. *The Anatomy Coloring Book*. New York: Canfield Press, 1977.

Kent, Raymond D. *The Speech Sciences*. San Diego: Singular Publishing Group, Inc., 1997.

Laban, Rudolf and F. C. Lawrence. *Effort*: *Economy of Human Movement*. Plymouth: Macdonald and Evans Ltd., 1974.

Laban, Rudolf. *The Mastery of Movement*. Boston: Plays, Inc., 1971.

_____. *A Vision of Dynamic Space*. Philadelphia: The Falmer Press, 1984.

Lessac, Arthur. *The Use and Training of the Human Voice*. New York: Drama Book Specialists, 1973.

Linklater, Kristin. *Freeing the Natural Voice*. New York: Drama Book Specialists, 1976.

Martin, Jacqueline. *Voice in Modern Theatre*. New York: Routledge, 1991.

Melton, Joan and Kenneth Tom. *One Voice: Integrating Singing Technique and Theatre Voice Training*. Portsmouth: Heinemann, 2003.

Moore, Keith, L. *Clinically Oriented Anatomy, Third Ed*. Baltimore: Williams and Wilkins, 1992.

Netter, Frank H. *Atlas of Human Anatomy*. Summit: CIBA-Geigy Corporation, 1989.

Pisk, Litz. *The Actor and His Body*. London: Harrap Limited, 1975.

Potter, Nicole, ed. *Movement for Actors*. New York: Allworth Press, 2002.

Redfern, Betty. *Introducing Laban Art of Movement*. London: Macdonald and Evans Ltd., 1965.

Rodenburg, Patsy. *The Need for Words*: *Voice and the Text*. New York: Theatre Arts Books, 1993.

Roy Hart Theatre Archives. *www.roy-hart.com*.

Schmidt, Paul, trans. and ed. *Meyerhold at Work*. New York: Applause, 1996.

Skinner, Edith. *Speak with Distinction*: *The Classic Skinner Method to Speech on the Stage*. Edited by Lilene Mansell. Revised, with new material by Timothy Monich and Lilene Mansell. New York: Applause, 1990.

Stone, Robert and Judith Stone. *Atlas of the Skeletal Muscles*. Dubuque: C. Brown Publishers, 1990.

Suzuki, Tadashi. *The Way of Acting*: *The Theatre Writings of Tadashi Suzuki*. New York: Theatre Communications Group, 2003.

Turner, J. Clifford. *Voice and Speech in the Theatre*, 3rd ed. Revised by Malcolm Morrison. London: Pitman Publishing Ltd., 1979.

Wangh, Steven. *An Acrobat of the Heart*. New York: Vintage Books, 2000.

Wells, Lynn K. *The Articulate Voice*: *An Introduction to Voice and Diction*. Needham Heights: Allyn and Bacon, 1999.

Wildman, Frank. *The Busy Person's Guide to Easier Movement*. Berkeley: The Intelligent Body Press, 2000.

INDEX

Books from Allworth Press

Allworth Press is an imprint of Allworth Communications, Inc. Selected titles are listed below.

Movement for Actors
edited by Nicole Potter (6 × 9, 288 pages, paperback, $19.95)

Improv for Actors
by Dan Diggles (6 × 9, 256 pages, paperback, $19.95)

How to Improvise a Full-Length Play: The Art of Spontaneous Theater
by Kenn Adams (5 1/2 × 8 1/2, 176 pages, paperback, $16.95)

Acting: Advanced Techniques for the Actor, Director, and Teacher
by Terry Schreiber (6 × 9, 256 pages, paperback, $19.95)

Clues to Acting Shakespeare, Second Edition
by Wesley Van Tassel (6 × 9, 288 pages, paperback, $18.95)

Acting the Song: Performance Skills for the Musical Theater
by Tracey Moore with Allison Bergman (6 × 9, 304 pages, paperback, $24.95)

Singing in Musical Theatre: The Training of Singers and Actors
by Joan Melton (6 × 9, 240 pages, paperback, $19.95)

Acting Teachers of America: A Vital Tradition
By Ronald Rand and Luigi Scorcia (6 x 9, 288 pages, paperback, 75 b&w illustrations, $19.95)

The Actor's Other Career Book: Using Your Chops to Survive and Thrive
by Lisa Mulcahy (6 × 9, 224 pages, paperback, $19.95)

Acting is a Job: Real Life Lessons about the Acting Business
by Jason Pugatch (6 × 9, 240 pages, paperback, $19.95)

Mastering Shakespeare: An Acting Class in Seven Scenes
by Scott Kaiser (6 × 9, 256 pages, paperback, $19.95)

To request a free catalog or order books by credit card, call 1-800-491-2808. To see our complete catalog on the World Wide Web, or to order online for a 20 percent discount, you can find us at **www.allworth.com**.